Surgeon On The China Seas

The Journal of Charles Courtney, Surgeon RN Recounting Experiences and Observations of the Second Opium War, 1856-1860

Edited and Introduced by
Michael Humphries

SURGEON ON THE CHINA SEAS

THE JOURNAL OF CHARLES COURTNEY,
SURGEON RN RECOUNTING EXPERIENCES AND
OBSERVATIONS OF THE SECOND OPIUM WAR, 1856-1860

Edited and Introduced by
Michael Humphries

Published by Atrabates Press, Hong Kong

with permission of

The National Archives, Kew, London

Introduction, and Notes, Edition Copyright © Michael Humphries 2012

ISBN:978-988-15417-1-0

Printed in Hong Kong by Corporate Press (HK) Limited

Cover picture: An itinerant doctor at Tien-Sing. Thomas Allom 1843 – 1847.

Michael Humphries is a physician and specialist in respiratory diseases who is currently engaged in clinical research and has lived in Hong Kong and China for nearly 30 years. He is Honorary Adjunct Professor in the Department of Microbiology, Faculty of Medicine, Chinese University of Hong Kong, Fellow of the Royal College of Physicians [London and Edinburgh] and Fellow of the Hong Kong College of Physicians and Hong Kong Academy of Medicine. This is his second book, the first being 'Ruttonjeee Sanatorium Life and Times', published in 1996.

Dedication

This book is dedicated to Peter John Humphries who in his 9th decade continues to lecture as an authority to fascinated audiences on a wide variety of subjects which include the history of medicine and the silk road.

Contents

	PAGE
Dedication	iii
Maps And Illustrations	v
Tables	vii
Acknowledgements	viii
Introduction	1
Forward The Courtney Journals	21
Journal Chapter Contents	22
Chapter 1 Canton	25
Chapter 2 Hong Kong	44
Chapter 3 Macao	47
Chapter 4 Swatow	48
Chapter 5 Amoy	50
Chapter 6 Fuchau	52
Chapter 7 Ningpo	54
Chapter 8 Chusan	56
Chapter 9 Shanghai	59
Chapter 10 Pekin	65
Chapter 11 Nagasaki	70
Chapter 12 Yedo	72
Chapter 13 Hakodadi	76
Chapter 14 An essay on the important diseases of China	84
Chapter 15 An essay on Chinese medical literature	110
Chapter 16 Translation of the Chinese anatomical maps	144
Chapter 17 An essay on the small feet of Chinese women	151
Chapter 18 An essay on opium smoking	154
Notes	166
Bibliography	176
Appendix 1	178
Details of Service Record Charles FA Courtney	
Appendix 2	180
Surgeon's account of the battle of Camperdown 1797 by Robert Young, Surgeon	
Appendix 3	182
Diseases on board HMS Highflyer	
Appendix 4	184
List of killed and wounded belonging to HMS Highflyer during the Peiho River Conflict	
Appendix 5	185
Clinical details and post-mortem findings of two patients who died of typhus fever	
Appendix 6	191
Clinical details and post-mortem findings of dysentery	

Maps

1. Voyages of HMS Highflyer 1857 – 1859
2. Tracking of a typhoon by HMS Pique during September 1857

Illustrations

1. Front page of the Courtney Journal
2. Detail of the Courtney Journal from Chapter 15, An essay on Chinese medical literature, which describes the history of smallpox vaccination in China
3. Surgeon's operating room on board HMS Vixen. Watercolour by Edward Cree, M Levien, The Cree Journals, 1981
4. Watercolour that shows improvement in '*Retinitis syphilitica*' following treatment. From the Journal of Surgeon Pierce Mansfield of HMS Racoon, 1868, The National Archives, London
5. Model of HMS Highflyer, the Science Museum, London
6. HMS Highflyer in action at Soujak Kaleh, Circassian coast of the Black Sea, 1855, the National Maritime Museum, London
7. Silk picture of HMS Highflyer made by crew member
8. Mandarin's boat at Hong Kong, 1843. Watercolour by Edward Cree, M Levien, The Cree Journals, 1981
9. Page from the Journal of Henry Walsh Mahon showing the effects of scurvy aboard HM Convict Ship Barrosa 1841, The National Archives, London
10. Picture of Dr Thomas Lind, Wellcome Library, London
11. The house of Sir Patrick Manson in Amoy [Xiamen], Wellcome Library, London
12. Manson's experiment with filariasis, Wellcome Library, London
13. River pagoda on the Pearl River near Canton, 1830's
14. Sampans on the Pearl River near Canton, 1830's
15. The fish market, Canton, Lithograph, Commodore Matthew Perry's 'Narrative of an expedition of an American Squadron to the China Seas and Japan', Washington, 1856
16. Foreign factories at Canton, 1850's, China National Maritime Museum
17. HMS Plover lying at anchor in Hong Kong in early 1859. The vessel was later sunk in the Peiho River campaign in June 1859
18. Praya Grande, Macao Bay, showing Portuguese Forts and St Francis Church c. 1830, George Chinnery
19. Chinese coastal craft 1830's, China National Maritime Museum
20. Hutung Fort and Beacon on the East China coast. Painting by Capt P Cracroft of HMS Niger, The National Archives, London
21. Stern of Fuchau pole junk. Painting by Ivon A Donelly, Chinese Junks and other native craft, 1924

22. Ningpo trading vessel. Painting by Ivon A Donelly, Chinese Junks and other native craft, 1924
23. Chusan archipelago fishing craft. Painting by Ivon A Donelly, Chinese Junks and other native craft, 1924
24. The Shanghai tea gardens, 1844. Watercolour by Edward Cree, M Levien, The Cree Journals, 1981
25. Near the north gate of Shanghai, 1844. Watercolour by Edward Cree, M Levien, The Cree Journals, 1981
26. The Customs House Shanghai. From the Standard Atlas and Gazetteer of the World. Standard Publishing Co. Chicago, 1888
27. Battle of the Peiho River 1859
28. Chinese fort on the east shore of the Peiho River 1859, Tang Gu Museum of History
29. Remains of the Taku Forts, Tang Gu, near Tianjin 2010
30. Map of Deshima Island
31. Map of Yedo (Tokyo) found in the Courtney Journal, 1850's
32. Painting of an unnamed American ship from Commander Perry's fleet in Japanese waters, Tokyo National Museum, 1850's.
33. Shimyoji Temple, Hakodate. The temple was the site of the first British Consulate in Hakodate which was visited by Courtney in 1859
34. Hand drawn map of excursions on the Hakodate peninsula by Mr and Mrs Hodgson, 1860, The National Archives, London
35. Statue of Commander Matthew Perry, Hakodate
36. Japanese painting of Chinese trading junk in Japanese waters, 1850's
37. A young Chinese patient with smallpox, (date unknown)
38. Thorny Elaeagnus (*Elaeagnus pungens*) as illustrated in the *Ben cao gang mu* by Li Shi Zhen, Wellcome Library, London
39. Effects of *Ma huang* to enhance the flow of blood and qi, Ming dynasty, Wellcome Library, London.
40. Woodcut from *Shenti sancai tuhui* by Wang Siyi, Ming dynasty, Wellcome Library, London
41. Illustration from William Harvey's *Exercitatio Anatomica de Motu Cordis et Sanguinins in Animalibus*, 1628
42. Zang Fu Ming Tang Tu. Explanatory map of the contents of the human body
43. Ce Ren Ming Tang Tu. Side view map of the human body
44. Zheng Ren Ming Tang Tu. Front view map of the human body
45. Fu Ren Ming Tang Tu. Back view map of the human body
46. First ever photograph of the result of foot binding [left] from John Thomson 1865 - 1868, Wellcome Library, London
47. Result of foot binding, Hong Kong, 1980's [Editor's collection]
48. Opium warehouse, Patna, India, Wellcome Library, London
49. Engraving of an opium den by Thomas Allom, 1843 - 1847

Tables

Table 1 List of casualties of the Marine and Naval Brigades of the 59th Regiment and the 38th Madras Native Infantry.
Table 2 Monthly statement of prevalent diseases in the Provisional Battalion from the 1st of January to the 30th of September 1858 at Canton.
Table 3 Census of Hong Kong 1859
Table 4 Medical statistics at Amoy 1858
Table 5 Medical statistics, Hospital at Ningpo 1852
Table 6 Medical statistics, Missionary Hospital Shanghai 1853 and 1856
Table 7 Summary of sailing activity of HMS Highflyer
Table 8 List of deaths on board HMS Highflyer during 1857 - 1859
Table 9 State of health of the Provisional Battalion of Marines 25th January 1858
Table 10 State of health of the Provisional Battalion of Marines 25th August 1858

Acknowledgements

This is a book of two journeys. The journey of Naval Surgeon Charles Courtney sailing Chinese waters and visiting Chinese cities in the nineteenth century and my own personal journey to bring his unique record to light. Our peripatetic surgeon tells his own story in subsequent pages, here I would like to share thoughts on my own journey and acknowledge the friends and experts who have helped me on this quest. The original journal was discovered by chance when following a reference to Chinese anatomical maps in The National Archives, London, some years ago. The box was brought from the bowels of the archive and on opening it I was surprised to find a substantial leather bound journal, written by Naval Surgeon Charles Courtney in longhand between 1857 and 1859. As is often the case with medical folk, the handwriting was a challenge to decipher and transcribing the original into type was a task that took a dedicated part-time team about a year to accomplish. Some words that seemed impossible to fathom or appeared to be spelling mistakes often turned out to be real words, such as sordes, greywacke, stinkpot, cyanche.

I then found myself in libraries and archives in London, Shanghai and Hong Kong trying to verify the records. It seemed initially a lonely task but I learned quickly that I was far from alone. There are thousands of fellow amateur researchers and scribblers examining obscure events, forgotten technologies, ancient documents and maps and most importantly of all, researching about people.

I was humbled by the generosity of fellow researchers and academics to share their insights and sources, whether in the coffee shops of archives or libraries or formally through societies and institutions [The National Archives, Royal Asiatic Society, Royal Geographical Society, Shanghai Library, Medical Library of Fudan University, Wellcome Library, National Maritime Museum, National Naval Historical Society]. Letters and emails that were fired off to senior academics were always greeted with courteous and helpful replies, from London, Boston, Cambridge, Baltimore and Melbourne. The realization dawned that I was part of a family and in common with all families there are unspoken rules and codes. The golden rule is to reply with as courteous and helpful response as you are able. And as many initially helped me, I was later able to direct others to archives or texts. What could be more joyful?

There are many I would like to thank who have joined me on this fascinating journey. I am grateful to Sir Christopher Hum [Former Master] and Anne Lyon [Development Director] of Gonville and Caius College, Cambridge, for their great enthusiasm and for introducing me to experts in the field. Professor Raphael Chan, Chairman of Microbiology at the Chinese University of Hong Kong provided valuable comments and Professor Christopher Cullen, Director of the Needham Institute, Cambridge, helped frame the historical context of the journal related to our current understanding of Traditional Chinese Medicine and guided me to the value that the journal brings as a historical and environmental reference.

Professor Lin Hongsheng, Oncology Department, Guang'anmen Hospital, China Academy of Chinese Medical Sciences, Beijing, Dr Zhao Yan and Dr Tu Yingmei provided invaluable expertise on the technical aspects of Traditional Chinese Medicine and also insights into the history of the first interest of Westerners in Chinese medicine. Professor Lin helped resolve the traditional issue of managing Chinese names and characters according to the different linguistic systems and we agreed a pragmatic solution. Courtney's text and place names [eg. Pekin, Hakodadi] have been transcribed as he penned them. However extensive work has been performed in Chapter 15, Essay on Chinese medical literature, to convert the Chinese characters to modern pinyin. The original Chinese anatomical maps discovered in the Courtney journal are not of sufficient quality to reproduce hence identical maps have been substituted by Professor Lin.

The staff of The National Archives, London were unfailingly helpful and polite, particularly Hugh Alexander who provided invaluable support based on his encyclopedic knowledge of ancient maps. Dr Lorraine Sterry of La Trobe University, Melbourne, solved a more than hundred year old mystery as to the identity of Mr Pemberton Hodgson's wife [Marie De Lahitte] who wrote fascinating letters about her time in Japan in the 1850's and 1860's.

I am especially grateful to Dr Lindsay Shen, Honorary Editor of the Journal of the Royal Asiatic Society in Shanghai for her boundless enthusiasm and for introducing me to the treasures of the Xujiahui Library. Professor Ian Gow, Dean of the Sino-British College Shanghai, opened my eyes to a multitude of excellent resources. Many friends and colleagues contributed specific advice or encouragement and I should like to thank John Jones, Alison Tan, Ma Ning, Liu Jie, Lilly Li, Robert Nield, William Stockley, Peter Calafiura, Professor Cecilia Chan and a special thanks to the team at Corporate Press (HK) Limited, especially Stanley Lin, Josephine Kor and Ken Ho.

Finally I should like to thank my father, Peter Humphries, for his unfailing support and enthusiasm and for transcribing a number of the chapters. This book is dedicated to him.

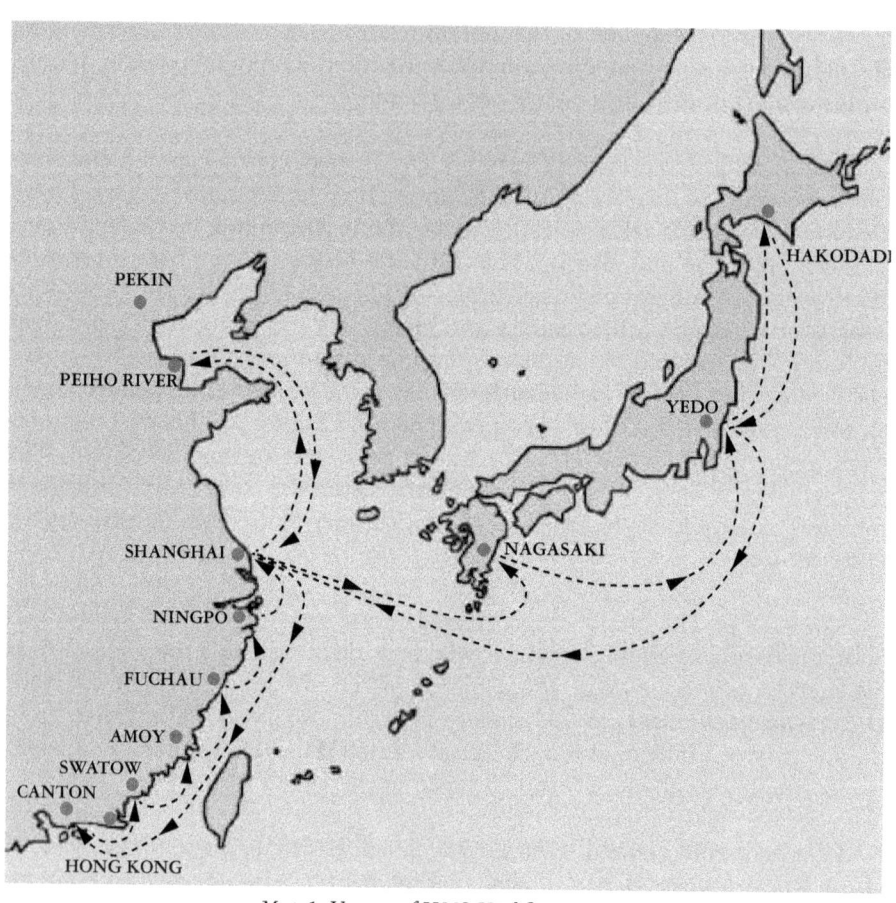

Map 1. Voyages of HMS Highflyer 1857-1859

Port of Call (Precise dates could not be obtained for all voyages)		
Canton*	November, December	1857
Hong Kong*	January, February, Depart 10th March	1858
Swatow, Amoy, Fuchau, Ningpo	11th March – 29th March	1858
Moored Ningpo	29th March – 14th April	1858
Shanghai**+	Arrived 17th April	1858
	Departed 18th June	1859
Peiho River	21st June – 5th July	1859
Shanghai	28th July – 17th August	1859
Nagasaki	12th – 16th September	1859
Yedo	21st – 27th September	1859
Hakodadi	6th – 15th October	1859
Yedo	20th October – 12th November	1859
Shanghai	25th November – 1st December	1859
Hong Kong***	6th – 15th December	1859

* A number of voyages between Canton and Hong Kong during these months
** A number of Yangtze River voyages during this period
*** HMS Highflyer departs for England
+ Courtney joins HMS Highflyer in December 1858

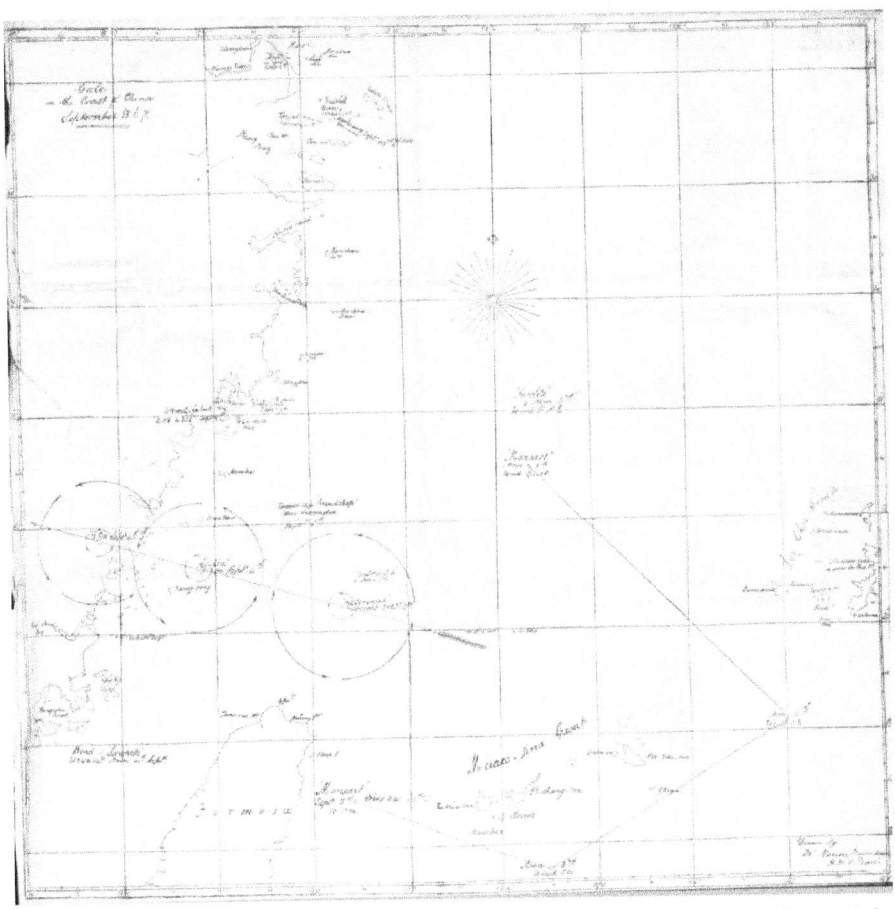

Map 2. Tracking of a typhoon by HMS Pique during September 1857. From 'On cyclones and the law of storms' by Sir F W Nicholson, Captain of HMS Pique. Journal of the Shanghai Literary and Scientific Society, No.1, Pages 17-43 June 1858. (Subsequently the North China Branch of the Royal Asiatic Society). Shanghai Library, Xujiahui.

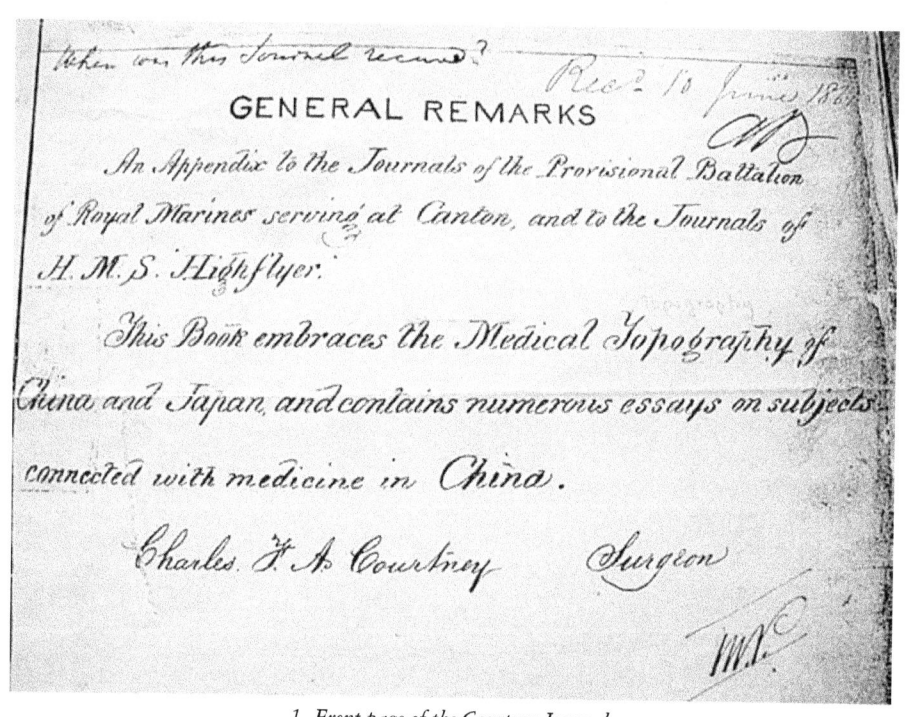

1. Front page of the Courtney Journal

2. Detail of the Courtney Journal from Chapter 15, An essay on Chinese medical literature, which describes the history of smallpox vaccination in China

INTRODUCTION

This is the journal of Royal Naval Surgeon, Charles Courtney who served in the China Squadron in the mid-nineteenth century and is a unique and hitherto unpublished account of his travels and observations in a rapidly changing era in Chinese history. In a brief three year period from 1857 to 1859, he witnessed military campaigns in Canton and the Peiho River and was required to manage dreadful injuries as well as a wide variety of illnesses, many of the more 'tropical' ones would initially be unfamiliar to him. He kept a meticulously written journal that describes in detail the topography, people and customs in China and also the medical conditions that he witnessed, finding time to write down his observations and essays despite onerous medical duties.

He wrote essays on opium smoking, foot binding and diseases particular to China. Quite unique is an essay on Chinese medical literature being one of the few reports by a westerner to catalogue the contributions of Chinese medicine to our overall understanding of the medical sciences. On some subjects he predates eminent twentieth century China scholars who wrote exhaustively on Chinese medical literature from primary sources.

The original journal is in the form of a leather bound book written in longhand that documents visits to ports along the China coast from Canton to Shanghai and also records a short visit to Japan. The journal was discovered by chance in The National Archives, London [1]. Subsequently the service records of Courtney were found in The National Archives after a search. [Appendix 1]. The journal is an eyewitness account of significant historical events including the Canton campaign of 1857 during the Second Opium War and of the failed assault in 1859 on the Taku forts which guard the mouth of the Peiho River.

There has been a requirement for centuries that the captain of a naval ship would keep an official log and for the surgeon to keep a journal, mostly to document the sick list but also to keep detailed observations of the weather. Surgeons' journals often contain colourful accounts of their observations both medical and of a general nature. A number of journals for medical officers in the Royal Navy are on record [1] many of which contain invaluable medical records and observations of the countries and environments in which they found themselves. Looking through accounts from various surgeons' journals, there are such diverse topics addressed as outbreaks of diarrhoea from drinking tainted water [in the Pearl River in Canton and also the Lewisham River in London], essays on syphilis 'pox' and gonorrhoea 'gleet' [both rife at the time], illness through badly salted meat, and the beneficial effects of dancing on sailors health. Infectious diseases such as malaria, typhus, leprosy, smallpox, yellow fever and many outbreaks of diarrhoea are described in detail including at attempt at diarrhoea prevention by ensuring all water on board ship was boiled. There are records of sailors being struck by lightning and tales of tarantula, shark and snake bites with serious and sometimes fatal outcomes.

Scurvy also was the subject of much attention as this malady was a particular menace. The usual ship-board diet consisted of biscuits and dried 'bully' beef, everything else [especially vegetables] rotted within days or weeks. A debate is recorded as to whether French cabbage as opposed to potatoes could prevent scurvy and the effectiveness of preserved vegetables to prevent the illness is also discussed. There were attempts to cure scurvy by burying patients up the neck in earth that was brought on board ship. There are also accounts of the stress and insanity caused by prolonged periods at sea including one record of a sailor who, in a desperate state, swallowed 14 knives. Accidents were common [falls from aloft, snagging by ropes and chains, crush injuries from barrels and cannon] and there were gun fights, mutinies, shipwrecks and numerous accounts of conflicts between captain and naval surgeon [on one occasion leading to a duel at the Royal Hospital at Martinique]. Rum and other forms of alcohol could prove troublesome as Naval Surgeon William Warner remarked "Drunkenness nowadays in the Royal Navy kills more men than the sword, I am sure of it". In one diary there is a private letter 'of an erotic nature, mainly about women who may be waiting to greet the officer on his anticipated retirement'.

The duties of a naval surgeon have traditionally been onerous. The ship's surgeon was not only expected to care for the health and welfare of the ship's crew but was also expected to keep detailed meteorological records. The surgeon was required to posses many skills and become adept at managing fevers, diarrhoea, sunstroke and infectious diseases. The work was often difficult and on occasions was undertaken in a battle environment which obviously could be rather dangerous. The surgeon's cockpit was usually situated below deck against the bulwark and was cramped, poorly lit, humid and with fetid air coming from the bilges. The surgeon often had to work under tremendous pressure, usually without an assistant and sometimes in a rolling sea or in a gale. Fires on board ship or accidents on the gun deck could produce horrific injuries and burns. During battle the surgeon had to operate quickly [usually without anaesthetic except for copious amounts of rum and a 'bit' between the patient's teeth]. He had to cope quickly with a deluge of casualties to minimize blood loss and save lives. Amputations of limbs shattered by gunshot were common; sometimes limbs were blown away by cannon shot altogether. The surgical and post-operative mortality was high. All this life saving work had to proceed despite the noise, confusion, smoke and smell of battle while avoiding cannon balls which could wreck havoc. The danger was not just the cannon shot but also flying wooden splinters which caused deep and horrific injuries due to their high speed and jagged edges. There are graphic details of battle recorded in a number of surgeons' journals. One account [2] describes 'fourteen or fifteen wretches tumbled down [into the

Introduction

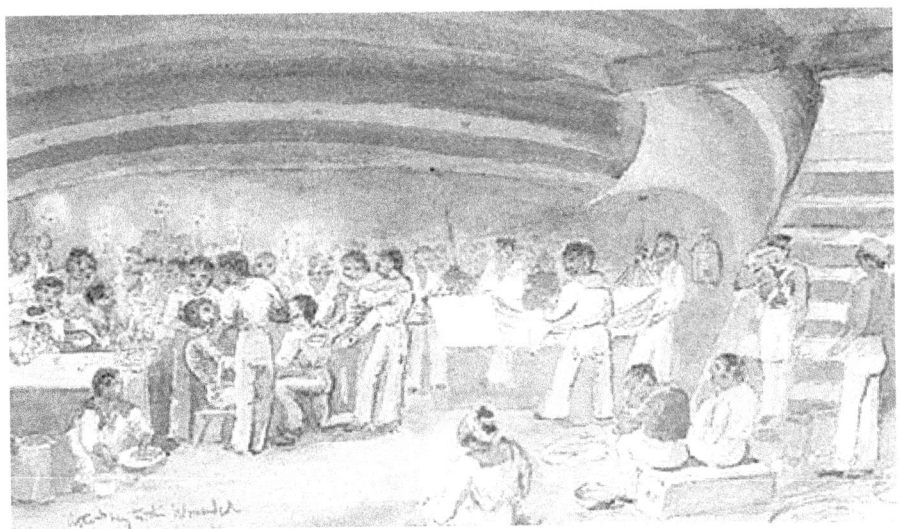

3. Surgeon's operating room on board HMS Vixen.
Watercolour by Edward Cree, M Levien, The Cree Journals, 1981

surgeon's cockpit] their faces as black as cinder, their clothes blown to tatters and their legs on fire'. [Appendix 2].

By the turn of the 19th century the position of naval surgeon was one of respect and competition for positions was keen. The surgeon was expected to be competent in many fields including general medicine, infectious diseases, surgery, pathology, dentistry and even midwifery. The position was seen as highly important as a crew in robust health was a critical success factor in naval operations while a sick crew would be practically useless. In many campaigns, disease claimed more lives than battle. The recommended training for a surgeon was significant, spanning 7 years which consisted of Anatomy (18 months), Surgery (18 months), Theory of Medicine (12 months), Practice of Medicine (12 months), Chemistry (6 months), Materia Medica (6 months), Midwifery (6 months), and Dissections of the human body (6 months) [3]. By 1814 there were 14 physicians, 850 surgeons and 500 assistant surgeons to care for 130,000 men on shore or at sea.

The pay however was modest. The base salary was five pounds per month and an additional five pounds for every hundred of cases of venereal diseases treated, usually gonorrhoea 'gleet' or syphilis 'pox'. Syphilis was treated with mercury powder hence the naval expression, 'one night with Venus then six weeks with Mercury'. On board ship each surgeon was equipped with a chest of surgical instruments [for which there was an allowance of 43 pounds] and although there was a six month training period in materia medica, the remedies available on board were relatively limited. Much use was made of ipecac, opium, turpentine, Dover's Powder and the 'Blue Pill'.

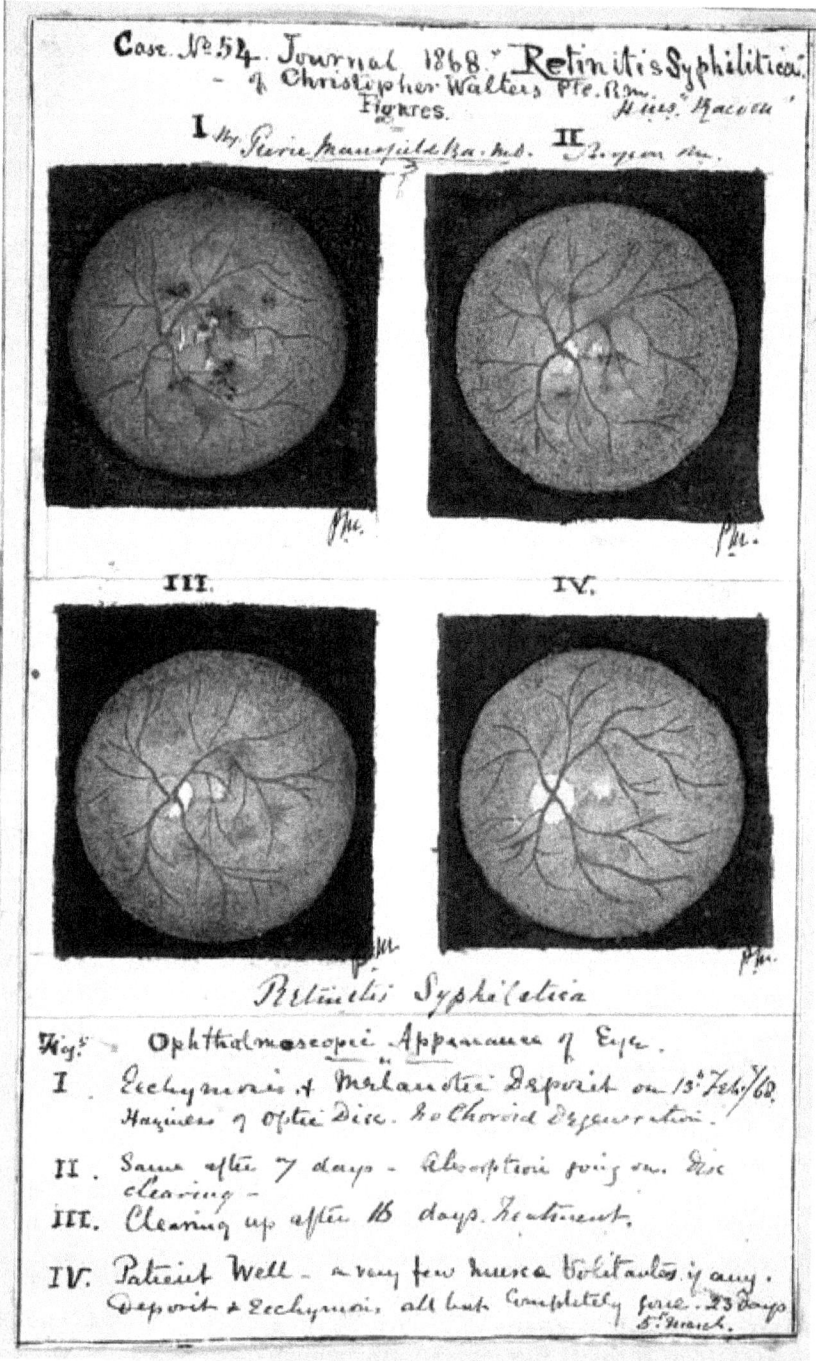

4. Watercolour that shows improvement in 'Retinitis syphilitica' following treatment.
From the Journal of Surgeon Pierce Mansfield of HMS Racoon, 1868,
The National Archives, London

Introduction

The techniques of blood letting, enemas and cold water hydrotherapy were commonly deployed. In general the treatments can be classified into emetics, antispasmodics, cathartics and narcotics.

Courtney had a fairly typical training and induction for a naval surgeon. He was the son of Abraham Courtney, (also a naval surgeon and enthusiastic proponent of hydrotherapy) [4] who recommended his son to the Royal Navy. Courtney graduated with the Diploma in Medicine, was confirmed as Assistant Naval Surgeon in July 1847 and became a Member of the Royal College of Surgeons of England [MRCS] and also a Licentiate of the Society of Apothecaries of London [LSA] in December the same year. Subsequently he passed the London Certificate of Medicine in April 1852 and was confirmed as Surgeon (of officer rank) in May 1852. On 6th November 1861 in Ireland he married Charlotte Gabbett who was the sixth of seven children of Joseph Gabbett and Anne Marshall. They had at least one child, a son, who also followed the family tradition and became a naval surgeon. Little else is known of Courtney's private or family life.

From September 1849 onwards Courtney served on a number of naval vessels before joining the Provisional Battalion of Marines, spending most of 1857 and 1858 in Canton. He was appointed as Surgeon to HMS Highflyer in October 1858 and joined the vessel probably in Shanghai in December of that year. The Highflyer was a wooden corvette that could be powered by a coal-fired steam engine or sail and was launched on 13th August 1851 at the C J Mare shipyard in Blackwall, London. She was an unusual ship, being one of the first with a propeller that could be lifted out of the water when the ship was under sail. The addition of a steam engine was a significant advantage, allowing the vessel to navigate deep into rivers where winds are often fickle and sailing difficult. The vessel was 192 feet long, displaced 1902 tons and

5. Model of HMS Highflyer, the Science Museum, London

6. HMS Highflyer in action at Soujak Kaleh, Circassian coast of the Black Sea, 1855, the National Maritime Museum, London

7. Silk picture of HMS Highflyer, made by a crew member

carried 21 guns. In 1852 and 1853 she saw service in North American waters and the East Indies and subsequently saw action in the Black Sea during the Russian war, engaging shore batteries at Soujak Kaleh in March 1855. In June 1857 under the command of Admiral Shadwell, HMS Highflyer took part in the second opium war and was involved in the battle of Fatshan Creek and subsequently in the assault on Canton in December 1857.

Throughout his naval career, there were high recommendations about Courtney's ability and conduct. "Mr Geiger, Surgeon of the HMS Encounter, spoke highly of Mr Courtney's general conduct and ability", "Mr Dalton, Surgeon of the HMS Sidow, stated that Mr Courtney served most diligently in his attendance to the sick both day and night during the situation of cholera on board", "Captain Shadwell certified very favorably of him" [Courtney attended to Shadwell when he was wounded during the Peiho River campaign of 1859]. Clearly the records indicate he was highly thought of as a capable and hard working surgeon.

Following service in Chinese coastal waters he served for ten more years from 1860-1870 at sea until he took a position at the Naval Hospital Haslar, the largest and most important shore hospital in the navy, situated at Portsmouth on the southwest coast of England. It is noted in his service record that he was admitted to hospital on 6th July 1871 "with a poisoned wound of the right thumb from the discharge of a scalp of a patient that he was dressing five days earlier. The hand and forearm were seen to be much inflamed". He died on 16th July 1871 from blood poisoning arising from the thumb wound. A note in his service records states "Their Lordships [of the Navy] expressed the melancholy of the intelligence of this officer's death". [5].

Courtney was required to keep records of the sick and wounded as part of his duties and detailed statistics are appended to the journal [Appendix 3]. However the journal of Courtney differs from many others as it captures not only an eyewitness account of historical events in China but also provides detailed accounts of the medical environment at the time in addition to containing unique and interesting essays.

Although for 1857-1859 most of the time the Highflyer was in the coastal waters of China, there was one voyage of just over three months from September to December 1859 to visit the Japanese ports of Yedo (Tokyo), Nagasaki and Hakodadi (Hakodate). This was just five years after Commodore Matthew Perry of the US Navy visited a number of ports with a squadron of warships to demand the opening of Japan to foreign trade. Following the Treaty of Kanagawa in 1854, a number of foreign consulates were established and Courtney's account of the installation of the first ever British Consul, Mr Hodgson, to Hakodate is an event of some historical interest. [6]. His account of Japan has detailed descriptions of housing, dress and habits of the inhabitants and the elaborate procedures to contain fires, an ever present danger given that almost the entire town was built of wood. The account of the landing at Hakodate, complete with honour guard and Marine band all decked in full regalia, is told with humour. At the outset none of the local officials agreed to meet the landing party at the dock and it took them some time to locate the meeting place.

The subsequent meetings with Japanese officials are told in detail with a keen eye for cultural nuance. As there was no suitable accommodation for the Consul, Mr Hodgson and family stayed in rooms at the Shomyoji Temple until the consulate building was completed in 1863. Hodgson and his wife Marie wrote a highly enlightening and often amusing book about their observations and travels while in Japan [Ch 13, 1]. The British Consulates in Hakodate have an unfortunate history. The first building was severely damaged by fire in 1865 after two years service and was then burned down almost completely in 1907. The structure was rebuilt in 1913 and was closed in 1934. It was restored as a Cultural Property in 1979 and is now a museum complete with tearooms where English afternoon tea is served on fine porcelain, overseen by a life-size model of a Scots piper replete with bag pipes, kilt and sporran!

Courtney was part of two major military actions, the occupation of Canton during the Second Opium War and also the assault on the Peiho River forts near the modern day Tianjin. In Canton Courtney described vividly the circumstances under which the campaign was fought, the dangers of sun stroke, excessive humidity, disease and battle injuries. Courtney made light of the risks of being in a battle zone and almost in passing recounts the sad fate of an unfortunate Midshipman who was killed "by being struck in the stomach by a rocket while at breakfast".

The Peiho River campaign of 25th June 1859 was an unsuccessful attempt by Rear Admiral James Hope to destroy the Taku Forts at the mouth on the Peiho River and force a passage up the river to secure an entry route to Tianjin. [7]. The attack started at 2pm and the defenders' guns responded with 'murderous accuracy'. Two ships were sunk and three others grounded. Troops landed from small boats onto the shallow estuary shoreline but were at a grave disadvantage as they were completely exposed to gunfire and quickly became bogged down in thick mud. Casualties were heavy and the decision was made to retreat to the ships. A number of the small boats with the survivors of the land attack were towed off the mud below the forts by sailors of the United States Navy, though technically neutral, who were present to support the English and French attack. The attack force withdrew the next day with the loss of 89 lives and 345 wounded. On the HMS Highflyer there were 9 killed and 17 others with significant injuries [Appendix 4]. There is a well documented account of Courtney treating the fracture caused by a bullet to the foot of Admiral Shadwell who was in command of the Highflyer. Courtney received significant praise for

Introduction

the surgery but Shadwell was left with a permanent limp. Courtney witnessed the action and tended to the casualties on the Highflyer however his journal account of this period is relatively brief, presumably because he was fully occupied dealing with the injured both during and also after the campaign when the fleet retreated in defeat. The fleet returned to Shanghai where all the wounded were transferred to one ship which proceeded directly to Hong Kong for medical treatment in the Royal Naval Hospital.

In was in Canton where Courtney penned his most detailed accounts of the medical environment. He documented the illnesses prevalent at that time with pertinent observations on the ravages of malaria, typhus, dysentery, sun stroke and many other potentially fatal maladies. There is a detailed account of the natural history of typhus, together with post-mortem findings, and a detailed clinical description of what was almost certainly meningococcal meningitis, a disease which is almost universally fatal if untreated with antibiotics, clearly not available at the time.

The medical environment in South China where Courtney was working had already been well recognized more than ten years earlier in Admiralty records from Hong Kong. An example from early records is as follows: "Sickness had already begun to prevail among our troops before they had reached Hong Kong. The eight days exposure that they had endured on the heights of Canton sowed the seeds of ague and dysentery which proved far more formidable enemies than any troops the Chinese could bring against us. The sickness spread among the men with alarming rapidity, so that at length, out of our small force, no less than 1100 men were upon the sick list at Hong Kong. Part of this alarming state of things must be attributed certainly to the pernicious influence of the atmosphere of Hong Kong itself at that time of year. But every allowance must be made for the exposure which the men had undergone at Canton and for the susceptibility and constitution produced by long confinement aboard ship. The germs of disease were planted in their bodies before the men returned to the harbour of Hong Kong, and therefore an undue stress was laid upon the unhealthiness of Hong Kong itself" [8].

In April 1841 the first ever Naval Court of Enquiry was held in Hong Kong to investigate the high death rates in seamen. Seamen were encouraged to spend most of their time onboard ship to avoid breathing the 'unhealthy air' and remained healthier if they did so. At the time this beneficial effect was attributed to the better circulation of air at anchor, however the surgeons were unaware that the likely reason to explain better health afloat is that the ships were probably outside the flying range of the Anopheles mosquito.

In the early 1840's the mortality from fever in Hong Kong was truly significant and earned the moniker 'Hong Kong Fever' [9]. In 1843 when fever killed 24% of the troops and 10% of all European civilians between May and October, the entire garrison was given orders to move out of barracks and onto the ships. General d'Aquilar, the first Commander of the British Forces remarked on the state of health of his troops 'To have 700 effective men in Hong Kong, it is necessary to maintain 1400". Other accounts recorded that "Deaths now [1841] became a frequent occurrence also among the European community and the first cemetery began to fill" and "Hong Kong proved a costly acquisition as in spite of good barracks and hospital the men continued to fall sick and die". The Illustrated London News had the following account "Its diseases are endemic fever, diarrhoea and dysentery, the graveyard was soon filled and another was required". In the early 1840's a number of naval surgeons perished while on duty on the China coast including John Weir from fever [1840], Henry Tracey and William Cumming from dysentery [1840] and Thomas Wallace who suddenly collapsed and died in 1841. The burial of one sailor in 1841 is illustrated in the diary of Naval Surgeon Edward Cree. [10].

This account has similar themes to those in Courtney's journal, in particular the frequent references to the bad air (mala-aria in Italian), miasmic [11] influence or 'malaria' as so named in the Courtney journal. Miasma refers to bad air, unhealthy vapours or pernicious atmospheres seeping through cracks in the earth seen as possible causes of often lethal fevers. In addition, rotting vegetation, animal matter, lavatories and swamps were postulated as possible sources of lethal fevers. It was also thought that fever was related to seasons, climate, and geographic location and could be driven by wind. This was the prevailing wisdom before the 'germ' theory as the origin of infectious diseases and fevers was later substantiated. At that time the mosquito as the vector for malaria had not been established [this was proven by Ronald Ross in 1897 who found the malaria parasite in the stomach of the Anopheles mosquito, confirming the earlier hypothesis of Alphonse Laveran who wrote the Treatise on Marsh Fevers in 1884.].

It is certain that most of these deaths in Hong Kong were due to malaria as much of the terrain was swampy at that time, the ideal breeding ground for mosquitoes. There is a long-standing story that the name 'Happy Valley' was so-called because of the delirium caused by fever in those who visited there. Also known at the time as the 'Vale of Death', Happy Valley was particularly unhealthy as being situated at the foot of ravines was difficult to drain. The risks for those wishing to live there were particularly serious "Last season five English gentlemen went to reside there; in a short time four of the number died from fever, the fifth scarcely escaped with his life, and the lodging, not without reason, has been abandoned". [12].

The theory that the fevers were due to rotting vegetation was elegantly proven to be a myth by Courtney. He spent some time in Canton observing the cycle of paddy planting and harvesting and documenting the incidence of fevers. There was no relationship between the incidence of fever and the amount of rotting vegetation lying on the fields. Moreover he noted that better drainage of paddy fields may be of benefit and indeed in Hong Kong most of the low lying swampy areas were subsequently drained, filled in or built over with a significant improvement in public health.

The situation in Hong Kong was very similar to the medical environment that Courtney found himself in Canton in 1857. Although he saw many cases of intermittent fever [almost certainly mostly malaria], typhus [13] and typhoid [14] he was particularly interested in a pernicious form of typhus which was prevalent and often fatal. Typhus, in common with malaria, was thought to be associated with unhealthy air although Courtney observed the close association of typhus with overcrowding and poor hygiene. For example, he noted that the disease was much more common in policemen who lived in the most densely populated parts of Canton.

It was some 50 years later that Howard Ricketts and Stanislaus Von Prowazek, two physicians, identified the body louse as the typhus vector, which would explain Courtney's and others' observations of the disease being closely associated with poor hygiene, infrequent changing and washing of clothes, close proximity to rats and overcrowding. New recruits, many pressed into service following release from prison [hence the other name for typhus – gaol fever], often arrived at the docks in rags and these clothes were often removed and burned and the recruits de-loused and re-clothed before boarding ship. Ricketts and Prowazek died from typhus in 1910 and 1915 respectively while studying the disease. Both physicians are immortalized as the offending pathogen is now named *Rickettsia prowazekii* in acknowledgement of their dedicated work to advance understanding of infectious diseases and typhus.

8. *Mandarin's boat at Hong Kong, 1843. Watercolour by Edward Cree,*
M Levien, *The Cree Journals, 1981*

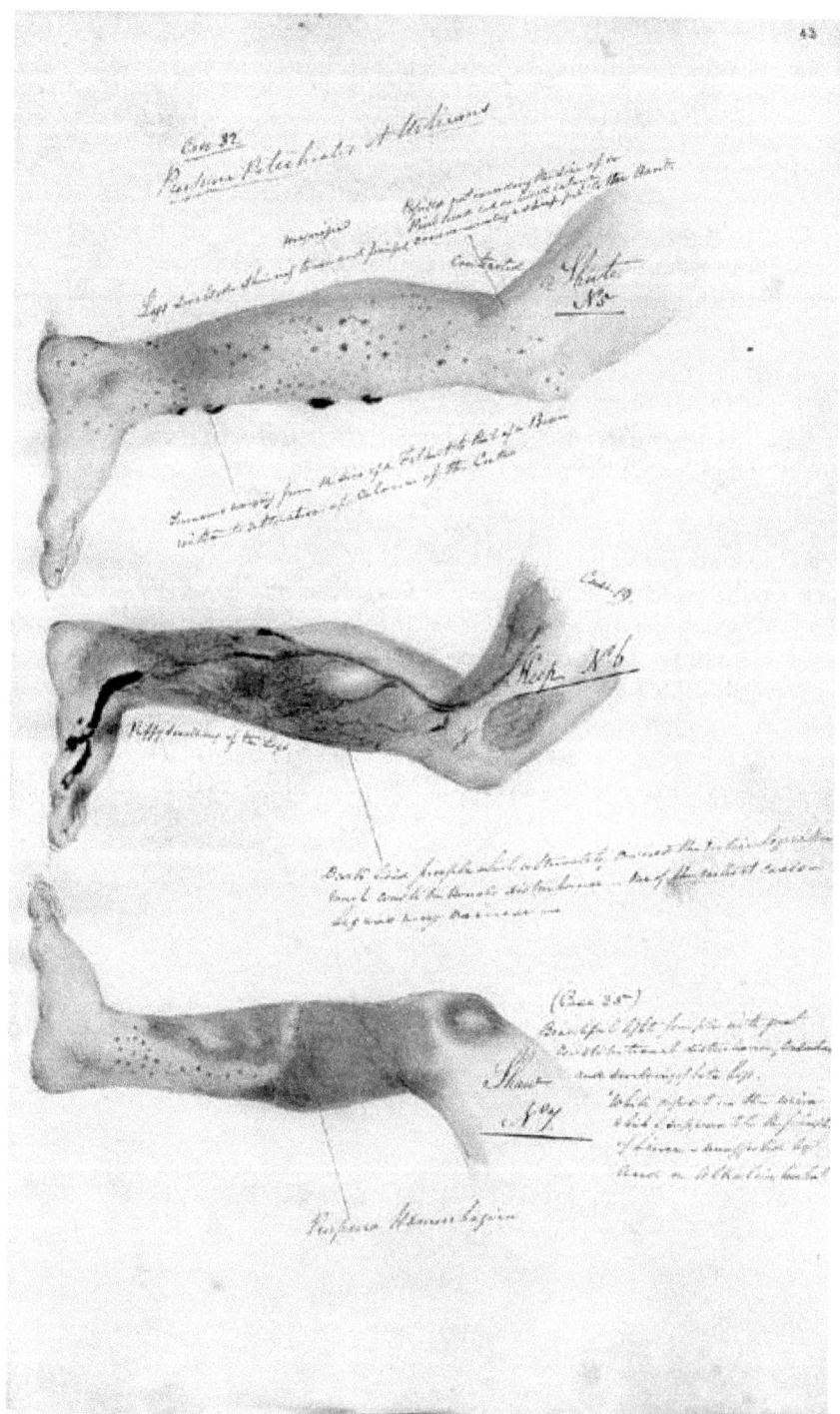

9. *Page from the Journal of Henry Walsh Mahon showing the effects of scurvy aboard HM Convict Ship Barrosa 1841, The National Archives, London*

Introduction

The role of body lice in the transmission of *Borrelia recurrentis*, the organism causing recurrent or relapsing fever, and of *Rickettsia prowazekii*, causing typhus, was not acknowledged by Courtney. It was inevitable that the crews and marines on board ship and ashore would be infested with lice given the long periods at sea or ashore in battle zones with little opportunity for regular hygiene necessary for the eradication of lice.

Courtney's role as naval surgeon included that of pathologist. The detailed post-mortem reports of two patients who died of typhus [Appendix 5] and dysentery [Appendix 6] highlight his skill at the autopsy table. It is clear that Courtney had a broad and significant knowledge in a number of disciplines including medicine, surgery, pathology, epidemiology, medical history and also public health.

Although Courtney spent most of his time on clinical practice, he also conducted a clinical experiment on the effectiveness of quinine to prevent [malaria] fevers. He observed the prevalence of intermittent fevers in the ship's crew for some time then divided them into those that were treated with quinine and others that were untreated.

Probably the earliest account of a controlled clinical trial comes from the early Chinese medical literature when physicians described two subjects, one of whom was given Ginseng and the other was not [the control patient] and then the effect was observed. [15]. Clinical experiments had also previously been conducted on ships, perhaps the most famous being conducted by James Lind in the early 1750's on the treatment of scurvy due to vitamin C deficiency [16]. Lind divided a group of twelve men suffering from scurvy into six pairs, giving each of them different supplements to their routine diet. The two sailors who were given oranges and lemons made a remarkable recovery. The benefits of using limes had already been well known, however this was not the only treatment that was being used. Lind definitively proved the benefits of all citrus fruits above all other supplements however it was some fifty years later, in 1795, before effective scurvy prophylaxis was adopted in the navy. The policy came rather late as years after Lind's experiment and publications, cases of scurvy continued to occur on board and are well documented. Lind also wrote a number of classic essays on hygiene in the tropics and emphasized that fresh air can be protective.

In the experiment conducted by Courtney, [Tables 9 and 10], after a period of observation quinine was given to just one of six cohorts of soldiers, No 2 Company, and one month later a summary of the health of the ships' company was undertaken. From the whole body of men, only those in No 2 Company were completely free of fever. Courtney concludes 'I therefore think myself justified in coming to the conclusion that the daily administration of quinine is a powerful preventive of disease and am of the opinion that its prophylactic power is very great.'

10. Picture of Dr Thomas Lind, Wellcome Library, London

This was an important observation as Courtney used an active treatment and an inactive control cohort of patients and as such conducted a controlled clinical trial. Although Lind had conducted a clinical trial on board ship some time before, the methods of Courtney can be considered ahead of the times. Currently it is standard practice in the evaluation of new medicines to compare active treatment to another active treatment or inactive controls. The observation of the benefits of quinine was not new. 'Peruvian bark' was first known in Europe in about 1630 and it is likely that the indigenous remedy widely used by Andean herbal physicians for centuries and its benefits were observed by Spanish missionaries. In Spain it became known as 'Jesuits powder'. Other naval surgeons had described the benefits of quinine wine in preventing fevers, particularly those ships active in West African waters in the 1840's. Indeed it is clear that quinine was so effective and important as its use enabled naval fleets to achieve many colonial ambitions in tropical climes that would not have been possible. Without quinine many fleets would have been decimated. There are clear descriptions where quinine was found to be more effective than blood letting or mercury compounds as a prophylactic, dating to at least 1841. What is important about Courtney's account is the research methodology and careful documentation of his findings.

In the journal Courtney also wrote a number of essays. One concerns the 'The most important diseases in China', there are also essays on opium smoking and on the bound feet of women [the first photograph to reach the west of the custom of foot binding was probably from John Thomson who traveled in China from 1865 to 1868. [17]. One contribution from Courtney of special interest is 'An essay on Chinese medical literature' where there is a catalogue of Chinese medical texts and his comments concerning the contents, often comparing the Chinese observations to contemporary medical science. A number of these observations stand out.

Smallpox had been a scourge in China for centuries. Courtney quotes from early Chinese references concluding that the Chinese physicians were vaccinating against smallpox for 'hundreds of years before the practice was introduced in Europe'. The history of smallpox vaccination in China has been documented from the primary sources in depth in the authoritative classic written by Joseph Needham. [18] Needham concluded that immunization by nasal inoculation for smallpox was documented around the year 1500 in China and the practice spread to Turkey and then to Europe by 1700, to be superseded by variolation about 1800 [19]. Needham speculates that immunization occurred in China around the year 1000 but was kept a secret by Taoism practitioners and was not recorded until 500 years later. These practices are more than 800 years earlier than vaccination in Europe. The introduction of variolation in Europe was probably by Mary Worley Montague in the mid eighteenth century and it was in the late eighteenth century that widespread vaccination was championed by Edward Jenner.

Another observation by Courtney concerned the circulation of the blood where the work of Liu Cong described the blood passing through the heart commencing in the 'middle region' of the heart, liver, spleen, lungs and kidneys to the extremities of the hands; from the extremities of the hands to the head, from head to the feet and from the feet to the abdomen. Regarding the nature of blood the texts are clear that nutrition is an important element. William Harvey in his classic treatise *Exercitatio Anatomica de Motu Cordis et Sanguinis in Animalibus* [1628] [20] was the first scientist to describe accurately the circulation of the blood throughout the body, the critical function of the heart, the role of the pulmonary arteries and veins and also the distinction between peripheral arteries and veins. Courtney concludes that "It would therefore appear from an impartial consideration of the subject that before the 14th century of the Christian era there was no nation upon earth that could boast of a better knowledge of the blood and its varied uses in the economy than the Chinese for a careful examination of their medical works gives convincing evidence that they have been from the earliest times been acquainted with the fact that the blood was a circulating fluid, that they were aware that the blood starting as it were from a given point , made the circuit of the body returning to the same point, that they even calculated the time it took to perform this circuit and calculated the relative frequency of the pulse as compared with the respirations. The Chinese have understood the true uses of the blood in the animal anatomy far better than any ancient Greek or Roman writer and that the knowledge of Hippocrates and Galen was very weak and imperfect compared with the knowledge of the Chinese authors".

Whereas Harvey was the first scientist in the world to correctly describe the heart as the centre of circulation, Chinese physicians, although theorizing a different circulatory route, give convincing evidence from earliest times of the awareness that the blood is a circulating fluid. There are early texts, for example the *Hu jing gong miaojue*, of breathing exercises to promote the free circulation of the blood and qi. Chinese physicians appreciated that the blood started from a given point, calculated the time taken to perform a circuit and calculated the relative frequencies of the pulse as compared to the respirations which were major advances ahead of physicians in other continents. However Courtney concluded that it was 'the most revered' Harvey who placed the heart at the centre of the circulation and documented the directional flows with anatomical perfection.

What is also remarkable about Courtney's essay on Chinese medical literature is that there were very few western physicians at that time who took an interest in Chinese medicine. Although the diaries of Courtney are not an exhaustive treatise on Chinese medicine, he produced important insights and an appreciation into the many unique and early achievements of Chinese physicians dating back 2000 years. Courtney freely admits that only about a third of the essay was entirely his own work. The other third he attributes to Dr Alexander Wylie, a missionary doctor and scholar who spent most of his life in China. Wylie, a respected sinologist and prolific writer, penned a significant number of books on diverse aspects of life in China and amassed a considerable library of books written by Chinese scholars and westerners writing about China. Much of Wylie's library is kept today in the Royal Asiatic Society collection in the Shanghai library at Xujiahui and there is another collection of Wylie's books in the Bodlean library, Oxford. Courtney may also have taken some ideas from an earlier essay on 'Chinese system of human anatomy and physiology by Dr W A Harland' [21] and also the books written by Dr Benjamin Hobson [22]. The essay on Chinese medical literature was almost certainly written during the sojourn of HMS Highflyer at Shanghai during 1858/1859.

So what is the contribution of the Courtney journal? Much of the interest of the journal comes from Courtney's acute powers of observation and his enquiring mind. He described very well the vagaries of infectious diseases such as malaria and typhus and through observation debunks the theory that rotting vegetation is a cause of malaria. He showed in a controlled clinical experiment that quinine prevents [malaria] fevers.

Courtney was a meticulous recorder of observations of signs and symptoms of his patients. Together with his training and knowledge he emerges as a remarkably effective clinician. He practiced at a time when medicine was on the threshold of great medical changes brought about by advances in technology. The discovery that many tropical fevers are caused by microorganisms [the germ theory] was only a few years away in the future. However Courtney's clinical descriptions are models of accuracy and his diagnoses were in some senses 'modern' and also remarkably consistent.

He came very close to associating malaria with the presence of mosquitoes, having discarded, through careful observation, the conventional wisdom of miasmas from rotting vegetation as being the cause. If only he had been aware of Giovanni Lancisi's insight which in 1717 led him to assert that 'malaria is caused by the injection of little animals by the bite of a mosquito' he would have made the link at once. He also used quinine as a prophylactic as well as prescribing it for the treatment of 'intermittent' fever. His attention to detail enabled him to distinguish tertian and quotidian [quartan] malaria, caused by different species of *Plasmodium*, referred to as 'intermittent' and 'remittent' fever by Courtney respectively.

At that time most encounters with tropical diseases occurred in the navy hence naval surgeons had considerably more experience than their peers who stayed in Europe. In terms of 'diseases in the tropics' he helped show the way for others to follow while not actually nailing down the root causes of disease. However he did capture the medical environment and made some valuable observations although it seems these were never published. He was one of the generation of naval surgeons who were adept at recognizing and treating tropical diseases and helped to promote the 'germ' theory of infectious diseases yet proof was still some years away to establish germs and vectors in the causality of infectious diseases. Surgeons contributed greatly to the understanding of tropical disease and medical knowledge and helped to establish the specialty of tropical medicine as a separate and important discipline in its own right. The clinical manifestations of many diseases were well documented a long time before the 'germ' theory of disease had been proven. He also recorded that leprosy was viewed by Chinese physicians as contagious which also supported the 'germ' theory of disease.

Courtney was active in treating tropical maladies in China just twenty years before a landmark discovery was made in China in 1877 by Patrick Manson that defined the genesis of tropical medicine as a medical specialty. Manson, by experimenting on a member of his household [a practice that would be unacceptable today], showed that a pathogenic parasite could be transmitted from man to mosquito. Manson conducted his experiment while working in Amoy [Xiamen] for the China Imperial Maritime Customs Service [23]. Manson is rightly known as 'the father of tropical medicine' and his later observations of malaria would pave the way for the elucidation of the malaria life cycle by Ronald Ross for which Ross was awarded the Nobel Prize.

Manson was co-founder of the London School of Hygiene and Tropical Medicine. It is not widely known that he worked in Hong Kong in private practice from 1883 – 1889 and played a major role in the founding of the Hong Kong College of Medicine for Chinese, a predecessor of the University of Hong Kong Faculty of Medicine, the first medical school in the territory. He also played an important role in the founding of The Alice Memorial Hospital 'mainly to serve the Chinese population' and was also involved in many other initiatives to strengthen medical education and infrastructure in Hong Kong.

11. The house of Sir Patrick Manson in Amoy {Xiamen}, Wellcome Library, London

What of the broader role of naval surgeons in tropical climates? While there were many important scientific and medical observations that were carried back to Europe, what was the benefit to the local medical practice in China? Medical missionaries built dispensaries and hospitals to treat the local population, translated western medical texts and were involved in medical education often sharing western medical concepts with local practitioners. By contrast, naval surgeons generally only looked after the ship's company and, like Courtney, did not appear to add major benefit to the local population in terms of offering medical treatment. There are records that during military campaigns Chinese soldiers and civilians were treated by foreign military surgeons and also records of treating the occasional interesting case in the local population, documented for a patient with elephantiasis for example. However this was the exception rather than the rule. The direct contribution to the local medical culture by naval surgeons was probably rather limited. However it was the knowledge and experience that was taken to Europe which paved the way for the establishment of tropical medicine as a specialty that would subsequently yield benefits for patients worldwide. Clearly a number of Western medical practitioners did appreciate the depth of Chinese medical history, literature and materia medica as witnessed by Courtney's detailed essay on the subject.

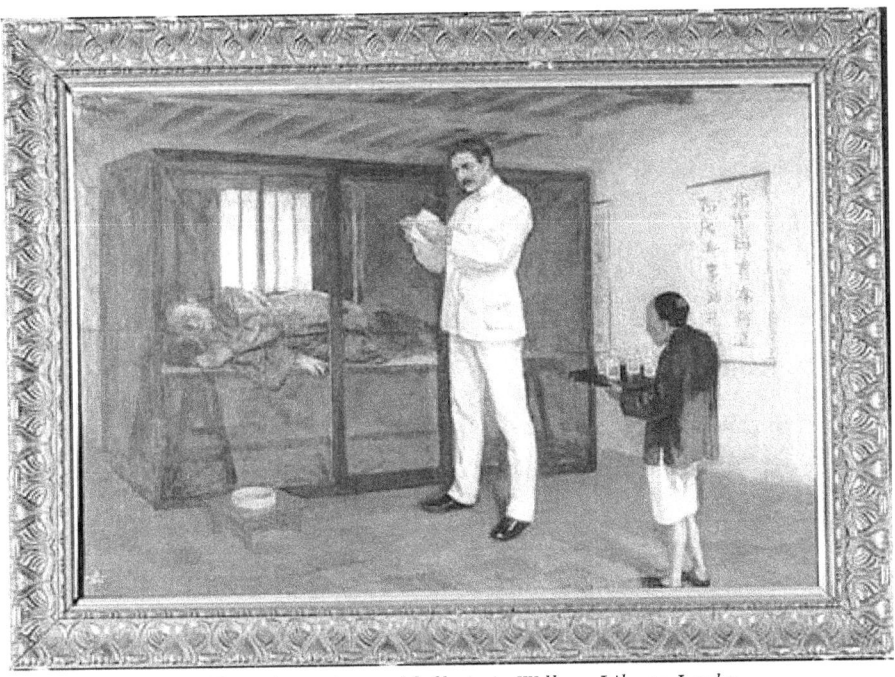

12. Manson's experiment with filariasis, Wellcome Library, London

During the Second Opium War when Courtney was on the China coast, he was in the service of a navy that was defending the opium trade yet there is no record of his conscience being exercised on being involved in a tawdry commercial enterprise that destroyed human life. He never reflected on the justness of naval actions, an issue that had caused angst to other naval surgeons, on rare occasions leading to suicide. There are reports of naval surgeons that worried little about collecting prize money for their actions but worried more about the plight which had befallen China's often helpless inhabitants [24]. If Courtney did experience anxiety in being involved in the opium trade, this was never recorded. Hence in Courtney there is a sense of detachment from the greater issues as he single-mindedly concentrated on his work and writing.

Naval surgeons had other responsibilities. Their non-medical duties included recording sea and ambient temperatures three times a day, describing the state of the sea and weather conditions such as rainfall, wind velocity and position of the vessel. Upon making landfall the surgeon was expected to record the terrain and find sources of fresh water and food. The meticulous meteorological observations recorded by Courtney are not reproduced here however they form a substantial part of Courtney's journal. The meteorological logs of a number of naval surgeon's diaries have now become objects of significant interest to researchers of climate change [25].

What do we know of Courtney the man and what can we deduce of his personality? From his journal and from the reports about him we can surmise that he was a highly dedicated surgeon who took his work very seriously. All of his clinical and post-mortem examinations are recorded in the most meticulous detail. There is very little humour in his writing and practically no mention of social events. Hence the impression is one of a dour and dedicated man who put his work and his patients above all other considerations. Clearly he was a very different personality from other surgeons for example Edward Cree who served in the China seas in the early 1840's. Cree is described as a 'dashing lady's man, dancing and flirting with the prettiest girls from Alexandria to Hong Kong'. [10]. Cree illustrated his journal with many high quality watercolours of China, Hong Kong and the Far East which are regarded as classic historical contributions.

Although probably not an extrovert or a very colourful character, Charles Courtney was clearly an outstanding surgeon and scientist who received unanimous praise from his superiors throughout his service in the Royal Navy. His premature and tragic death from such a mundane injury cut short a career that held much promise of greater things to come. We are fortunate to have his journal, almost intact, as a fitting memorial.

Forward

The Courtney Journals

An Appendix to the Journal of the Provisional Battalion of Royal Marines serving at Canton, and the Journals of HMS Highflyer.

This Book embraces the Medical Topography of China and Japan and contains numerous essays on subjects connected with medicine in China.

During the time that the writer was in China he directed his attention to a very great variety of subjects connected with the country. Taking great interest in China, he laboured hard to acquire as much information as his time and opportunities would allow. Although he did not give his undivided attention to medical subjects he did not forget that as a Medical Officer of Her Majesty's Navy it was his duty to obtain a knowledge of the Medical Topography and course of the seasons of the several ports and countries that he had the opportunity of visiting, as also of the most prevalent diseases and the general method of healing them.

This Book of Remarks contains the principal portion of the medical knowledge that the writer was able to collect concerning China and Japan. Nearly the whole of it is original with the exception of the essay on Chinese medical literature: about one third of that essay is the writer's own composition; about another third is compilation from a variety of sources; and for the remaining third he is indebted to the extreme kindness of his friend Mr Wylie of Shanghai whose profound knowledge of the language and extensive researches in its literature vouch for the accuracy of the information therein contained.

Charles Frederic A Courtney
Surgeon

Journal Chapter Contents

Chapter 1 • Canton
Description of the city and suburbs. Geology. City wall. Character of the buildings. Principal temples. State of education. Charitable institutions.

Chapter 2 • Hong Kong
Geographical position. General description of the island. Geological nature of the soil. Sanitary condition of the island. Striking proof of its insalubrity. Prevalent diseases. Census of 1859.

Chapter 3 • Macao
Geographical position. Description of the town. Hospital for lepers. Diseases. A summer retreat for the merchants of Canton and Hong Kong.

Chapter 4 • Swatow
Geographical position. Description of the town. Origin of the present prosperity of Swatow. Double Island described. Chinese superstitions.

Chapter 5 • Amoy
Geographical position. Description of the island. Geological nature of the soil. Meteorological remarks. Productions of the island. Population. Unhealthiness of the British troops at Amoy in 1841 and its probable cause. Prevalent diseases. Cholera at Amoy in 1858.

Chapter 6 • Fuchau
Geographical position. Description of the River Min and the city of Fuchau. Pagoda Island described. Variety of fruits at Fuchau. Asylum for lepers. Hot sulphur springs. Prevalent diseases.

Chapter 7 • Ningpo
Geographical position. Description of the city and surrounding neighbourhood. Prevalent diseases.

Chapter 8 • Chusan
Geographical position. Description of the island. Geological nature of the soil. The harbour described. Occupation of the island by the British forces in 1840. Unhealthiness of the troops and its probable causes.

Chapter 9 • Shanghai
Geographical position. Description of the Chinese city and the foreign settlement. Public institutions. Earthquakes. Woosung anchorage recommended during the hot months. A cruise to Japan or among the islands of the Chusan archipelago recommended when there is much sickness among the ships. Prevalent diseases. Epidemic of catarrhal ophthalmia. The

climate of Shanghai and Canton compared. Tabular statement of diseases treated at the Shanghai dispensary. Comparative return of the European Hospital.

CHAPTER 10 • PEKIN
Geographical position. Description of the city. Temples and palaces. Account of the action off the Peiho River on the 25th June 1859. List of killed and wounded. History of the wounded on board. H.M. Temporary Hospital Ship Assistance.

CHAPTER 11 • NAGASAKI
Geographical position. Description of the town. Population. Chief public buildings. Island of Deshima. Coal mines. Nagasaki recommended as a sanatarium for the residents of Southern China.

CHAPTER 12 • YEDO
Geographical position. Description of the city. Fire engines. Fire proof buildings. Width of the streets. Observations on the Japanese. Bay of Yedo described. Account of the great eruption of the volcano Fusiama in 1783. Yokohama, the port of Yedo, described.

CHAPTER 13 • HAKODADI
Geographical position. Description of the town. Installation of Mr Hodgson as 1st British Consul. Lead mines. Exports of Hakodadi. Flora. Prevalent diseases.

CHAPTER 14
An essay on the important diseases of China. Continued fever, Intermittent fever, ephemeral fever, smallpox, measles, epilepsy, insanity, coup de soleil, bronchitis, pleuritis and pneumonia, phthisis, dysentery and chronic diarrhoea, cholera, hepatitis, diseases of the eye, rheumatism, scrofula, cutaneous diseases, hydrophobia.

CHAPTER 15
An essay on Chinese medical literature.

CHAPTER 16
Translation of the Chinese anatomical maps.

CHAPTER 17
An essay on the small feet of Chinese women, origin of the custom, its' effect upon health.

CHAPTER 18
An essay on opium smoking.

CHAPTER 1   CANTON

Description of the city and suburbs. Geology. City wall. Character of the buildings. Principal temples. State of education. Charitable institutions.

Canton, principal city of the Chinese province of the same name, is situated on the north bank of the Pearl River. It is about 70 miles from the sea. The geology of the country between the city of Canton and the ocean seems simple and requires but few remarks. The general characteristics are primitive and the usual accompaniment of the presence of such rocks are seen in the isolated and barren peaks which line the coast on the north side of the river. The country rises into hills which are formed of a compact greywacke [1], probably belonging to the lower secondary class of rocks. It is finely grained and contains a large quantity of quartz. Lying immediately below the greywacke is the old red sandstone. This stratum is found varying from a bright red fine grained rock to a coarse conglomerate full of large pebbles of quartz. It is seen cropping out in the middle of the river a short distance below the site of the old factories. Below the sandstone is found the granite. This rock outcrops more and more as the river descends towards the sea and below the Bogue Fort, it is the only structure.

That part of the city which is surrounded by a wall is built nearly in the form of a square and is divided by a wall, running from east to west, into two parts. The northern, which is much the largest part, is called the old city; the southern part is called the new city. The entire circuit of the walls is about 7 miles. At a quick step the whole distance may be walked in an hour and forty-five minutes. On the south side the wall runs nearly parallel with the river. The gates of the city are 16 in number; 4 lead through the wall which separates the old from the new city, so that there are 12 outer gates. The walls vary in height from 25 to 35 or 40 feet and are composed partly of coarse reddish sandstone and partly of brick. They are highest and most substantial on the northern side.

The neighbouring country is very charming, hilly towards the north and northeast and presenting in every other quarter, a beautiful prospect. The country being level, populous and highly cultivated southwards from the city as far as the eye can see. The water covers a considerable portion, perhaps a third part of the whole surface. Rice fields and gardens occupy the low lands with only here and there a few little hills and small groves of trees rising up to diversify the otherwise unbroken surface. Only about two thirds of the space enclosed by the city walls is covered with buildings. The rest being occupied with pleasure gardens and fish ponds so that Canton looks like a forest and city combined. On the buildings of Canton we have doubtless so great a variety of structure and style and as fair specimens of Chinese taste and wit as can be found in the whole empire.

A large portion of the city and suburbs is built on low ground or flats. Special care, therefore, is requisite in order to secure the houses and temples a solid basis. Near the river and in all the most loose and muddy situations, houses are raised on wooden piles that make the foundations as secure as brick or stone, and perhaps even more so. In some cases the piles rise above the surface of the ground, and then the buildings, constructed of wood, rest directly on them; but in other instances the piles reach only within a few feet of the surface, and the remaining part of the foundation is made of mud brick or stone. Bricks are in most general use for the walls of houses; perhaps three fifths of the whole city is built of this material: of the remaining part a very large proportion is constructed of mud. Windows are small and rarely supplied with glass; paper, mica or shell, or some other similar translucent material taking its place.

The houses are mostly of one storey, the rooms being mostly of the whole height of the fabric without any concealment of the rafters of the roof; the beams being often carved, and as well as the rafters and tiles, painted. In Canton and its neighbourhood there are three pagodas, one of which is a Mohammedan mosque.

There are four temples deserving of special notice, viz, the Temple of 500 Gods, the Emperors Temple, Temple of the five Genii and the Temple of Honan. The Temple of the 500 Gods is in the western suburbs and is so called by Europeans because it has that number of idols in the interior. It is a Buddhist temple. The gods which are of great size and arranged in rows are in an exceedingly good state of preservation. Before each divinity is an immense incense pot and on great occasions every one of these has its lighted incense-stick diffusing clouds of incense before its particular divinity.

The Emperors Temple is in the city. It is dedicated to the Emperors of China and in it the Emperors throne is erected. The temple is supported by red pillars and the roof is of the imperial yellow colour. Ornamental representations of dragons adorn the walls of the building. On New Years Day and on the birthdays of the Emperor and Empress the temple is visited by the Mandarins who come to pay their homage to the throne.

The Temple of the Five Genii is a Taoist place of worship and is dedicated to the memory of the five genii who according to legend in a very early period of history alighted at this spot and were transformed into rams and became the founders of the city of Canton. Whence it arises that Canton is often called "the City of Rams". In an apartment adjoining the temple the impressions of the footprints of the five genii are shown to the faithful.

In the neighbouring suburb of Honan is a celebrated and ancient Buddhist temple. It is an extensive range of buildings or halls containing idols of enormous dimensions. This temple is much frequented by Europeans on account of its size and the large gardens attached to it. Independently of the large halls alluded to there is a range of smaller apartments on either side for the monks, a kitchen, and a large dining room. In several parts of the premises are small places set apart for the lodgment of animals such as pigs, goats, fowl etc which are attended to with peculiar care by the priests. The holy swine are not objects of worship as many foreigners suppose. The Buddhist faith includes the doctrine of metempsychosis ascribing immortality to the souls of animals and consequently preaches the doctrine of humanity and kindness towards the brute creatures. The result of this belief is that it is considered a virtuous and meritorious act to preserve the life of animals or to give them their liberty. Hence a Chinese will buy a bird for the sake of giving it its liberty, or will give his pig or his goat to a Buddhist monastery, there to spend its life under the charge and superintendence of the priesthood. Fish are also placed in a pond for a similar purpose. In the grounds attached to the temple are many curious dwarf plants, and there also vegetables grown for the use of the clergy. In this locality there is a mausoleum wherein the ashes of the burnt priests are, once a year, deposited, and also a furnace for burning the dead bodies, and a little cell in which the jars containing their ashes are kept until the annual season for opening the mausoleum returns. There are likewise tombs for those who leave money for their burial. The priests are supported in part by property belonging to the establishment and partly by their private resources.

13. River pagoda on the Pearl River near Canton, 1830's

14. Sampans on the Pearl River near Canton, 1830's

Of the whole population of Canton, it is estimated that about one half are able to read. Perhaps not one boy in ten is left entirely destitute of education; yet of the other sex not one in ten ever learns to read or write. There is scarcely a public school for girls in the whole city. Public sentiment here is against the education of females; immemorial usage is against it, many passages in the Chinese classics are against it; and the consequence is they are left uninstructed, and sink far below that point in the scale of being for which they are fitted and ought ever to hold. The degradation into which the fairest half of the human species is here thrown affords cause of complaint against the wisdom and philosophy of the sages and legislators of the Celestial Empire.

There are no tombs or places of interment within the city of Canton, but the hills beyond, and in every direction around the city are covered with monuments and hillocks which mark the places of the sleeping dead. Thither the lifeless bodies of the poor are carried out and buried, usually, we believe at the public charge. Of the charitable institutions of Canton there are three deserving of especial notice, viz the Foundling Hospital, the Institution for the Blind and the Hospital for Lepers. The Foundling Hospital was founded in 1693 and was rebuilt and considerably enlarged in 1732. It stands without the walls of the city, on the east; and has accommodation for two or three hundred children. It is supported by Imperial patronage. The Yangtse Yuen is a retreat for the poor aged and infirm or blind people, who have no friends to support them. It stands near the Foundling Hospital and like it enjoys Imperial patronage.

The Ma Fung Yuen or hospital for lepers is also at the east of the city. The average number of patients is about three hundred. In the year 1828 a dispensary was opened at Canton by the missionaries for the poor natives of every description.

The most common diseases among the natives seem to be of a chronic character viz ophthalmia, chronic rheumatism, pectoral complaints, dyspepsia, diarrhoea, dysentery, ulcers and diseases of the skin, dropsy, intermittent fever, and glandular swellings especially of the neck.

Allied French and English Occupation of the City of Canton

On the outbreak of the rebellion in India in 1857 all the troops ordered for China were diverted from their original destination and dispatched with all expedition to Calcutta. Among these were 300 Marines under the command of Colonel Lemon who arrived at Hong Kong in HMS Sanspareil but were immediately re-embarked on board HMS Shannon and sent on to Calcutta. At the latter place they remained in garrison at Fort William, and here also they lost several men by cholera. On the 4th November 1857 they again embarked on HM Troop ship Assistance and arrived in China 280 strong, the remaining 20 being dead or in hospital.

On the 12th December 1857 I joined the Provisional Battalion under Colonel Lemon on board HMS Assistance and on the 18th of the same month disembarked at Honan Island a distance of about 600 yards from Canton, the narrow river intervening. The 1st and 2nd Battalions of Marines had already arrived here and were quartered in the large and lofty warehouses of the Hong merchants. The quarters were tolerable but being surrounded by swamps and paddy fields were exposed to miasmatic influence.

The season of the year however was favourable and prevented any deleterious effect the situation may have had on the troops. From about three days after our disembarkation the Battalion was receiving fresh accessions from the ships in the river, the whole of their Marines being ordered on shore and placed under Colonel Lemon's command. By these additions we became the largest battalion being upwards of 800 strong. The men were in very good spirits, but I cannot say so much for their health. Among those disembarked were men who had been three years on the station, and almost all had spent the summer on the river. Of these at least two thirds had had intermittent fever [2, 3] and were thus predisposed to miasmatic affections.

The voyage from Calcutta had considerably improved the health of Colonel Lemon's party. We remained at Honan till the 28th December, and in the meantime had fitted up a Temporary Hospital, where the sick were removed from the noise of the barrack rooms and had comfortable beds to sleep on. A number of cases of diarrhoea occurred while quartered here, but very few cases of fever. There were also a great many cases of ulcer which had just been healed before leaving their ships but had broken out again. As the river water was supposed to be the principal cause of the diarrhoea, filters were fitted up at convenient places sufficient to supply drinking water to all hands.

On the 28th December we were all embarked on board gunboats for a passage to the Canton side of the river having previously provided every man with a blanket, waterproof sheet , 4 days cooked rations and water bottles filled with filtered water. Before starting we sent our sick, 14 in number, to HMS Assistance which was set aside as a Hospital ship for the Provisional Battalion. There were also 50 of the weaker men left behind from the Marines to form a guard for stores.

Immediately on landing the provisional battalion pushed on towards Fort Lin where the 59th Naval Brigade was in action. The march was hurried but only extended for a few miles. The 1st and 2nd Battalions remained near the beach as a reserve. During this day only one man of the Provisional Battalion fell out, and he was immediately sent on board ship again. It was only a case of intermittent fever, and the wonder is we had not more considering how long some of the men had been exposed to this debilitating climate. Several trifling cases of diarrhoea occurred and were attended to in the field, but none such as to prevent those attacked continuing in the ranks.

As yet none of the Marines had been in action. The French, 59th and Naval Brigade being the only ones that had fired a shot. Of the Naval Brigade several were wounded and conveyed to Fort Lin in the evening where now the 1st Battalion with Dr Turnbull, staff surgeon, had established themselves. All this time a heavy bombardment was kept up, the ships off the city which were doing immense damage. Fort Lin being taken and the country cleared by our various skirmishing parties, orders were given to bivouac for the night. We accordingly advanced in the dusk of the evening to within 500 or 600 yards of the walls and found shelter behind some trees, where the men piled arms and lay down in their companies ready at a moments notice to stand to their arms. The night was rather cold and as we were directly exposed to the fire from the walls, no fires were allowed to be lighted and consequently everyone was obliged to content himself with cold rations.

The other parts of the force were more fortunate being more in the rear and better sheltered and consequently were enabled to have tea made. At 3 o'clock. the next morning all were under arms and after a march of about 1 hour over very irregular ground we halted at a large Joss house [4] about 600 yards from the city wall and within range of the gun in Goughs Fort. As the wall was to be scaled at this place the medical staff established themselves in the Joss house, as the most convenient situation for the reception of the wounded.

A hill intervening between the Joss house and the city wall, the Provisional Battalion and Naval Brigade deployed there till 9 o'clock am when the assault was to be made. The firing all this time was very brisk both from the city walls and Goughs Fort. A large body of Chinese took the field below Goughs Fort, and several companies of the Provisional Battalion were sent out to drive them back. At this time the 1st Battalion was also advancing and threw out two companies to support those engaged. In this skirmish Lieut. Dodson was wounded and brought into the Joss house. He had a ball through the right arm fracturing the radius.

Mr Thompson, Midshipman of the Sanspareil was also mortally wounded, being struck by a rocket in the abdomen whilst at breakfast. The body of Captain Bate was also brought in at this time. The Marines & Royal Artillery with two companies of the Provisional Battalion having been keeping up a steady fire on the walls, the guns there were silenced and at 9 o'clock am the parties with scaling ladders advanced and placed them without opposition. The French, 59th and Naval Brigade and Marines were soon on the walls, clearing away every resistance both the right and left. No opposition was offered except at the gates and Magazine Hill.

Once within the walls there was no use for the Medical Department stopping in the Joss house [4] and the Medical Officers with their stores entered the city. During the whole attack there was an assistant surgeon with each division, and when without the walls sent the sick to the Joss house, and when inside the city to a temporary hospital on Magazine Hill. This evening the whole of our force with the exception of the 2nd Battalion slept in Canton, the latter having been left at Fort Lin to keep the road to the landing-place clear.

Table 1: List of casualties of the Marine and Naval Brigades of the 59th Regiment and the 38th Madras Native Infantry

Casualties of the Marine Brigade

Battalion	Officers	Men	Total	Slightly	Wounded Severely	Mortally
Provisional Battalion		10	10	8	2	
1st Battalion	1	4	5	1	4	
2nd Battalion	0	0	0			
R.M. Artillery	1. Col.	3	4	2	2	
Total	2	17	19	11	8	0

Casualties of the Naval Brigade

Ship	Officers		Men	Total	Wounded			Killed
					Slightly	Severely	Mortally	
Actaeon	1	Captain	0	1	1			1[1]
Calcutta	1	Lieut[2]	4	5	2	3		
Cruiser	1	Comdr	3	4	3	1		
Elk			2	2	1	1		
Esk			1	1				1[3]
Furious			1	1	1			
Highflyer			3	3	2		1	
Hornet	2		1	3	1	2		
Inflexible			1	1		1		
Nankin			5	5	3	1	1	
Niger			1	1				
Racehorse			1	1	1			
Sanspareil	1	Mid	4	5	3	1	1	1[4]
Sybille			6	6	4	1	1	
Total	6		33	39	22	11	4	3

[1] *Captain Bates* [2] *Viscount Gifford* [3] *Thorax wound* [4] *Mr Henry Thompson*

Other Casualties

		Total
59th Regiment	1 Officer killed, one wounded	2
	1 Private killed, 16 wounded	17
38th Madras Native Infantry	1 Halvidar wounded	1

	Total killed and wounded in the Allied Force
English	12 Officers and 84 men
French	34 Officers and men in total

On the 31st December there was an accidental explosion of a Chinese magazine by which 17 men belonging to the Naval Brigade were most severely burnt and 4 died very soon afterwards.

Though we had possession of the walls and Canton was at our mercy it was deemed advisable to remain on the walls for the present. Accordingly all bivouacked on the ramparts, being the second night in the open air. A small house was set apart for the sick, several of whom began now to drop in. The night passed quietly, and next morning, the 30th December, our services were very much sought after. The cold night air, constant marching and irregularity in meal hours began to tell on the more debilitated, the principal complaints being dysentery, diarrhoea and intermittent fever and these occurring, for the most part, among those who had been some time on the station. The small building set apart for the sick became soon filled and preparation was made to send the worst cases away next morning.

Arrangements had been previously made by Dr Deas, Inspector of Hospitals and Fleets, for the transfer of the sick from Canton, the want of accommodation there having been anticipated. These arrangements were very perfect. A gunboat started every morning from the landing-place with the sick to temporary hospitals prepared for them. These hospitals were the transports which had brought the Marines out. The HMS Assistance a well ventilated roomy ship being set apart for the Provisional Battalion, the HMS Imperador and HMS Imperatrice for the 1st and 2nd Battalions, accordingly, on the 31st December 1857, 18 men were sent away.

For the first week in January 1858 we remained on the walls, the men having no shelter and there being very little accommodation for the sick. The weather during this time was most inclement, raining almost incessantly. Great numbers were consequently under the sick list. At length we were ordered to move into a series of buildings below Magazine Hill which was supposed to be large enough to hold the whole Battalion, but not only was it too small, the roofs had been very much damaged by the bombardment and were still not repaired. The rooms were partially flooded from the water pouring down the side of the hill and there was not a dry spot in the whole cluster. Thus there was certainly very little improvement on our old station on the walls. The want of room being so apparent, the buildings at the north-east gate were given to us and two companies moved to them. These buildings, though water proof, were anything but perfect being all open and quite exposed to every breeze which at that season was very cold.

The crowded state of the rooms was thus partially remedied but it was some time before the roofs were repaired, so much was required to be done to make the quarters comfortable so that the men were for a long time much exposed. We had consequently much sickness during this period, and many were sent to HMS Assistance. A large temple in good repair and in a convenient airy situation was set aside for our hospital but the accommodation was not nearly sufficient for our large sick list. Before the end of the month however, we had settled down in pretty comfortable quarters.

The 1st Battalion removed into the city to the Governor-General's yamun and there quarters were given over to the Provisional Battalion. The north-east gate was then evacuated by us and was occupied by the 59th. The Battalion was thus all close together in the large joss houses on Magazine Hill.

Such is the early history of the Provisional Battalion of which I had medical charge, and during this period was so much engaged and was so far removed from the other parts of our force as to be in a great measure unaware of their movements. As soon however, as we were settled in Canton we were all so closely quartered together that I became cognizant of everything that took place and am thus enabled in a great degree to give their medical history during the early part of their stay in the Celestial City.

I take this liberty with the other Battalions as I consider that the larger the number of men, the more correct will any statistical account be: and the more important conclusions can be arrived at as regard the prevalence and severity of disease, the effects of climate and the influence of locality. This duty would naturally have devolved on the late Dr Turnbull, our lamented Staff Surgeon, who from his knowledge of the statistics of the Brigade would probably have given important information on the health of the troops and from the constant attention he bestowed on the hygiene of the garrison, was fully competent to write a medical history of the Marine Brigade during its sojourn at Canton, which would not only have been of interest as a history, but might have been a guide to the medical officers of any future force. I cannot expect to give such an extensive account of the garrison as Dr Turnbull might have done , my attention having been principally engaged by my own Battalion, and as there have been a good many changes among the medical officers of the Brigade and

I had the fortune to remain always in the same place for 10 months. I shall endeavour as far as possible to give an account of the movements and sanitary condition of the whole Brigade during that period of our occupation of this city. Before doing so, however, it will be requisite to give the antecedents of the Battalions before their settling in Canton.

On the original force being diverted to India it was determined to employ a portion of the Marine force for the subjugation of Canton, as that force was then pretty strong at home. Accordingly two Battalions were ordered to be formed under the command of Colonel Holloway as Brigadier. Three first class steamers, viz HMS Adelaide, Imperador and Imperatrice were employed for their transport. On the 17th August 1857 they left England and after a speedy passage arrived safely in China. The HMS Imperador having lost two men, the Imperatrice and the Adelaide none. In fact such a force could not have been brought from England with less inconvenience and less sickness than in this case. Upwards of 1500 men were thus brought to China in good health and spirits and ready for any campaign.

As we were now able to commence operations an ultimatum was sent to the Chinese and while waiting for an answer the ships with Marines on board remained at Wantung where several companies went on shore every day for exercise. The negotiations being unsuccessful, on the 15th of December a movement was made up the river and by means of gunboats the whole of the Royal Marines and Marine artillery were landed at Honan Island on the 19th December. Here they were in exactly the same position as the Provisional Battalion with the exception that being first landed they had the best quarters and procured the best rooms for their hospitals. The whole Marine force at this time including Marine artillery and Provisional Battalion was about 2500 strong.

On the 28th December they landed below the French Folly for the attack on Canton but were kept in reserve that day. In the evening they advanced to Fort Lin and part of the 1st Battalion was, as already stated, in action with the braves from Goughs Fort, and had one of their officers (Lieut. Dodson) badly wounded in the arm. On the opening of the gates the 1st Battalion marched in and occupied the heights known as Magazine Hill on the night of the 29th while the 2nd Battalion remained outside at Fort Lin. Here these last remained for a week, when they also joined the force within the walls and took quarters in a large temple at the foot of Magazine Hill. The 1st Battalion was under shelter immediately they entered the city and escaped the severe weather to which the Provisional Battalion was exposed. About a week after our entering the city, quarters were secured so all the Battalions, the 2nd Battalion and Provisional Battalion being round Magazine Hill and the 1st Battalion in the Governor General's yamun [5] - a large series of buildings in the centre of the city occupied by the three Commissioners appointed by the Allies for the administration of affairs in Canton. At first, the rooms appropriated for the men were rather crowded, but day by day improvements were made and more accommodation was provided until eventually the space allotted to each man was sufficient. Thus crowding was not so much of consequence in the winter months, and was not so much felt at first occupation, so many men being employed every night on guard or piquet.

As the weather got warmer our affairs looked more tranquil. The Marines were gradually withdrawn, the majority of them having embarked before the end of March 1858, the HMS Sanspareil men alone remaining until the month of September. By the withdrawal of all these men we had increased space for the remainder, only about 500 instead of 800 occupying the rooms. Since the first settling down on the heights, the Provisional Battalion never shifted its quarters. Not so, however, the 2nd Battalion: their barracks being so low, in the hollow of a hill, seemed to be the cause of much sickness among the men. Accordingly, on the 59th Regiment being sent north, the 2nd Battalion was shifted to the huts on the top of the hill, without, however, providing, I am sorry to say, any great improvement in the health of the force. These huts were built of wood and occupied every available spot on the heights, the purpose being to get as many men as possible accommodated without our fortified position. The first Battalion remained the whole time in the yamun and was generally the healthiest of the lot. Their quarters were magnificent and though in the centre of the town, were so surrounded by trees and gardens as to be quite secluded.

Having given a particular history of our movements I next intend to describe our position as accurately as possible and to specify the diseases most prevalent at different seasons. The following table shows plainly that in this climate the most unhealthy season is the summer. This is what one would naturally expect and the prevalence of affections of the mucous membranes shown in the number of catarrhal, dysenteric and diarrhoea cases in the spring might also be looked for when we consider the unsettled state of the weather and the exposure to which our men were subject. Fever, of course, is more prevalent in the summer and it will be seen that this disease became more virulent as the season advanced.

In January there was by far the greatest amount of sickness but still the averages not so great as in June for in the first month of our occupation of the city we had about 800 in the Battalion while in June there was not more than 200. The diseases which occurred in this month were principally diseases of the mucous membrane, diarrhoea and dysentery forming more than one half of the list. Of these affections of the bowels only one or two were serious and these were sent to HMS Assistance.

Table 2: Monthly statement of prevalent diseases in the Provisional Battalion from the 1st of January to the 30th of September 1858 at Canton

	January	February	March	April	May	June	July	August	September
Continued fever			1	1	1	14	6		
Intermittent fever	42	43	20	18	25	75	54	70	61
Remittent fever		2	6		5	14	24	13	
Ephemeral fever					5	25	29	17	
Pulmonary affect.	21	14	7	8	6	3	10	7	8
Coup de Soleil*						5	2	3	
Dysentery	17	12	1	1	1	1	6	3	2
Diarrhoea	134	55	35	20	22	28	38	28	16
Cholera						1	2		
Rheumatism	15	6	2	1	2		1	2	3
Incidental	42	33	43	36	31	33	47	53	40
Total	271	155	115	85	98	199	219	196	130

*Sunstroke

Pulmonary affections were rather frequent but there was only one case in which the bronchial mucous membrane was much affected. That case of bronchitis was also sent to HMS Assistance. Catarrh and cyanche tonsillitis were the principal affections. That more inflammatory affections of the chest did not occur is rather surprising as our men were so much exposed to wet and for nearly a fortnight had no change of clothing. Rheumatism also is a considerable item in the return, a natural consequence of the season. Altogether the number of cases sent to hospital this month was much greater than any succeeding one, for the reason already assigned; that we had no accommodation for sick at that time and every facility was offered for their removal.

Those cases in the column of incidental diseases include wounds, phlegmas and all those diseases which have no relation to climatic or miasmatic influences, and those which were of rare occurrence. Syphilis I have also included in this column as it was, comparatively speaking, a rare disease. Among the 42 there is one case of anasarca, one of epilepsy and one of scrofula, and one of conjunctivitis.

January. The amount of rain fallen during this month was considerable but there was no means of ascertaining the quantity. It was, however, greater than for several succeeding months. The thermometer ranges from 29 to 74 degrees, a temperature more felt by us during the first fortnight, having no beds and no change of clothing. There, fortunately however, was plenty of firewood and it was made very free use of. Our greatest inconvenience this month being the dampness of the houses; none of the roofs were perfect and none of the floors dry. Trusses and doors were picked up by most of the men so that they were raised from the floor but it was not till two months later that these were served out by the military authorities. Our greatest comfort during this month was the water-proof sheet than which nothing could be more useful serving as a comfortable warm wrapper at night, and an excellent cloak when walking during the rain in the day time.

February. This month shows that there has been nearly 120 fewer sick than the previous one and this is to be ascribed principally to the better accommodation of the men, to the more favourable state of the weather and to the increased comfort the men enjoyed by having their kit with them, thus enabling them to change clothing when required. About the end of this month also the men belonging to the smaller ships embarked reducing our numbers and increasing the space for those that remained. The principal disease this month occurred among the dysentery and diarrhoea cases, but still the number was large although there was a considerable diminution in the severity of the complaint. While affections of the bowels diminished, cases of fever increased. There was not that exclusiveness either so marked last month. Several men who had only been 2 months in China were attacked by intermittent fever. We had also a few rather obstinate cases; and for the first time I observed two of the cases to be remittent.

The proportion of pulmonary affections has slightly decreased but still was sufficiently frequent to make them an important item in the returns. Rheumatism also was much more rare. The weather during this month, though cold, was not such as to be unpleasant. A fair proportion of rain fell, but the majority of the roofs had been repaired and a dry place was at all events found to sleep in. The temperature varied from 38 to 78 degrees and the north east monsoon blew occasionally rather fresh. Very few men were sent to hospital during the month. The regimental hospitals having been so much improved, beds having been supplied, cooking houses built, and a competent staff of attendants appointed there was not the same necessity to send men away, those only being sent who would probably be a long time under treatment or would most likely be invalided.

March. There was again a marked improvement this month; the sick list being still further reduced. This reduction has principally occurred among affections of the bowels and intermittent fever. Our complement, however, was still further reduced by the withdrawal of some more of the ships marines. Only one case of dysentery occurred and the number of diarrhoea cases was less by 20 than last month. Indeed , though this disease formed a large item in the returns at this time, it is not to be at all dreaded, for unless in chronic cases it is easily checked, and indeed the diarrhoea is generally of the irritative form and not so much depending on climatic influences; a purgative of castor oil being about the best remedy. The early part of the month was rather rainy and to that some of the diarrhoea cases may have been attributed, but during that time scarcely a case of diarrhoea occurred; the majority occurring in the latter part of the month when the weather was remarkably fine, clearly showing that exposure to wet was not the cause of the disease. For my own part, I attributed it more to the unripe fruit men had access to at this time. The cases of intermittent fever also decreased in number this month, but increased in severity. Six cases of remittent fever occurred of so severe a character that three of them had afterwards to be sent to hospital, and one was invalided for debility and palpitations.

A new feature showed itself among the fevers in the shape of a continued maculated fever. As this was the first time I had seen such cases in China I attached considerable importance to it. The patient was a young man of sanguine temperament and who had been remarkably healthy previously. On admission to hospital he was rather feverish, but I did not pay any particular attention to this case for the first few days. Finding, however, the fever did not abate under the treatment employed I examined him more narrowly and found his whole body covered with a rose coloured eruption, quite distinct from the eruption of prickly heat with which also he was covered. The eruption disappeared on pressure at first, but afterwards became quite persistent. The pulse never was above a hundred. Patient lay for several days almost constantly on his back, and had to have everything put into his mouth. Mouth quite dry, and clogged up with sordes. A low muttering delirium was present for several days. About the 12th or 14th day he appeared to be improving but there was no marked crisis of any sort. Patient was very sleepy about that time and slept day and night except when drinking or eating. Appetite always appeared good, that is, he took whatever was offered him without any demur. As he improved, the eruption disappeared, the mouth became clean, the fur left the tongue and the appetite became ravenous. On six weeks from his first attack he was again at duty. This case, there could be no doubt, was one of typhus fever, and how it originated is not so easy to say.

The man's rooms were not crowded; in fact he lived in one of the most airy situations on the side of the hill. His food was liberal and certainly his personal appearance showed that he was anything but ill fed, being rather adipose than otherwise. And as this is the first case that has been noticed by anyone in the garrison, contagion could not be put down as the cause. I could only assume that he had been exposed to the offensive emanations of cesspools or drains, which had the effect of producing typhus fever in him.

I had one case of fracture of the patella this month, which, from the great effusions into the knee joint, prevented any appliances being used for several days. It was a transverse fracture and did well. Fewer have been sent to the hospital that in any of the previous months, indeed towards the end of the month, we had the smallest sick list we have had yet.

April. This month shows the smallest sick list of any, only 85 having been added. The greatest decrease as in the amount of the diarrhoea cases, these diarrhoea cases are of much the same class as last month and require no remark. Another case of fever was added and I am very sorry to report that with a fatal result. This was the case of a very powerful man brought in from the Police Force. He was taken ill the day before admission and was quite prostrate the second day. About the 3rd day a coloured eruption appeared on body, and remained persistent until his death. Delirium set in about the 6th day and merged into a coma on the 9th day, carried him off. This was another undoubted case of typhus fever but in this instance I had not the same difficulty in assigning a cause, as the man was in the habit of constantly patrolling the filthiest and closest parts of the city. Their quarters were also in crowded places, so that either on the theory of foul air, or even contagion, could be a hypothesis for the attack. He was generally supposed to be a very temperate man, but the mucous membrane of his stomach showed the peculiar characteristics of gastritis chronica potatorum which of course lessened his chances of escape when attacked of such a disease as typhus fever.

Leave is now granted to the men to go into the city and the effects of this indulgence are beginning to show themselves, no less than ten having been added for venereal afflictions. Whether from the change of season or not I cannot say, but coughs and cases of ophthalmia are rather common, none of them however, serious. The weather has been remarkably pleasant.

May. There was a slight increase in the sick list this month, the augmentation arising from the greater amount of fever cases. It was now a very common thing for men to be relieved from sentry with severe headache, and general febrile symptoms; in fact, presenting a very alarming appearance, but next day finding themselves quite well. These cases I have attributed principally to the effects of the sun and these cases which had no second attack I have classed as ephemeral fever, while those that had a recurrence of pyrexia either the next day or the following one, I have styled intermittent. These last were by far the most common, and have led me to consider the sun's rays as one of the most powerful exciting causes of ague, once the body has been predisposed by exposure to malaria. To protect the men as much as possible, bamboo sheds were built for them to walk under; the lightest possible clothing with no necktie whatever was ordered to be worn. Still, with all precautions the weather had a most debilitating effect, and not only did more cases of fever occur, but they were in general more obstinate, and several of them assumed the remittent type. One case of typhus fever recurred, and no cause could be traced for its' appearance. The patient was the General's orderly, and was by no means exposed to exhalations of a crowded room.

June. This has as yet been the unhealthiest month of the year. Fever cases are much on the increase. Continued, remittent, intermittent cases have become very common. The number of typhus fever cases was particularly alarming. They came from all the barracks so that whatever was the cause of it one room was no more a fault than the others. Orders were given to whitewash all the places, to make more windows, and increase ventilation, and all drains to be cleaned, but as yet with little apparent benefit. Three of the fever cases, I am sorry to say, proved fatal. All presented the maculae on the surface and death generally ensued from the 6th to the 9th day. Cases of coup de soleil also occurred showing clearly the risk of exposure to the sun at this season. Only one of these cases died. They all occurred at the expedition to the White Cloud Mountain, when Dr Turnbull unfortunately lost his life. The suns rays were particularly strong and the men had a long march of it. Several cases of fever occurred among the men of this expedition also but not so much an extent as to be marked, nor that could say the exposure there was the cause of the sickness, nearly an equal ratio of sickness having occurred among those that remained behind. The vast increase of fevers, however, this month is very conspicuous and very alarming. I don't know that any means more than those employed could have been used. There never has been any needless exposure to the sun. The men were only on one hour on sentry duty at a time. The men however had very little sleep on account of the heat. They were in the habit of sleeping outside whenever they could get a breath of wind, and no precautions could prevent this as it was really impossible to get any sleep in those warm rooms. There is very little increase in affections of the bowels, and the affections of the chest have considerably diminished. Rheumatism has disappeared altogether.

July. This has been by far the most sickly month since our occupation of Canton, the great increase being in fever cases, principally remittent and intermittent. A greater number of deaths have also occurred, the largest proportion being cases of continued fever. But though so many deaths occurred from the disease yet there have been fewer new cases than in the preceding months. All the cases died early in the month.

Cholera made its' appearance among the Police Force living in the centre of the city in close rooms where they were required to be constantly on the watch against surprise. One died a few hours after being brought into hospital, another survived the stage of collapse but died of fever and a third recovered. Two cases of coup de soleil are recorded; they seemed to arise from the effects of the hot sun acting on a disordered stomach. I am happy to report they did well. One case of gunshot wound is reported as having died, Robert Elson having been shot by a party lying in ambush when patrolling the streets in the Western part of the city. Two cases of burn also occurred, it having become a common trick to heave a bag of powder or a stinkpot [6] at passing parties of men. They were severely burnt, the whole body having been singed. The streets in which these dastardly attempts were made were always severely punished which soon put a stop to that kind of work. Quinine wine [7] was given every morning to the men who appeared most debilitated.

August. During the month the effects of the long continued heat of the summer began to exert a marked influence on the general appearance of the men as indicated by the sallowness of the complexion of very many of them, and the instability of gait and feebleness of the whole frame in others. The continued form of fever appeared, but remittent and intermittent were very prevalent. There was nothing remarkable about any of them except it may be the suddenness with which some were attacked, scarcely a day passing without someone requiring be relieved of sentry duty. This state of things may always be looked for at this season and being very alarming to the other men it required the constant effort of the Medical Officers to give prompt attendance to these cases and reassure others of the harmlessness of the complaint, an assurance which they are not long in acquiring as the frequent occurrence of the disease and their knowledge that the attendance to them is prompt gives them the greatest confidence. Quinine wine was liberally served out to large bodies of men during this month.

An expedition to Namtow occurred this month. Namtow is a large walled town not far from Hong Kong and in the Canton River. The town was assaulted and taken. Captain Lambert of the Royal Engineers and Ensign Danvers were killed on this occasion, and Commander Madden was wounded. Walter Kelly, a Private belonging to the Provisional Battalion was also killed. Three cases of Coup de Soleil happened among the detachment of the Provisional Battalion; these cases all did well. The only death during the month was one from dysentery. The patient was a strong powerfully built man who withstood the disease for upwards of two months and at last sunk exhausted from the continuous drain.

September. This month was still very warm, but there was occasionally a certain coolness in the evening which was very refreshing. The amount of serious disease diminished. Continued and remittent fever disappeared altogether. Intermittent fever, however, became remarkably frequent which may perhaps be accounted for by the change between the diurnal and nocturnal temperature. Diarrhoea was also a very common complaint and was probably owing to the same cause. There were many cases of pure debility; these were cases of men with clean tongues, small pulses, no evident symptoms of disease, yet who were scarcely able to walk merely from the enervating effects of the climate and previous sickness.

The Provisional Battalion of Marines was broken up in September 1858, and I was appointed soon afterwards to the HMS Highflyer and was consequently unable to continue these remarks so as to complete a twelvemonth.

15. *The fish market Canton, Lithograph, Commodore Matthew Perry's 'Narrative of an expedition of an American Squadron to the China Seas and Japan,' Washington, 1856*

16. *Foreign factories at Canton, 1850's, China National Maritime Museum*

Chapter 2   Hong Kong

Geographical position. General description of the island. Geological nature of the soil. Sanitary condition of the island. Striking proof of its insalubrity. Prevalent diseases. Census of 1859.

Hong Kong is in latitude 22°16.27 north, longitude 114°11.48 east. The length of the island from east to west is about 8 miles. The utmost breadth is not above 5 miles. When seen from the harbour Hong Kong has a pleasing and somewhat picturesque appearance. The north and north-east side of the island are separated from the south and south-west by a continuous range of hills on no place less than 500 feet and in some parts upwards of 1000 feet in height. The highest pinnacle which reaches an altitude of 2000 feet is called Victoria Peak. Small streams run down the ravines which, in the driest seasons of year, never fail to furnish water and in the wet season when swollen by the heavy rains become torrents.

The island of Hong Kong is composed of granite [1] in all its geological change, some of which is well adapted for building purposes, but other specimens of the mineral are found in the state which the French name "maladie de granite"; viz. that state in which there is want of coherence of the materials forming the rock, without any visible sign of decomposition. The rock looks fresh but the slightest blow is sufficient to reduce it to the state of sand, in which all the different ingredients of the rock (quartz, mica and feldspar) are distinct. The decomposed granite is in many places covered with vegetable mould which in some localities is two or three feet thick.

Everything connected with the sanitary condition of the colony is of importance inasmuch as it is yearly rising. To greater consequence, my visits to Hong Kong have afforded me an opportunity of observing the inconvenience of a tropical land-locked harbour from a sanitary point of view, the more objectionable from the position of the town itself, which like the harbour, is flanked by hills of an altitude of between 1000 and 2000 feet completely excluding the south-west monsoon. This objectionable feature may be corrected to some extent by anchoring close to the mainland. The superiority of Kowloon and other points opposite to Hong Kong clearly point them out as the most suitable for a hospital.

Hong Kong has for many years been noted for the insalubrity of its climate, and as a proof of its unhealthiness and the impropriety of retaining it as a military establishment, one fact with regard to the 59th Regiment which left the colony in 1858, after being located in the island for nearly 8 years is of most startling import. Upwards of 1800 men were buried or invalided during that time. On the 8th July 1857, of the 600 men who formed the strength of the Regiment, 150 were in hospital. The barracks are situated at the foot of the largest and deepest ravine, both sides being enclosed by high mountainous projecting hills, a stream of water perpetually running down this ravine washing down during the rains. The ravine forms a collection of small pools and swamps which are extremely favourable for the development of miasma, the interference of moderate currents (of air) being prevented by the hills. The diffusion of miasma will take place in a horizontal and downward direction. In many other parts of the island, however, there is not the same inconvenience inasmuch as these periodical floods are the most efficient means of thoroughly cleaning the place without danger which usually attended similar processes in other tropical climates where the water, perhaps impregnated with the filth of the place, remains stagnant in various parts.

The most prevalent diseases are intermittent, remittent and continued fevers, sloughing boils, diarrhea and dysentery and hepatic affections. Intermittent fever is very common about the equinoxes, and in the cooler weather. Dysentery is common during the whole year but particularly after sudden changes of weather.

With regard to the fever termed 'Hong Kong Fever' [2], much difference of opinion has existed concerning the nature of this very fatal disease. It is generally classed as a remittent fever, but it would appear that it frequently commences as a fever of intermittent types and that not seldom it assumes a typhoid character, and then has very imperfect intermissions. In some years it has been looked upon as an idiopathic continued fever. Doubtless the change of type in different seasons has given rise to the mystification which seems to exist with regards to its true nature.

Hong Kong Fever seems to me a low remittent fever with congestion of the brain and lungs attended in some instances with ulceration of the bowels. Sometimes there is a maculated eruption on the skin. The convalescence from the disease is very slow particularly in those who remain in the locality amidst the predisposing and exciting causes. Deaths from the disease are by no means rare as it is always a very serious complaint either to have or to treat it. It is called *par excellence* the Hong Kong Fever as that is the place whence all bad things and people are recommended to hail from.

Of late years it would appear that the island has become more healthy than it was formerly which may, perhaps, be attributed to the planting of numerous trees which by their foliage afford shelter from the solar heat; the clearing away of the paddy fields, and a better system of drainage.

In concluding these remarks on the climate of Hong Kong I must say that from all I have seen, heard and read, I consider it the most unhealthy locality inhabited by Europeans in China. Indeed, the town can never be as healthy as the mainland opposite, viz. Kowloon, and it seems probable now that this has been ceded to the British government that Hong Kong will ultimately be evacuated by the troops, and that invalids will remove to the mainland for the benefit of their health. To conclude this article, I subjoin the last census [3]. (Table 3)

Table 3: Census of Hong Kong 1859

	No. of Houses	No. of Boats	Population				Total
			Adults		Children		
			Male	Female	Male	Female	
Europeans & Americans			665	178	100	101	1034
Goa, Manila, Indians and Others of mixed blood			448	18	5	6	477
Aliens, chiefly seamen and temporary residents			150				150
Chinese in employ of Europeans			2,893	148	34	91	3,166
Chinese residing in Victoria			28,725	9,249	3,930	3,149	45,053
Chinese residing in villages			2,989	822	442	321	4,574
Boat population in Victoria		1,981	6,922	3,002	2,960	1,817	14,701
Other than Victoria		1,805	6,996	3,535	3,305	2,300	16,136
Vagrants			1,500				1,500
Emigrants			150				150
Totals	4,261*	3,786	51,428	16,952	10,776	7,785	86,941

*In Victoria and villages

17. *HMS Plover lying at anchor in Hong Kong in early 1859. The vessel was later sunk in the Peiho River campaign in June 1859*

CHAPTER 3   MACAO

Geographical position. Description of the town. Hospital for lepers. A summer retreat for the merchants of Canton and Hong Kong.

Macao: This Portuguese settlement is situated 40 miles to the westward of Hong Kong and about the same distance from Canton, and is a peninsula about 8 miles in circuit. It is attached to the south-east point of a large island, the connecting bund being a narrow isthmus which, in the native topography, is designated the stalk of the water-lily.

The natural site of the town is picturesque. It climbs up the sides and through the ravines of a group of hills the summits of which are topped by old castles and convents. There are two harbours, an outer one and an inner one. The Portuguese poet Camoens [1], the author of The Lusiads lived here and Chinnery [2] the painter expired here at the venerable age of 85. The salubrity of Macao is principally owing to its being open to both the south-west and north-east monsoons. The Praya Grande where the Governor's resident and the principal houses are situated is open to the south-west monsoon.

Outside the Campo gate there is a hospital for lepers, both male and female; this establishment is not a government affair, but is left up to the people. The patients are kept separate and there is a chapel outside the hospital. During the last two years the French have had a temporary naval and military hospital on the hill for the sick and wounded of their forces in China and Cochin China, to which three medical officers are appointed. The climate being pleasant and healthy, Macao is the chosen retreat of the business-worn merchants of Canton and Hong Kong.

18. *Praya Grande, Macau Bay, showing Portuguese Forts and St Francis Church c. 1830, George Chinnery*

CHAPTER 4   **SWATOW**

Geographical position. Description of the town. Origin of the present prosperity of Swatow. Double Island described. Chinese superstitions.

Swatow (i.e. Tail of Land) in latitude 23°21 north, longitude 116.39° east is situated on the north bank of River Han and also is the seaport of a large town called Chinhai being distant about 2 miles. Swatow has about 10,000 inhabitants, and being built on a small low neck of sandy soil, the kongs and houses are very closely packed. The country in the immediate vicinity is low and soil very rich and highly cultivated with numerous villages and towns all of which are very thickly populated. The people hereabouts subsist by agriculture and fishing and are, generally speaking, a rough hardy set of men, tall, robust with intelligent expressions. Large quantities of rice, with sugar cane and tobacco are grown in the vicinity and, as the country is completely intersected with fine deep canals, the means of transit to and from Swatow is both cheap and expeditious. The Chinese are in the habit of traveling from Swatow to Chungchow in the environs of Amoy by these canals, a distance of 120 miles.

The opium ships are the real foundation of the present flourishing trade of Swatow, they having moved into their present position off Double Island in 1850, and were the first ships in the River Han. From their intercourse and transactions with the merchants of the place who are both numerous and wealthy, have in a measure, brought the trade to its present flourishing condition.

The entrance to the River Han is round the Cape of Good Hope, leaving two small islets called the Bill, and squat rocks on the port hand: from them your course is north westerly to Sugar Loaf Island, 3 miles from the east end of which a reef extends. Thence your course is westerly into river, on the bar of which close to Sugar Loaf Island the depth is only 15 feet at low water with a most irregular and uncertain rise and fall of tide. Three-quarters of a mile north-west from Sugar Loaf lays Double Island; having passed which your course is west to Swatow on the north bank of the river and about 4 miles from Double Island. Soon after leaving Swatow the river narrows and has numerous sand banks and shoals so that it is only manageable for vessels of very light draft.

In 1851 there was but one house on Double Island; now the whole of the western side is completely occupied with kongs and houses, with a large and apparently thriving Chinese population. At present there are from 20 to 30 Europeans located on shore, some of whom are concerned in the coolie trade which has done a great injury to foreign interests in this part of country. Until 1857, Double Island anchorage was considered perfectly safe, never having been visited by typhoons, but in the past two years very heavy typhoons have been experienced. These have done a great deal of damage to shipping and property on shore [1].

The import trade here consists of all kinds of Straits produce, with but small quantities of cotton and opium. The exports are sugar and tobacco. When this trade is properly developed, it is thought it will materially interfere with the sale of cotton goods at Amoy.

When HMS Highflyer was at Swatow in 1858, I was told that the Chinese considered Double Island to resemble a peacock with outstretched wings. The superstition of the people attributes the occurrence of typhoons to the fact that a European has built a lighthouse in the eye of the peacock so that the bird can no longer see.

Double Island, where the Europeans reside has been occupied by too few people, and for too short a time to venture to give a decided opinion upon the salubrity of the climate. From its position and nature of soil etc, it seems probable that fevers are infrequent.

19. Chinese coastal craft 1830's, China National Maritime Museum

Chapter 5   **Amoy**

Geographical position. Description of island. Geological nature of the soil. Productions of the island. Population. Unhealthiness of the British troops at Amoy in 1841 and its probable cause. Prevalent diseases. Cholera at Amoy in 1858.

Amoy: This seaport which is situated in the Province of Fokien on the western side of an island of the same name, in a bay of the China Sea opposite Formosa at latitude 24°10 north, longitude 118°13 east.

The island is separated from the mainland by a narrow channel varying from one to two miles in breadth. It is about 22 miles in circumference and 10 miles across and somewhat circular in form. The southern and western portions are much broken by a range of granite hills. The principal use to which the sides of these rocky hills are appropriated is to supply burial places for the dead. The soil of the island is naturally thin and unproductive except in the small valleys where water is found and where the mould of higher regions has been collected by mountain torrents. The industry has, however, in some measure overcome the original barrenness of the ground and now secures tolerable good crops. The production consists chiefly of sweet-potatoes, paddy, wheat, sugar-cane, ground nuts and garden vegetables. The prevailing feature of the island, except where the land of cultivation is constantly employed, is naked barrenness. The eye searches in vain except in a few favoured spots for the larger species of the vegetable kingdom. On the tops of some of the hills a few scattered firs are growing. The markets are chiefly supplied with vegetables and meat from the mainland. The population of the island is computed to be between 350,000 and 400,000. Of this number, the numerous villages are said to contain nearly 100,000, the rest being the city population.

When Amoy was first occupied by the British in 1841, a large portion of the force perished from disease but the excessive mortality was in a great measure owing to the over indulgence of the troops in ardent spirits, inattention to the quality of the water drank, and the bad state of the commissariat department. At a subsequent period when more attention was paid to hygiene measures the health of the men was very much improved.

With regard to disease among the Chinese population, ophthalmic complaints seen here as elsewhere in China, appear to be very numerous. Affections of the organs of respiration are remarkably common; most of coughs resulting from slight bronchial irritations. Asthma is a common complaint and rheumatism is very prevalent. The number of cases of ague seems to be large as in most parts of China. Dr Hepburn who has charge for several years of a dispensary at Amoy states that phthisis is by no means uncommon among the native population, but thinks it is not so frequent as in Europe or America. During one of the years in which he had charge of this institution he classified the diseases which came under his notice in the following manner.

Table 4: Medical statistics at Amoy 1858

Affections of the eyes	571
Affections of the organs of respiration	244
Affections of the organs of digestion	393
Affections of the organs of generation	120
Affections of the skin	175
Miscellaneous	359
Total	1862

Numerous cases of cholera occurred at Amoy in the summer of 1858 among the native population, and there were a few fatal cases among the European residents. Several cases occurred on board HMS Acorn and two of them proved fatal [1].

Dr Duggan, a medical gentleman with whom I became acquainted at Shanghai, told me that after a residence of nine months at Amoy, and three years and a half at Fuchau, he arrived at the conclusion that the former city was more unhealthy than the latter.

20. *Hutung Fort and Beacon on the East China coast. Painting by Capt P Cracroft of HMS Niger, The National Archives, London*

Chapter 6   **Fuchau**

Geographical position. Description of the River Min and the city of Fuchau. Pagoda Island described. Variety of Fuchau. Asylum for lepers. Hot sulphur springs. Prevalent diseases.

Fuchau, the capital of Fokien, stands on the north bank of the River Min, about 30 miles from the mouth. After entering fully within the river you find yourself between two ranges of mountains whose bases approach often to the margin of the stream. The valley between these mountainous ridges forms the bed of the Min, even to the city itself, and it is said for a long distance beyond it.

Between the city and the river mouth are several small villages, but much of the way the mountains approach too near the river to allow favourable sites for large settlements. The sides of the mountains are cultivated nearly to their summits, ground being laid out in terraces rising one above another till they reach an elevation difficult to be distinctly traced with the unassisted eye. Not far below the city, the mountains on the north bank of the Min diverge from the shore, leaving between it and them the large and fertile plain on which stands Fuchau with its extensive suburbs.

The anchorage for the shipping is Pagoda Island which is about 9 miles below the city. It is about 3 miles from circumference and rather hilly centre. The island takes its name from a 7 storied pagoda which stands on its summit. The pagoda is built of coarse grained granite.

The loquat and the lichi blossom in January; the first is ripe about the 25th of April; the second about the end of June. The (Lungyer) is in flower from the 1st of April to the 15th, and ripens in the latter half of August. The Chinese olive (Canarium) flowers in April, and is ripe in September, it bears a high price and is sent to Soochow. The Arbutus or Yang Mei (Myrica) is ripe in May. The komquat orange flowers in January and ripens in November. Pomegranates, grapes, pommeloes and guavas are ripe in August; the peach, pear and plum come to market from the last of May to the first of July. The apple is small but rather pleasant and ripen in December. The mandarin and coolie oranges are also very common, the former attain a large size.

It is said that there are several asylums for leprous individuals where they are fed and sustained, for they are not allowed to roam at large. The number of these miserable beings gathered into these retreats is said to be near 1000: the disease is here considered to be contagious and being loathsome and incurable, is the object of great terror and dread. In the immediate neighbourhood of Fuchau are several hot sulphur springs which are used by the Chinese for medicinal purposes. The water is hot and clear and, not only rises from the ground, but bubbles up out of the beds of streams in the neighbourhood [1].

Regarding the climate of Fuchau, it may be observed that those who have resided there consider it a very healthy one. February, May and September are the most rainy months. The winters are sufficiently long to afford an invigorating and very agreeable change after the close of the hot season, the thermometer sometimes falling to 38°, and frost and ice not being uncommon. During the hottest weeks the thermometer rises occasionally to 90°, but during the summer months cool breezes from the hills contribute to the salubrity of the city.

Dr Duggan, a medical gentleman, who had resided for three years at Fuchau, tells me that out of about 100 Europeans residing there he had only two deaths during the whole time: one was the case of a lady who died of chronic dysentery which she had contracted at Aden on her passage out to China, and the other was case of a gentleman who died of delirium tremens. Therefore, it appears that he had no deaths from any disease contracted at Fuchau.

HMS Sampson was at anchor for several months opposite Pagoda Island (the usual anchorage for men of war) in the year 1858. Dr Hastings told me that the ship was remarkably healthy during the whole time.

21. Stern of Fuchau pole junk. Painting by Ivon A Donelly, Chinese Junks and other native craft, 1924

CHAPTER 7   **NINGPO**

Geographical position. Description of city and surrounding neighbourhood. Prevalent diseases.

Ningpo is a large city situated at the confluence of two rivers, nearly in the center of a large alluvial plain varying from about 10 to 15 miles in breadth and 2 to 25 miles in length, enclosed on all sided by hills latitude 29.58° North, longitude 120.18 East. The plain is intersected in every direction by canals which serve for draining, irrigation and transportation. The soil is very productive and presents an aspect of teeming fertility. In the city there is large pagoda: it is 12 storied and 164 feet in height.

The climatic features of the department in which Ningpo is situated, exhibit great extremes of heat and cold. For three months in summer the heat is excessive. The thermometer has frequently been known to range from 96° to 102° for many days in succession. In general terms it may be said that there is a hot and cold season, of three months each, with intervening agreeable periods of the same duration. The winters may be compared with those of Paris and summers, for short seasons, to those of Calcutta. During all seasons of the year the average temperature of Ningpo is somewhat below Shanghai.

This alluvial, marshy district is fruitful in fevers of nearly every type. In the spring and summer of 1849, after a season of almost unprecedented moisture, fevers of a violent intermittent form first appeared, and subsequently those of a low typhoid character. The latter cases were particularly fatal, many villages decimated, and of those who took the disease, very few recovered. Foreigners suffered also but none fell victim to the malady. Intermittent fever is, however, very common at all seasons of the year.

Dr Macgowan [1], who was attached as medical missionary to the hospital at Ningpo during the year 1852, took some trouble in collecting the medical statistics of the city. He gave me the following summary of the cases which came into his charge.

Table 5: Medical statistics, Hospital at Ningpo 1852

Ophthalmic cases	3856
Diseases of the ear	15
Surgical diseases	725
Cutaneous affections	1989
Intermittent fever	411
Remittent fever	105
Diseases of the chest	219
Diseases of the digestive organs	554
Miscellaneous	82
Total	7956

The filthy condition of the city, the stagnant canals, exposure of nameless ordures, the number of dead left in coffins above ground in vacant spaces, would seem to render this, like other towns, the very focus of malaria; but while this state of things is unfavourable to longevity, it has not, so far as observation extends, caused them to be peculiarly obnoxious to epidemics. Cases of small pox and measles are not, however, infrequent, particularly in the spring and summer months. The city seems to enjoy a great exemption from pulmonary affections. Phthisis appears to be a very rare disease. In this respect Ningpo differs greatly from Amoy and Shanghai, for in the latter cities, diseases of the respiratory organs are very common. Rheumatism is, however, a very common complaint.

In the year 1820 Ningpo was visited by cholera, and during the summer of that and the following year, suffered severely. Since the last named period, it has prevailed epidemically, though few years pass by without the occurrence of sporadic cases.

Foreigners are very subject to diarrhoea; it is said that a few hours sailing among the islands of the Chusan archipelago is almost sure to arrest the disease. Towards the end of the hot season natives as well as foreigners are liable to be affected by boils.

22. *Ningpo trading vessel. Painting by Ivon A Donelly, Chinese Junks and other native craft, 1924*

Chaper 8 Chusan

Geographical position. Description of the island. Geological nature of the island. The harbour described. Occupation of the island by the British forces in 1840. Unhealthiness of the troops and it's probable causes.

Chusan is an island, 5½ miles long and 20¾ miles in circumference. The greatest breadth is 10½ miles and narrowest 6 miles. The direction of the island is from north-east to south-west. The general aspect, and that of all the neighbouring islands and coasts, is ridges of lofty hills, very steep and occasionally running into peaks. The ranges of hills enclose beautiful and fertile valleys; some of them in the interior of the island are almost completely sheltered by the hills, but the greater number run from the interior towards the sea. All the larger valleys have a stream of water running through them but none of them are sufficiently large to merit the name of rivers.

The principal portion of island is composed of porphyritic clay stone [1]. Assuming in some places a columnar or in others, a laminated structure. The soil in the valleys is dark alluvial mould. There is no limestone in the island. The harbour in Chusan is well situated either for the purpose of war or commerce. It is superior to that of Hong Kong being more easy of access and egress in all winds and safer in a typhoon. As a military position it is well placed, being midway between the northern and southern portions of the empire, and only 60 miles to the south of the entrance of the great river Yangtse Kiang.

The climate of Chusan is subject to a great range of temperature. The range of temperature during the 24 hours sometimes varies remarkably: a change of 30 degrees has been noticed. During the south-west monsoon the weather is hot and sometimes oppressive, the thermometer in the shade frequently standing at 90° during the day: the average of the night being about 72°. During the north-east monsoon the weather is generally very cold with fine clear days. During December, January and February the thermometer is as low as 25° or 26° during the night. During the cold weather there is frequently ice upon the ponds. Snow occasionally falls during the winter but seldom in sufficient quantities to cover the plain. The hills around the city are sometimes capped with snow.

The mortality among the British troops which landed here in 1840-41 was excessive. The 26th Cameronians landed 860 strong in Chusan in about October 1840 and such was the mortality among them that could not muster 200 effective men leaving their compound in the March following. Thus, in four short months, bad water and worse food carried off nearly 700 of the best and most seasoned troops sent there from India.

It may be asked, seeing the favourable position of the island and the comparative mildness of the climate, does much disease exist among the natives themselves or was it from particular causes alone that the British troops suffered so severely in the years 1840-41 when located there. It would seem that there could be no doubt that malaria exists to a powerful degree in nearly the whole of the valleys, arising from the excessive moisture in which the surface of the ground is kept by the banking up of the streams from the hills. During the wet weather the canals and dykes overflow and the country is flooded with water. During the summer months the days are very hot, and at night the dews are exceedingly heavy, so that if any one be exposed at this time, their clothes soon become saturated with moisture.

As to the reasons to be assigned for the degree of sickness that prevailed among the troops while at Chusan, it may be observed that the most prominent causes were the laborious but unavoidable duties which the men had to perform, their exposure to the sun by day and to the heavy dews by night, united to which was the want of fresh provisions which could not at first be procured. When the strength of the men was worn down, being exposed to the malaria of the locality in which they were, fever seized upon them, followed by severe and almost incurable dysentery, which proved fatal to a most fearful extent. To so great a degree did these diseases prevail, that of the whole force very few of the men escaped more or less severe attacks.

The disadvantages of the island seem, however, to have been of our making, although it must be confessed that fever, particularly of the intermittent type, is common enough among the inhabitants. Although the deaths among the men were numerous, very few officers suffered severely and there were only one or two instances of any of them dying from the climate. They had generally healthy nourishment and exposed themselves less to the enervating heat than the troops on shore. By better management and cautions no such distressing sickness would have occurred although living in swamps in any part of the world must be productive of fever and dysentery.

Elephantiasis is said to be more common in Chusan than many other parts of China known to Europeans [2]. As compared with Hong Kong this island is healthy. During the war of 1840-41 the deaths among the troops stationed at Hong Kong was 1 in 3½; at Chusan it was 1 in 29½. Chusan is generally considered more favourable to health than Shanghai, Ningpo or Nanking. The reason probably is that the latter cities are situated on a flat alluvial plain without any mountains and sea-breeze to temper the atmosphere during the intense heat of the summer months.

23. *Chusan archipelago fishing craft. Painting by Ivon A Donelly, Chinese Junks and other native craft, 1924*

CHAPTER 9   SHANGHAI

Geographical position. Description of the Chinese city and the foreign settlement. Public institutions. Earthquakes. Woosung anchorage recommended during hot months. A cruise to Japan or among the islands of the Chusan Archipelago recommended when there is much sickness on board the ships. Prevalent diseases. Epidemic or catarrhal ophthalmia. The climate of Shanghai and Canton compared. Tabular statement of diseases treated at the Shanghai dispensary. Comparative return of the European hospital.

Shanghai is a large city situated in latitude 31, 15 north and longitude 121, 29 east at nearly 70 miles from the island of Gutzlaff [1] at the embouchure of the great river Yangtse Kiang. On the north branch of the Woosung branch of the river, the town of Shanghai rears its weathered mature and noble foreign structures in the midst of a soil wholly alluvial. The Chinese city lies to the East of the European settlement and is large, busy, dirty, uncomfortable and dangerous. Within and without the walls, the city is cut up by innumerable ditches and moats. There are in the city of Shanghai a Public Dispensary, a Humane Society, a Foundling Hospital, an Alms House for the aged and infirm, a Poor Fund, and a fund for the providing of coffins. The Humane Society or Kew Sang Kewh (establishment for saving life) is situated on the bank of the river outside the great East gate of the city: its object is to save the lives of those who fall into the river. The bodies of any thus rescued are taken to the establishment, where efforts are made to restore life, but from the list of persons receiving, it would seem that the chief duty of the superintendent consists of furnishing coffins for his patients.

This is done at the expense of the institution which like the Jung Jin Tang Hall of United Benevolence, is supported by public subscription. Among the plans adopted for the rescue, one is to place the patient on his back, and then invert a large iron boiler, commonly used for cooking rice, over the abdomen. This they ply and on the account of the cohesion between the empty space and the distended abdomen causes the ejection of water from the nose. Another plan is to suspend the patient by his feet from the shoulders of a man standing erect, stopping up the anus by a wad of cotton to prevent the passing of a motion that would be filthy. This will soon be followed by the flowing of water from the mouth, and the patient's life will be spared. The public dispensary has attached to it 15 practitioners for internal diseases, 4 for infantile diseases, 2 for ophthalmic diseases and 4 for performing acupuncture.

The Hall of United Benevolence. Its office is in the city where the officers and committee meet for the management of all the details of business. Outside the South Gate, it has a large cemetery, where the poor are buried and coffins are also given, with certain restrictions to those who are unable to purchase them for their diseased relatives. Money is also distributed to the poor. Outside the North

Gate it has a large and commodious building appropriated as a hospital for the aged and infirm who have no relatives to maintain them and who are committed on the recommendation of the subscribers and supporters of the institution.

The Foundling Hospital. This institution is supported by public subscription and receives all the sick children as are sent to it. They are placed by their relatives in a box near the front of the gate, and a bell is struck to give notice to the gate-keeper, who transfers the little ones to the care of the matrons. Some of the children are sent out to nurse; others are kept in the hospital under the charge of two wet nurses hired for the purpose. Each of these women has two children to feed, and if at any time she cannot afford them sufficient nourishment, she gives them flour and water which is kept in readiness. The establishment appears to be tolerably well managed. The rooms are as clean as Chinese rooms commonly are; the children seem to be well fed and the nurses are healthy looking strong women.

From the above statements concerning the charitable institutions, it will be seen that the charge brought against the Chinese in common with all other healthier nations that among all are found no hospitals or other institutions for the relief of the sick and destitute is not correct.

The foreign settlement which is very extensive is in the westward of the Chinese city. The streets are wide, and the houses large, commodious and elegant. There is a wide pleasant promenade and carriage drive along the riverbank called the Bund. The residents support a public library, a hospital for the Chinese, and a sailors home. Dr Sibbald, a resident medical practitioner has a hospital for the benefit of the merchant fleet where sailors receive medical treatment at a moderate charge. This hospital frequently proves of service to men of war frequenting this port as it affords a quiet retreat for serious cases of disease.

During the time Shanghai has been occupied by Europeans several shocks of earthquake have been felt. The prognostics observed were a highly electric state of the atmosphere, a long drought, excessive heat, and what seemed like a stagnation of all nature. Within the past few years there have also been several falls of dust. The putrid shower consists of infinitesimally fine powder, sometimes black, occasionally yellow.

As consequence of the great heat of the summer months in Shanghai, I should recommend that the ships situation here during the hot months should remove to the anchorage at Woosung which is 10 miles due north of Woosung. On account of the large fleet of ships in Shanghai and the close proximity of the houses, the atmosphere is doubtless polluted by offensive smells arising from the city and the suffocation of air obstructed. The temperature of Woosung will be found more agreeable and the emanations from the surrounding country not so rebellious to health.

24. *The Shanghai tea gardens, 1844. Watercolour by Edward Cree, M Levien, The Cree Journals, 1981*

25. *Near the north gate of Shanghai, 1844. Watercolour by Edward Cree, M Levien, The Cree Journals, 1981*

I feel that I am doing the navy in China a service by calling attention to the importance of authorising the captains of ships of war whenever there should be much serious sickness on board to make course to the Japan islands. The harbour at Nagasaki is 3 days easy steaming and affords a useful change from the alluvial coast which our vessels frequently need. The Chusan islands afford a change, but of comparatively small variety. The case of a large American frigate which left Shanghai in 1857 with a very heavy lot of serious cases of disease affords an illustration by soon after reaching Japan every case recovered. The most persistent complaints are diarrhoea, dysentery, intermittent fever, remittent and typhoid fevers, pulmonary complaints, rheumatism and cutaneous diseases. Diarrhoea and dysentery occur at all seasons of the year, but more in the summer and autumn.

Table 6: *Medical statistics Missionary Hospital Shanghai 1853 and 1856*

	1853	1856
Intermittent fever	570	580
Cough	690	486
Asthma	164	130
Haemoptysis + Phthisis	48 / 37	70
Dyspepsia	980	698
Diarrhoea	280	300
Dysentery	166	212
Psora + Psoriasis	480 / 280	1930*

* Including Leprosy

Intermittent fever is remarkably frequent as might be expected from the grassy nature of the surrounding district. This is a form of ague which has been noticed in a few cases. The patient has every day, or on the alternate days, a slight cold stage, followed by the hot; then the hands and feet alone begin to perspire most profusely, the water standing in beads on the skin, and even running off the hands when held down, the rest of the body being quite dry: This species of ague, with it confined local perspiration, is accompanied with intense headache, and more general discomfort and suffering than normally occur during common ague.

A fatal form of petechial fever has occasionally prevailed at Shanghai among the inhabitants of the city and has proven very fatal. Those who have had opportunities of observing this fever state that from the commencement of the attack, the patient is much prostrated, the skin burning hot, the pulse quick and feeble, with extreme pain in the head accompanied by frequent vomiting and in the worse cases excessive diarrhoea and even dysentery. The petechiae make their appearance on the 3rd or 4th day; the body becoming then covered with the usual purple spots in patches, and when these came freely out there was less danger in the issue of the case. In fatal cases death generally occurs on the 7th or 10th day. In those that were not fatal the patients had a long and tedious convalescence, suffering much from extreme debility [2].

Bronchitis, pleurisy and pneumonia are common complaints in this part of China. Cutaneous lesions are very common among the natives owing to the lack of cleanliness. Cases of smallpox occur almost every spring, and Europeans occasionally fall victims to the disease. In the city of Shanghai, there is a temple dedicated to the god of cutaneous diseases, such temples are not uncommon in Chinese cities [3]. A few cases of cholera occur almost every summer. In the summer of 1859, there were several cases on board the men of war and the merchant ships.

During the summer of 1859 there was an epidemic of catarrhal opthalmia [4] at Shanghai. The disease was very common among both natives and foreigners. On board HMS Highflyer we had upwards of 50 cases of the disease and it was found necessary to place 34 of them on the sick list. The complaint seldom lasted more than 7 or 8 days. Men were seldom kept from duty more than three or four days. The consummation of mild aperients, the local application of cold and warm formulations, together with seclusion from the glare of the sun were the chief remedial measures employed and they were in all cases successful. Though the disease is amenable to the treatment in the beginning of the attack, still many cases have occurred among the Chinese, where the patient has not been attended to at once and with regularity, in which the result has been material injury or even destruction of one or both eyes.

Dr Hobson [5] who spent several years in both Canton and Shanghai and had ample opportunities of comparing the two climates came to the following conclusions.

1st That a far larger proportion of diseases among the inhabitants of this vast plain (where irrigation is greater than in any other part) are of an intermittent or periodic character arising from malaria. Canton and Macao are nearly entirely free from marsh effluvia, and hence intermittent fevers, neuralgia, dysentery and nervous depression are much less common in those parts than here.

2nd That inflammatory afflictions of the healthy organs are far more frequent in this part of China; whooping cough and croup are unknown, and acute bronchitis, pleurisy, and pneumonia are very rarely seen in the South of China and observe no difference in sanguinous discharges, tropical effusions and pulmonary consumption.

3rd This climate is more trying for young children, especially during teething. It is also unsuitable from its sudden alterations in temperature, and increased cold and dampness, to persons with weak lungs, or of a rheumatic diathesis. It is also disagreeable and at first for residents who have been acclimatized to the tropics, especially those of nervous excitable temperament, or liable to intermittent fever. Children can remain much longer in China than they can do in any part of India.

4th Cutaneous diseases among the natives here are much more frequent and severe owing to the lack of frequent ablution, and from wearing the same underclothes for months together, and even for successive years during the winter months, without washing the undergarments. Scrofulous enlargement of the glands and leprosy, are however much more common in Canton than Shanghai probably from the excess of heat.

In the year 1853 there were 11,028 patients in 1856 there were 11, 595 patients attended at the missionary hospital.

26. *The Customs House Shanghai. From the Standard Altas and Gazetteer of the World. Standard Publishing Co. Chicago, 1888*

Chapter 10 **Pekin**

Geographical position. Description of the city. Temples and palaces. Account of the action off the Peiho River of 25th June 1859. List of killed or wounded. HMS Temporary Hospital Ship Assistance.

Pekin. The capital of China is situated 40 degrees of the northern latitude in a sandy and very fertile plain between the Peiho River and its affluence 100 miles North-west of the mouth of the former river or a canal which is said to join the Yangtse Kiang with the Peiho River but to those who visited Pekin in 1860, did not appear to have been much used of late. It is 50 miles south of the Great Wall of China. Pekin forms a square and is divided into two cities; the northern one is named Sin Ching, or the new city, in the centre of which is the Imperial Palace. Its circumference is estimated at 7 miles. It is inhabited by Tartars [1]. The streets are wide and straight, cutting one another at right angles. They are very sandy, and some of them have rows of trees before the houses, which are principally of one story.

The other city is called Lau Ching, or the old city, and is separate from the other by a large wall. The greater part of the inhabitants are Chinese, it has an appearance very similar to the towns in South China having narrow paved dusty streets. The circumference of the two cities is estimated to be 18 miles. The wall of Pekin is about 60 feet in height and 80 feet in breadth having 8 or 9 large gates over each of which barracks or guard houses are built 4 or 5 stories high. These are the only remarkable objects that strike the eye when approaching Pekin, as there are very few high pagodas in the city or the neighbourhood. The suburbs on the east and north-east side of Pekin do not lay at the foot of the wall, but with the exception of a few streets which are close to the gates are some distance off, some as much a two miles, and appear to have been summer residences or large store-houses, very few shops being seen there.

The principle temples were the Temple of Heaven inside the city, the Temple of the Earth at the south-east end of the Tartar city, and the Lama Temple in the north-east suburb. The summer palace of the emperor is about 8 miles from the nearest gate and occupies a space of about 7 square miles. From a pagoda on the top of the hill belonging to the summer palace the Great Wall of China can be seen in the distance. Pekin is not a commercial city. The inhabitants get their wants principally supplied from Tung Chow [2] (15 miles from Pekin on above-mentioned canal near the Peiho) and Tientsin through the canals from the south. The country is flat, and a great deal less inhabited than the borders of the lower part of the Peiho River around Tientsin. The temperature of Pekin is very hot in summer, and very cold in winter, particularly during northerly winds, which blow down from the mountains of Tartary, which in October 1860 were observed to be already covered with snow.

I am sorry to say that I have failed to obtain accurate information regarding the most prevalent diseases of Pekin.

To conclude these remarks I subjoin a description of the fight at the Peiho River on the 25th June 1859, the most important of all as regards the severity of the action and the numbers killed and wounded, and the only one of which I was present [3].

On the 25th June 1859 the Hon T Bruce arrived at the mouth of the Peiho where the British squadron under Admiral Hope had previously settled. Negotiations were immediately entered into with the Chinese authorities relative to the Bruce's landing and reception. These were treated in an evasive manner by the Chinese who pretended that Mr Bruce would not be received there, but it was necessary that the boats go to a river about 10 miles further north, the Pehtang, where they said orders had been given to receive him. Admiral Hope treated these as mere evasions and required that the stakes, booms and other obstructions of the river should forthwith be removed to enable our small vessels to pass into the river and hence onwards to Tientsin. The Chinese replied that the fort at the mouth of the river and the defenses of the river itself were only intended against pirates and rebels and not against us and that they would not remove them at the request of a foreign authority. Admiral Hope replied by allowing them a certain time to remove them, informing them that if they were not removed he would remove them himself.

On the 24th June the Marines and landing party, having been placed on board the gunboats, moved in and took up a position inside the bar where HMS Nimrod and HMS Cormorant had already placed themselves. Some junks were seized and taken possession of, to afford temporary quarters for the marine battalion. On the morning of the 25th June the gunboats placed themselves in position opposite the fort in the river below the barrier. About 2 o'clock, Admiral Hope moved up the river in HMS Plover, supported by the Opossum and Attempter to pass through the first line of obstruction, namely strong spiked stakes passed across the river. On this the Chinese immediately opened fire from the forts whereon the signal was made to engage and the action immediately became general. Our ships were the HMS Nimrod, Cormorant, Opossum, Plover, Banterer, Janus, Kestrel, Haughty, Starling and Forester. The fire of the enemy forts distant from 500 – 800 yards was directed with great precision and with great effect. Many of the shots fired were of heavier calibre than usual and altogether the batteries worked in a style very different from the Chinese warfare therefore. Admiral Hope was soon obliged to retire with the Opossum and Plover, both of which together with HMS Lee which had been sent to their assistance were very much cut up. About 5 o'clock Admiral Hope was severely wounded and taken to the Cormorant. Subsequently the fire of the enemy having slackened and being apparently silenced, it was determined to land and endevour to take possession of them.

Accordingly, at 7 o'clock, the attempt was made, but the enemy returned to their guns, and re-opened their fire with murderous accuracy and vehemence. Our men, although much impeded in their advance by the soft nature of the ground being up to their ankles in mud, advanced with great energy to the front, although momentarily some of their numbers were mown down by enemy fire. Captain Vansilland, second in command, being struck by a round shot in the leg was carried to the rear. Captain Shadwell in charge of the landing party was wounded by a musket ball in the foot, but managed notwithstanding to reach the first ditch. Our men in position in the first ditch with the advanced party holding the second, vainly endeavored to make further way and scale the walls. The enemy's fire however, continued so deadly and the mud was so deep that it was impossible to overcome the difficulties of the position. Added to this, very few had been able to keep their ammunition dry. As our case was now hopeless, the order was given to retire. In effecting the retreat many lives were lost for the Chinese kept up an incessant fire and our men were shot down in great numbers and several were drowned in the attempt to get off to the boats. The ships Plover, Lee, Kestrel, Haughty and Cormorant were all sunk by the enemy fire.

27. Battle of the Peiho River 1859

Among the officers wounded were Admiral Hope, Captain Shadwell and, Captain Vansillant. Among the killed were Lieut Graves, Lieut Clutterbuck, Lieut Herbert, Lieut Inglis, Lieut Woolridge and Colonel Lemon.

The Casomandel was made a temporary hospital. It was nearly one o'clock in the morning before the last boatload of men was brought off to her, and long ere that hour she was crowded with the mutilated and the dying. The number of killed and wounded was 434. The 1st battalion of marines alone, which landed barely 400 strong, lost altogether 172 killed and wounded, the Chesapeake had 26 killed and 34 wounded, the Highflyer 9 killed and 18 wounded [Appendix 4] and the gunboats 90 killed and wounded.

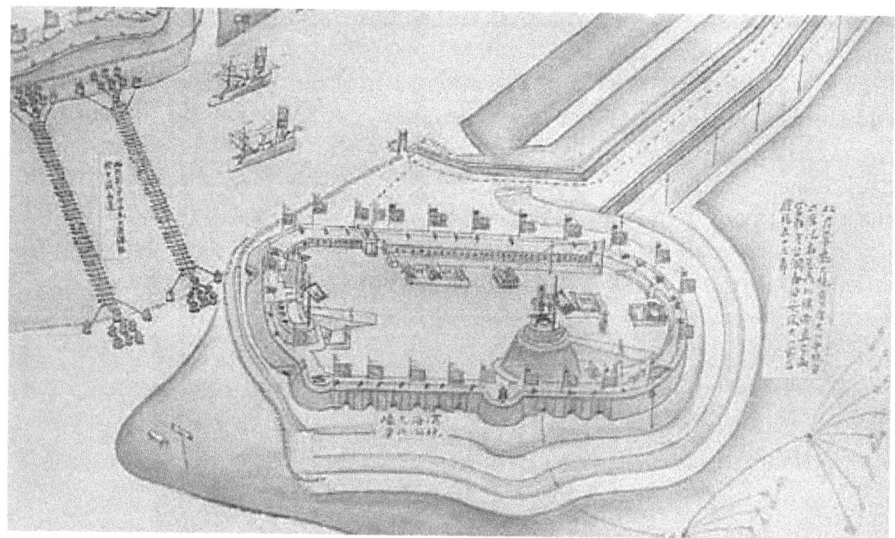

28. *Chinese fort on the east shore of the Peiho River 1859, Tang Gu Museum of History*

29. *Remains of the Taku Forts, Tang Gu, near Tianjin, 2010*

A few days after the defeat at the Peiho Forts, the troop ship HMS Assistance was converted into a temporary hospital for the occupation of the wounded from the fleet. The marines from the Battalion of Engineers were received on board immediately after the attack. Afterwards the seamen and marines belonging to the ships engaged. All embarked on the 5th July, when the Assistance sailed in the afternoon for King Lang Island. She arrived, and anchored midway between the island and the main land. This was supposed to be a very healthy locality. Provisions of medical comforts were procurable; the anchorage being about 10 miles from Ningpo and 12 hours run from Shanghai.

The nature of the wounds consisted principally of bullet wounds, simple fractures and a few compound fractures and several cases of arrow wounds. There were also a few with severe contusions with burns caused by the explosion of gunpowder. On the 9th, 10th and 11th July 1859 the weather became very sultry with a damp atmosphere. The patients began to suffer much from the heat and some of the wounds in the forepart of the ship took on an unhealthy action. The patients complaining of prickly pain of heat in the seal of the wound accompanied with small fever, thirst and constipation of the bowels. On the 12th July the first decided case of gangrene made its appearance when the disease rapidly spread on both sides of the deck to the after part of the ship although every precaution was taken by the removal of the cases as they occurred to the upper deck, one side of which was appropriated to the use of the sick until the disease became so prevalent that numbers were obliged to be kept on the lower deck. But as some cases of death occurred from haemorrhage on the upper deck, the patients had a strong objection to being removed above.

Several cases of amputation were performed in hope of removing the disease at first, but it invariably presented itself again in the stump with more malignancy. The treatment found most efficacious in removing the plague consisted in the application of nitric acid. At times a solution of sulphate of copper was applied but was found not to answer so well. In slight cases, oil of turpentine did well, and partly did away with the fetid smell. At the same time the strength of the patient was kept up as much as possible by wine porter and nutritious food. By the latter part of August and beginning of September the disease was very much abutted and then the HMS Assistance received orders to proceed to Hong Kong as soon as it was thought advisable without injury to the patients. No cases occurring for 15 days, HMS Assistance left King Lang on the 17th September and arrived in Hong Kong on the 25th September, 1859.

CHPATER 11   **NAGASAKI**

Geographical position. Description of the town. Population. Chief public buildings. Island of Deshima. Coal mines. Nagasaki recommended as a sanatorium for the residents of Southern China.

Nagasaki is a situated at the southwestern part of Kiusiu, latitude 32° 43' longitude 130°11.47 east. It is nearly in the same latitude as Malta. The approach to the town is particularly fine, a ship having to pass between a succession of lovely islands before arriving at the bay which forms the harbour of Nagasaki. The whole of the surrounding country is noted for its picturesque beauty presenting to view alternate hills and valleys clothed to their summits with oaks, cedars and laurels and richly cultivated with traced field and gardens of brightest green.

The greater part of the town is built on a low level slip of land at the extremity of the harbour, but many houses stand on slope of the hills. Ships lie a very short distance off the town protected from all winds. The population is said to be about 60,000. While the conclusion of the late treaty was that Nagasaki be the only port at which foreigners were allowed to trade, for the two centuries during which any intercourse has been allowed to them. The town is well-built. The streets are guarded by light wooden gates at which watchmen are stationed. They are short and wide and kept very clean by being frequently watered. Swept gutters and sewers drain the refuse water and feed into the harbour. The height of the houses is regulated by government. They seldom exceed one story to which is added in some a sort of cockloft and in others a low cellar. Most of them are build of wood, but many are constructed of a framework of bamboo tried together with rope and then covered with a tenacious mud which when dry is again covered with a coat of plaster. In the rear of a large proportion of the houses are small yards or gardens containing a few flowers and generally a tub for washing and bathing. The floors of the rooms are covered with mats which are kept scrupulously clean as squatting; not sitting is the usual practices there. Oiled paper supplies the place of glass, and the windows are further protected from the weather by external wooden shutters and venetian blinds.

The chief public buildings are the palace of the governor and grandee of the empire and the temples. Most of the edifices occupy a large extent of ground. Tea houses are remarkably numerous. The artificial island of Deshima [1], to which the Dutch merchants were formerly rigorously confined is about 600 feet in Length and 240 feet in breadths, a few yards from the shore close to which stands the town.

Nagasaki seems destined to derive an accession of trade from neighbouring coal deposits which are numerous and perhaps extensive. The coal, however, is for the most part of an inferior quality, abounding in sulphur and leaving a large residuum of soot, ashes, and clinkers. It appears to be surface coal. Scientific mining might prove more satisfactory. Vegetable-wax has lately become an important article of export. Silk, isinglass, seaweed, camphor and copper are also articles of export.

During the summer months the temperature of Nagasaki is an average 85 of degrees. The thermometer occasionally reaches 95 or 98 degrees. The heat is, however, somewhat modified by the sea breeze. In the winter season the thermometer sometimes descends as low as 25°. The weather is changeable and rain is abundant all the year round. The rainy season occurs in June and July.

Nagasaki, on account of its proximity to Shanghai holds out special inducements to the foreign residents of that city as a sanatorium, particularly during the summer months. Its exemption from miasmatic discourses will render the change from any of the alluvial districts of China very beneficial. Consumption, however, is said to be a common disease among the native inhabitants. The writer must however observe that although the change from Shanghai and other parts of China during the summer months would doubtless prove beneficial to most invalids, he would recommend some more northern part to those who can afford the time and extra expense where the heat is somewhat less and the weather is of a more bracing character.

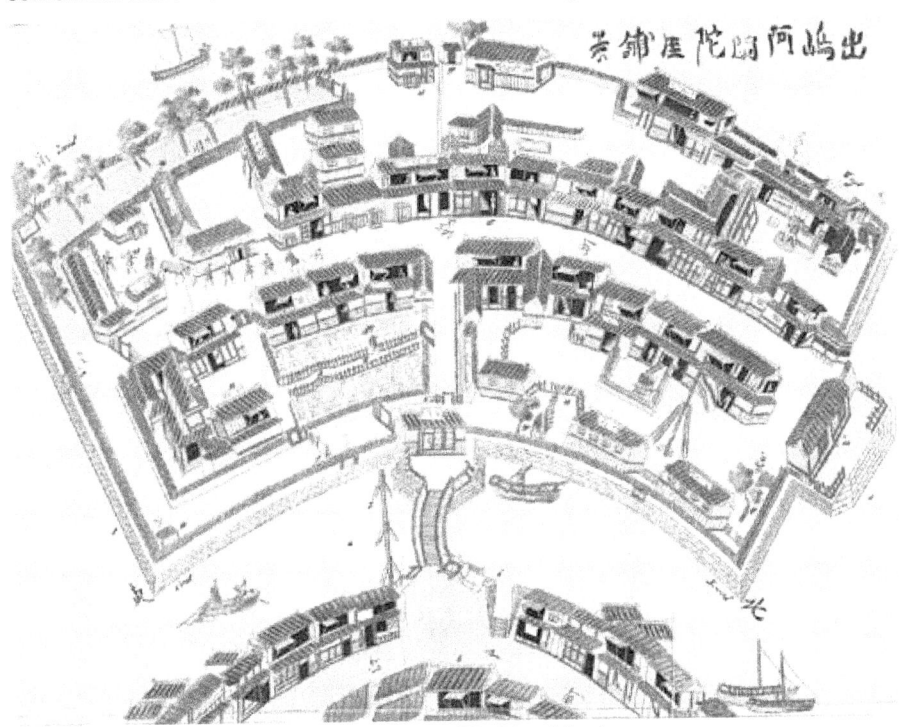

30. Map of Deshima Island

Chapter 12   Yedo

Geographical position Description of the city, Fire engines. Fire proof buildings. Width of the streets. Observations on the Japanese Bay of Yedo described. Account of the great eruption of the volcano Fusiama in 1783. Yokohama, the port of Yedo, described

Yedo the capital of Japan is situated at the head of a bay or estuary round which it extends in a crescent like shape. Latitude 35.40 N and Longitude 139.40. In consequence of the extensive flats which border that part of the bay in which the city of Yedo is situated, ships are obliged to anchor at a distance of 5 or 6 miles from shore, off the suburb called Sinagawa, an hours pull leaving to the right the five large square forts which defend the approach to the city. One lands at the Tokado or great high road which traverses the whole island. From the landing place to the city proper, it is a walk of some half an hour, through densely populated streets consisting generally of two storied houses scrupulously clean though the absence of all paint is certainly no improvement to the look of the place.

Yedo not being yet open to the world only a few privileged persons can visit it, and in leaving ones residence to take a walk through the streets one is immediately surrounded by officers who are responsible for the safety of the strangers under their care. The procession is headed by two men with long poles furnished at the top with half a dozen iron rings, which as the other end stamped at the ground at every step keep up a musical jingle. The business part of the town is separated from the official by a large bridge, the Nippon Bas [1], and as this part contains the most attraction for strangers it is the part most frequently visited. At regular distances of 30 or 40 houses the street is divided by gates where the men with the ring-staffs are relieved. Here too the crowd, which always flocks out at the sound of the ring-poles, is kept back.

At each of these gates there is a ladder reaching up to a large bronze bell which serves as an alarm in case of fire, while a fire-engine is always ready on the opposite side. These fire-engines soon drew my attention and I examined them attentively. They are excellent specimens of the old model of fire-engine. In each of these streets, or rather wards, is also one, sometimes two fire-proof buildings to which we were told, the inhabitants carried their valuables in case of alarm. From all these precautions fires must be very prevalent, though it is difficult to imagine how a fire can ever be extinguished should it begin in such a crowded place where every house is build of wood. Yet fires are of frequent occurrence and do not spread far, for in every quarter we see the ravages being repaired and they did not seem to have extended further than at most to a couple of houses. The greater part of the city of Yedo is built with extreme regularity, the streets cutting each other at right angles. Temples, monasteries, and other religions buildings abound, many of them are situated in conspicuous places with gardens and ponds beautifully laid out.

31. Map of Yedo (Tokyo) found in the Courtney Journal, 1850's

The city of Yedo is not enclosed by a wall, nor are any of the cities of Japan for the government being feudal the system adopted is that of fortified castles {2}. Canals intersect the city in every direction. The Emperors Palace is an immense range of buildings with extensive grounds intended for the court and its armed retainers. It is of an irregular figure roughly in a circle. The imperial residence embraces two castles in front as one may call them, the innermost or third castle which is properly the residence of the Emperor and two other strong well fortified but smaller castles at the side. Each castle is enclosed with walls and ditches.

The streets are all wide and well macadamized. Many of the shops too, particularly the silk shops, are as large if not larger than any in either London or Paris. Of the extent of the town it is difficult to say, or to form any idea. On the occasion of our visit we went on for 4 hours in a straight line and might have gone on still further for I could see no end to the street. When walking along, I must confess that one is constantly struck by proof of the high state of civilisation of this people. They appear to be a people contented with their lot, respecting their government, able to supply all their wants within themselves. There are no houses falling to ruins, no people in rags and no cripples. Not only in Yedo but throughout the country, one sees nothing but contentment and prosperity.

In the city and neighbourhood are many gardens adorned with trees and flowers among them. I noticed maples, varieties of laurel, bay box camphor, willows, pines, cedars, a few palms, juniper, and a great variety of hibiscus. The *Camilla Japonica* becomes a tree sometimes 35 feet high.

From the city and Bay of Yedo a beautiful view may be obtained of the celebrated mountain Fusiama which rises in a regular cone to the height of nearly 12,000 feet. This magnificent mountain forms a favorite subject for embellishing the wares of the Japanese and identifies articles with that country.

Shocks of earthquake are exceedingly common at Yedo. At the British Consulate at Yedo in the summer of 1859 scarcely a day passed without some slight tremor. It was at Yedo in the year 1783 that one of the most frightful earthquakes on record occurred. It seems to have exceeded in its horrors and wide distinction the earthquake of Lisbon. The accounts state that at 8 o'clock in the morning of the 27th of July of that year, a great wind got up, accompanied by subterranean muttering of thunder, which continued augmenting from day to day, in seeming menace of some frightful catastrophe until the 1st of August. On that day an earthquake, with loud thunder, shook all the houses to their foundation, the intensity of the shocks each moment increasing until the summit of the mountain was rent open, and fire and flame appeared, followed by such an avalanche of sand and stones, tossed high into the air, and carried to incredible distances, that the darkness of night come on, the only light being the lurid glare of burning lava and devastating flames. Vast chasms opened before the affrighted inhabitants in their flight, into which thousands, in the darkness and panic, urged on by the streams of fire and showers of stone and ashes are said to have been perished. The shocks did not entirely cease until the 12th day and were felt over a space of 30 leagues. Twenty seven towns and villages were destroyed, and the rivers boiling and overflowing inundated the whole country to complete the work of destruction. My inquiries to the effect of earthquakes on the magnetic needle have led to no definite conclusion.

The sun during the hottest days of summer is very much less intense in its heat than on the neighbouring coast of China. The thermometer ranges in the shade from 70 to 85 degrees and average 80 degrees between the morning and evening, while it is sometimes below 70 degrees at night. This is a climate, therefore, which does not make mere existence a burden and an effort, as it often does in India and the South of China. The highest temperature registered at Yedo in 1859 was 85 degrees. May, June, July and September are the most raining months.

As to its suitability and freedom from disease, it is yet too soon to give a very decided opinion. The Japanese are, however, a clean people, wash often, wear little clothing, live in houses open to the air and have wide and well ventilated streets when nothing offensive is allowed to rest. It is said that cholera made its first visitation to Japan in 1818. Its record visitation was in 1850. In this last instance some declare that it was the United States Frigate Mississippi that brought it over and others that it was HMS Retribution.

No meteorological observations extending over any considerable period of time have as yet been taken at Yedo and I therefore subjoin the following remarks on the weather the result of observations made at Simoda, a town lying near the entrance of the Bay of Yedo. The information was supplied me by Mr Harris, the American Minister [3, 4].

Yokohama, a small town situated on the western shore of the Bay of Yedo is the common anchorage ground for men of war and merchantmen. It is the Port of Yedo. There are extensive marshes in the immediate neighbourhood. Intermittent fever and diarrhoea were very prevalent during the time the Highflyer was at anchor in this locality for one month. The weather, however, was very fine, the atmosphere being impeccably clear and serene.

32. *Painting of an unnamed American ship from Commander Perry's fleet in Japanese waters, Tokyo National Museum, 1850's*

Chapter 13   **Hakodadi**

Geographical position. Description of the town. Installation of Mr Hodgson as 1st British Consul. Lead mines. Exports of Hakodadi. Flora. Prevalent diseases

Hakodadi is situated on the north-east slope of a promontory which forms the eastern boundary of a spacious and beautiful bay at the south of the island of Yesso. The position is on the north side of the Strait of Tsugaru which is here about 15 miles broad. It is the largest town on the island with the exception of Matsmai. The Bay of Hakodadi is about 4 miles wide at the entrance and 5 miles deep. The harbour is on the south eastern arm of the bay, is completely sheltered with regular sounding and excellent holding ground. The extreme rise and full of the tide is 3 feet. The promontory on which the town is built has three peaks, the highest of which is 1131 feet high and is connected with the mainland by a low sandy isthmus. The general appearance of the place reminds one of Hong Kong and Gibraltar, all three places having a striking resemblance to each other.

The town extends for about one mile and a half along the sea-shore and consists of one broad main street and several others of lesser length running in the same direction. These are connected with cross streets some of which ascend nearly half a mile up the side of the hill. Immediately above the central portion of the town there is a large plantation of pines, cypresses, and maples.

In the month of October 1859 HMS Highflyer conveyed Mr Alcock, HM British Minister and Mr Hodgson. HM Consul to Hakodadi for the purpose of installing the latter gentleman as the first British Consul at the town [1]. As this event was one of some little importance, I here describe the installation on the 7th of October being appointed for an official audience, Mr Alcock was minister, Mr Hodgson our Consul, and Mr Cowan interpreter went ashore accompanied by as many of the officers as could be spared from the ship together with the Marines as a guard headed by a brass band. The interpreter had been told several times in the morning that there must be some proper person to meet us at the landing-place, but notwithstanding there we found no one to receive us though the authorities must have been aware of our approach from hearing the salute fired as Mr Alcock left the Highflyer. Fortunately Mr Cowan happened to know the way as he had been at the temple the day before. No one was at the gate and it was only at the end of one of the passages of the Temple that we were met by the Governor, an old grey headed gentleman to whom Mr Alcock introduced us, who then desired us to be seated at a long row of tables along one side of the room while he himself and his colleagues faced us man for man.

The Japanese who had visited us in the morning had been very anxious to know how many of the officers of the ship would accompany the Consul, but as it was impossible to give them an exact answer, so that they had reckoned, it seems upon two less than we were. The two last ones were however faced by two Japanese summoned its seemed on the spur of the moment for that purpose, but I must say we should not have noticed the circumference had it not been that these unfortunate gentlemen were not supplied with anything to eat or drink, as only a certain number of dishes were prepared.

The entertainment was an exact copy of what is generally seen on such occasions: a tobacco box, chaffing dish, ash pot and two long pipes on a 4 footed tray. Then a cup of weak tea placed before each person, a tray with sponge cake, and a large tray supplied with several different Japanese delicacies, some nice, some palatable, others nasty, at least to my taste. While the repast was going on the conference was progressing simultaneously, that is to say the tea introduced the compliments and as the dishes became more numerous we plunged more into business.

The Governor hoped he saw the Minister well; the British Minister was happy to say that he felt himself remarkably well. The Governor thanked his Excellency for bringing him some treasure from Yedo by the Highflyer and was afraid he had given himself much trouble with it. Mr Alcock lost no opportunity of turning anything to account, so that when the Governor complimented him upon his coming in person to Hakodadi, he answered that this in itself was a proof of how much importance he attached to the establishment of a Consulate in that place. He having come such a distance for the express purpose of seeing the Consul settled there, observing that two months ago he had written to the Minister for Foreign Affairs requesting him to have a proper residence prepared for the Consul, and that he was sorry to find that the house shown him the day before was not one fit for a British Consul. It might indeed do for Mr Cowan who was a single man, but Mr Hodgson had brought his wife and child and would require a house with at least 4 large rooms of thirty mats, and 5 or 6 smaller ones.

The Governor replied that if the house we had seen was too small he was prepared to have some extra rooms built. To this proposal Mr Alcock offered insuperable objections, for in the first place it was necessary that the Consul should be housed before he left Hakodadi, that he was pressed for time and must speedily return to Yedo, and proposed that as the temple in which we were received was in every respect fitted for a temporary residence, that Mr Hodgson should be accommodated in it until a new Consulate was built. To this the Governor replied that the temple was a place set apart for official visits, that a new Governor was expected soon and that the temple must be kept in readiness for his reception [2]. As Mr Alcock, however, insisted upon the propriety of having the temple as a temporary residence for the Consul, the Governor replied that he could once more take the matter into consideration and then give an answer. Mr Alcock was content to agree provided the answer came the next day. After some reflection the proposition was accepted by the Governor.

33. Shimyoji Temple, Hakodate. The temple was the site of the first British Consulate in Hakodate which was visited by Courtney in 1859

Matters being thus arranged the Governor was asked whether he would like to hear our band play and upon his expressing the pleasure he should feel in hearing it, the musicians were marched into the garden and played us several tunes, to the great delight of the Japanese, many of whom, the governor among the number, had never heard European music. The first notes seemed to have a magical effect and to break up all the formality of the meeting. The Japanese rose in a body and took down the screens which shut the verandah from the garden, and went and fraternized with them, such a thing having I believed never occurred before at any official interview. In a pause between the tunes the Governor was invited to pay a visit on board HMS Highflyer, and he in his turn invited us to come and see him at his residence the next day. The visitation was accepted on condition that we have an answer to our request about the house, and also that these should be a proper officer at the landing place to receive us. The Governor expressed his regret that there was not one there today, and we promised him that we would not deprive him of the honour of a visit, and took leave.

Some six leagues from the Bay of Hakodadi are lead mines worked by the Japanese and said to be particularly rich in ore with a considerable percentage of silver. The road to them lies along the eastern shore for a distance of ten or twelve miles when it enters the hilly country which everywhere forms a background to the Bay. Several of us took an opportunity of visiting these mines. The first part of the road was good enough and of great breadth but as soon as the traveler turns inland it narrows while at every hundred yards there is a water course to be crossed on the most dilapidated planks; it had rained during the night also so that we soon found ourselves in a beautiful specimen of a Corduroy road with a facing of mud. Only instead of being made of wooden sleepers the regular ridges were result as I discovered on our progress while watching the horses in front, by every four footed animal with pertinacious identity of pace and measurement setting their feet into the same furrows, leaving of course the ridge just as they found it between their hoofs.

One has heard of Japanese stereotyped character, customs and habits from one age to another, but it had not entered into any traveler's conception that this peculiarity extended to the quadrupeds. The ride through the hills was of the roughest therefore and also of the wettest description for the traveler has to across a broad and rapid stream and tributary streams innumerable. It was a fine October day, however, the sun a little overclouded and the heat tempered. The wooded hills and mountain streams not without beauty although the timber was none of it very fine and largely mixed with scrub of willow and pine and dwarf oak. Here and there the wide vine twisted itself over the branches of the trees in fantastic garlands. Occasionally a woodman with his load of wood or horses laden with charcoal passed on their way, but the people we met seemed by no means to correspond to the ploughed up state of the road.

After a ride of five or six miles we began more abruptly to ascend and presently saw the huts and other signs of entrance to the mines. Having an order from the Governor we were quickly invested with miners dress and began with torches made of dried bamboo to grope our way through the low, narrow and wet galleries to which we gained access by what in Cornwall they term an adit, a horizontal passage carved through the hill to strike a vein. We soon came to several of these which they were engaged in working and they bore every appearance of being rich in metal.

The galleries are much like our own with wooden support and rafters. They have also shafts descending perpendicularly, but as they have no steam machinery or other efficient appliances for emptying the water they can scarcely descend deeper than the horizontal adits will allow for the drainage. Their crushing and washing, and melting and casting processes are all of the most primitive kind and on a comparatively small scale. There was no means of ascertaining the yearly produce. On asking the Governor if they had none for export he replied in the negative and to the question what could possibly required the whole produce of such an extensive mine for, he replied it was all for home consumption for canon and rifle ball practice!

Not certainly to defend the poor fishing village of Hakodadi this with all its advantages of a noble bay, scarcely seemed to promise any elements of a great trade. Eatables for the Chinese, Beche de Mer [3], sea-weed and dried mushrooms, delicacies they delight in may make a beginning. Bear and fox and deer skins, also abundant, will help. Sulphur too which can never be difficult to find in these sorts of active volcanoes will in time no doubt come into play.

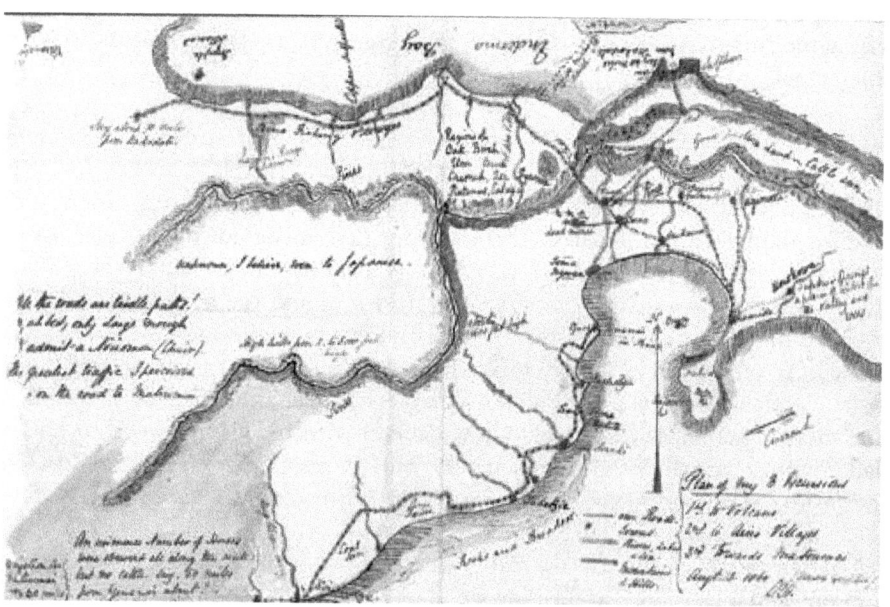

34. *Hand drawn map of excursions on the Hakodate peninsula by Mr and Mrs Hodgson, 1860, The National Archives, London*

The flora of Hakodadi is not a rich one. It is that of the northern temperate zone. Among the flowers I have observed in my rambles are the plantain, bindweed, dandelion, lily of the valley, *Iris japonica, Sambucus japonica, Lilium japonica, Capsella bursa-pastoris* (shepherd's purse), *Dianthus Chinensis* (Chinese pink), *Caltha pakustris* (Marsh marigold) and *Torilis japonica*.

During our short visit to Hakodadi, it was not possible to obtain many statistics with regard to the diseases of the place, but Dr Albrecht [5], a Russian Physician who had resided a short time at Hakodadi informed me that pectoral affections, diarrhoea, rheumatism, and intermittent fever were common complaints. Hakodadi is a rendezvous for whale ships. The crews of these ships are generally very healthy. Pectoral affections and rheumatism are the chief diseases among them.

The weather of Hakodadi though healthy is perhaps too severe during the winter months to those accustomed to the climate of the south of China. The winter is severe with perpetual snow during five months. In June, July, August and September there are heavy and continuous rains. Fogs are very prevalent from May till August. Easterly winds prevail during the whole summer; westerly winds begin in September and continue till April.

35. Statue of Commander Matthew Perry, Hakodate

SUMMARY OF SAILING ACTIVITY OF HMS HIGHFLYER

The history of HMS Highflyer is that of a man of war with a compliment of 240 men commissioned on the 1st of August 1856 and paid off on the 31st of May 1861 a period of nearly 5 years. Of this time 42 months and 8 days were spent in Chinese waters. For nearly three years the ship was at anchor in the Canton River and the Woosung branch of the Yangtse Kiang. The following table will give a pretty accurate idea of the proceedings of the ship during the entire commission.

Table 7: Summary of sailing activity of HMS Highflyer

Year	Steam			Steam And Sail			Sail			At Anchor			Distance
From 1st August 1856	D	H	M	D	M	M	D	H	M	D	H	M	Miles
1st Year	23	4	30	8	2	30	160	13		173	4		20,774
2nd Year	4	22	30				14	20	30	345	5		2,363
3rd Year	3	1	30	21	30		20	14	30	340	10	30	2,239
4th Year	6	20		21			55	2		302	5		7,969
5th Year to 31st May 1861	10			2	4		85	20		159			14,771

From the above statement it may be noticed that if the days were deducted for the long passage out to China (7 months) and the long voyage home (3 months and 13 days) it becomes evident that nearly the whole of time the ship was in China was spent at anchor. The effect of remaining for such a lengthened period of time in rivers with low alluvial banks and much marshy ground was very perceptible on the health of the ships company. From the beginning to the end of the time, the sick list was always large, the number of patients being frequently as great as that of a battle ship on the home or Mediterranean stations.

As compared with many other ships on the China station more favourably situated, I find from inquires that the number of sick was large. The Surgeon of the Esk, a sister ship about the same time in commission informs me that his list was very rarely as large as mine, but on the contrary generally much lower. The principal diseases, as may be easily surmised, were those incidental to the climate viz ague, dysentery, diarrhea, and sloughing boils. The stokers were the most unhealthy part of the crew. Why such should have been the case, I do not know for the number of days the ship was under steam was remarkably small.

The following statement will give a good idea of the amount of disease on board during the ships commission. The numbers do not include men belonging to gunboats and others who were sent by me to hospital but who formed no part of the ships compliment. They are: sent to hospital (62), invalided to hospital (74), killed in action (11), died on board (14), died in hospital (8), and drowned (2) [Appendix 3].

Table 8: List of deaths on board HMS Highflyer during 1857 to 1859

NAMES	AGE	DATE OF DEATH	DISEASE
Thomas Folther	23	20th August 1857	Remittent Fever
John Bowles	22	9th August 1857	Remittent Fever
John Layton	28	4th November 1857	Remittent Fever
James Snipe	26	22nd December 1857	Continued Fever
Joseph Garrett	25	18th July 1858	Remittent Fever
John Carty	22	31st August 1858	Continued Fever
James Reed	23	31st August 1858	Remittent Fever
Canduis Harrigan	21	20th October 1858	Remittent Fever
George Mantle	20	20th October 1858	Remittent Fever
Alfred Curtis	20	20th October 1858	Remittent Fever
Blaxland Transom	35	4th November 1858	Pneumonia
John Wilbee	22	13th May 1859	Continued Fever
John Beesley	30	25th August 1859	Cholera
James Prince	28	5th November 1859	Dysentery

36. *Japanese painting of a Chinese trading junk in Japanese waters, 1850's*

Chapter 14 An Essay On The Important Diseases Of China

Continued Fever

As already mentioned the first case of this disease which came under my notice occurred in the latter end of March, and attracted considerable attention from the typhoid character it assumed and more especially from the maculated eruption which was profusely scattered over the whole body, a feature so peculiar in fevers of this climate as to warrant the conclusion that a disease of a different type from what is usually seen was appearing among us. That disease also presenting a typhus character rendered it doubly important as the ravages it commits among large bodies of men have in many cases been so dreadful as to almost decimate an army. Our experience of the Crimea was sufficient to make all anxious, and to endeavour to discover what hygienic means were required to check its course, if it should assume an epidemic character. No cause, however, could be assigned for the appearance of this disease. The rooms were not overcrowded, great attention was paid to cleanliness, new drains were made and others cleaned out, but in Chinese buildings it is extremely difficult to prevent all effluvia, and occasionally noses were greeted with a perfume not at all agreeable, and what was worse without knowing exactly were it came from.

Every precaution was taken not only in regard to the barracks, but in the hospital itself acting on the supposition, that the disease might be contagious, the solution of chloride of the zinc was freely sprinkled over the different parts of the hospital during the prevalence of the complaint. I must confess, however, that in no single instance could I trace the origin of the complaint to contagion. Fortunately, however, we had no epidemic. During the whole year 23 cases were admitted into the Provisional Battalion Hospital. Of these nine died, showing how very fatal the disease was, and how thankful we ought to be that our exertions were successful in staying the progress of such a dreadful malady.

The commencement of this disease was so various it was impossible for the first few days to decide its character. In one case the patient first suffered from headache, his back and limbs ached with occasional chills followed by heats, and in this state he may go on for two or three days without applying for relief till at last he is obliged to take to his bed and then the disease steadily advances to its termination. In another case the commencement is traced to a distinct rigor followed by heat but accompanied with severe headache and so much prostration that patient is knocked down at once. Or again a man may apply and say he had the shakes which means generally that he passed through the cold stage of ague, you find him as you suppose in the hot stage, and accordingly put him to bed and endeavour to induce the sweating. You are most likely successful in your endeavour and next morning the patient expresses himself as much better. His skin certainly is cooler, and the pulse is not much excited but still there remains a suspicious thirst and pains in the limbs and headache. In fact the case is taken as one of remittent fever. Another accession of fever, however, comes on and from its persistence the true type is at once detected.

As the disease advances all the pyrexial symptoms increase. The skin continues hot and dry. There is great thirst, complete loss of appetite, and extreme prostration. The tongue which in general is at first while furred becomes dry and brown and gradually black sordes in almost all of cases is deposited round the teeth and gums sometimes indeed to such an extent that frequent cleaning the mouth is required before the patient could take anything. The pulse is never very high at any time, generally from 90 to 96 and even as low as 84, but towards the termination of the disease whether that be by death or by a crisis it rises to 120 and even higher. The character is probably at first full and strong but very soon becomes soft and compressible and sometimes is very small indeed.

For the first few days the patient complains of severe headache, pains in back and legs and symptoms, however, which almost invariably left him and he complained of no pain whatever. By this time delirium had set in, there was suffusion of the eyes, a restless frightened manner, but yet he was apparently very sensible when spoken to. The delirium was of that low muttering form, resembling greatly delirium tremens, and often spoken of as typhomania.

It occasionally set in very early though more generally it was not noticed fill the 4 or 5th day. The patient is constantly talking to himself, picking at the bedclothes, and occasionally getting out of bed without any apparent reason. He is, however, very obedient doing everything he is told, and even answering rationally when spoken to. The disease appears to have an effect on the brain for even some of those cases which recovered remained for a long time weak in the intellect. During the severity of the disease great attention has to be paid to the urinary organs as the catheter has frequently to be used, the patient having lost all power over the bladder.

The urine when examined was generally found alkaline, of normal specific gravity, and frequently contained abundant discharges of urates of soda and ammonia. The appetite for food was greatly impaired, but yet the patient when more delirious would generally swallow any fluid placed to his lips.

The most remarkable feature in this fever and the one which seems to distinguish it from all other is the appearance of maculae on the surface of the body. It certainly was not a universal symptom, but was present in at least 4/5 of the cases, and those cases in which no eruption appeared were less severe than the others. This eruption generally appeared from the 2nd to the 4th day, and on first appearance was apparently evanescent on pressure, but certainly on the 2nd day it was persistent. The term of its duration was very uncertain. In one or two cases it was visible after death, but in far the majority of cases it disappeared from the 4th to the 7th day. In some it was very thinly scattered over the body; while on others it was so diffuse as to give an almost universal blush to the skin.

The maculae were certainly larger than those seen in typhus fever cases in England, being generally from 1 to 2 lines in diameter. Petechiae I have very rarely seen. Up to the end of July not a single patient presented that eruption but later in the year it became more common. Such were the general symptoms of the cases I had under my charge and they were universal, of course many had complications but the above account I consider to be really the fever itself. The eruption, the delirium the state of the tongue etc, being decidedly characteristic of the typhus type. The duration of this disease was also well defined. From the 12th to the 15th days an improvement generally begins to appear, but the change is marked by no appreciable crisis, it is gradual and the advancement to convalescence steady but slow. Death in most cases occurred from the 7th to the 9th day, but in one case was as early in the 6th and in another as late as the 15th. This fatal issue generally happened by coma, very few by asthenia. The recoveries in many cases were very unsatisfactory; in some cases the patients being as long as three months before being again fit for duty. The powers of mind were temporary enfeebled. The prostration of strength was the more remarkable as most of the patients were young and previously very robust and healthy. Deafness generally supervened toward the termination of the disease. It was looked upon as a good sign and as evidence that the complaint had taken a favourable turn.

In this disease the mucous membrane of the lungs is generally more or less affected, indeed that is sometimes the most troublesome symptom as the fit of coughing increases the headache. Patients complain very much of it; and strong measures are required to alleviate the congestion. This complication rarely advances farther than simple catarrh, but bronchitis and even pneumonia may be present making the case of the course far more serious, and requiring more active treatment. In a few cases in which the lungs were much affected, there was no cough indicative of the disease for the patients sensibility being impaired the complaint did not cause sufficient irritation to induce either cough or expectoration, so that one was compelled to rely entirely on percussion and the stethoscopic signs.

Without careful observation extensive mischief may creep on slowly and insidiously, the complaint assuming a latent character. Diarrhea, splenitis and hepatitis may be mentioned as complications. With regard to the treatment it may be observed that it required modification according to the peculiar circumstances of each individual case, but in no one single instance, however violent the headache or delirium might be or however great the suffusion of the eyes, was it thought necessary to abstract blood from the arm.

In some instance local depletion was had recourse to by means of leeches but this measure seemed productive of more harm than good for in every case in which leeches were applied the patient became worse. Nay even the topical application of a blister to the head seemed productive of mischief. The disease being very serious every kind of treatment was had recourse to in the endeavour to ascertain which was best suited to the complaint. Antiphlogistic measures were invariably attended by bad results. The only treatment that seemed to be generally beneficial was a moderate supply of nourishment in the shape of sago arrowroot and beef tea and wine and the exhibition of small dozes of mercurial diaphoretics, lemonade, soda water, quinine and spirits.

Although the above account of typhus fever in China is founded on my observation of cases which occurred in the Provisional Battalion of Marines stationed at Canton in the year 1858, it is right to observe, however, that I noticed several similar at Shanghai in the year 1859. Two patients died on board HMS Highflyer. The complaint appeared in every respect identical although no cutaneous eruption was observed in either of the two fatal cases. As I consider this a most important disease, I here append two of the cases most typical of the complaint [Appendix 5].

This disease which is very common in the south of China during the hot months of the years is I believed only a modification fever. It appears to me to arise from the same cause and that there is no real difference in the ultimate nature of the complaint. At the outset of the complaint it is almost impossible to distinguish it from ague. This however, may be said of continued fever which I allow to be a complaint differing in very essential particular. But although to distinguish between these three fevers in their earliest stages during the hot months is at first difficult, a few hours generally sets the matters at rest. For a distinct remission, an accurate diagnostic sign, although the pulse continues high, gives evidence of the true nature of the malady. As compared with intermittent fever the cold stage is shorter and the hot stage longer. Indeed in many instance after the first rigor no other follows: there is continued heat of skin with a great aggravation of it at certain times.

Exposure to the sun during such weather is very likely to produce the disease. Like intermittent fever it not infrequently shows itself at sea many days or even weeks after a ship has left harbour. We had one well marked case on board HMS Highflyer on the passage home. The sick-bayman, a young man of twenty years of age was the patient. He was attacked during March 1860. During the 4 years that he had spent in China he had suffered occasionally but not frequently from intermittent fever.

The fever termed Hong Kong Fever [1] appears to be low remittent fever with congestion of the brain and lungs attended in some instance with ulceration of the bowels sometimes there is a maculated eruption on the skin. In the worst cases of the disease there is extreme prostration of strength. The convalescence from this form of fever is very slow particularly in those who remain in the locality amidst the predisposing and exciting cause. Although there are generally distinctly marked remissions and exacerbations such is not always the case and from the various types the complaint has assumed in different years various observers have given very different descriptions of the disease.

In some years it has been looked upon as an idiopathic continued fever and in others as typhus fever, occasionally the symptoms have assumed a choleric character. Dr Wilson in his "Medical Notes on China", [2] states that "some cases which occurred in 1842, on a cursory view might have been mistaken for cholera". The writer of these pages has never seen such a case. In this fever the duration of which is very uncertain there is a strong tendency to relapse. In several instances which have come to the writers knowledge when the patient had apparently made a favourable recovery a little indiscretion in eating or drinking or undue exposure to the solar rays, has brought on a second and more dangerous attack which in some cases has terminated in a fatal issue.

In the treatment of a disease which varies so much in severity and in its type as remittent fever, must be regulated in a great measure according to the nature of each individual case. That which I have ordinarily employed and most successfully has been to give at the outset of the complaint, particularly when there is much headache giddiness and disorder of the stomach, two Calomel and rhubarb pills followed by small doses of quinine and sulphate of magnesia, liquor ammonia acetate, and saline effervescing draughts. The hair was at the same time cut close and cold evaporating lotions applied to the head. Should there be any tendency to extreme prostration of strength, cordials and stimulants will prove useful and necessary adjuncts to the treatment.

INTERMITTENT FEVER

According to my individual experience intermittent fever is the most common complaint in China. Next in order of frequency and closely associated with it is diarrhoea. This statement is founded on the result of my practice in the Provisional Battalion of Marines and two years on board the Highflyer viz from the 1st of January 1859 to the 31st of December 1860. The two compared give the following results, namely intermittent fever 616 cases, diarrhoea, 554 cases.

My own experience also seems to show that the complaint is less rife during the Quarters commencing on the 1st of January and terminating on the 31st of March than during the other three Quarters. On comparing the Quarters for two years of my practice on board HMS Highflyer I find that there occurred the following number of cases. From 1st of January to 31st March, 25 cases; from 1st April to 30th June, 54 cases; from 1st July to 30th September, 67 cases; from 1st to December 31st, 63 cases.

As above stated intermittent fever and diarrhoea seem to be mutually related as regards the frequency of their occurrence. They also more frequently coexist in the same individual than any other two diseases. It has rarely fallen to my lot to treat any very severe case of chronic diarrhoea or dysentery in a patient who has not suffered more or less at some former period from ague.

Although there can be no doubt that low marshy humid localities, more especially where the soil is alluvial give rise to a condition of the atmosphere favourable for the production of ague it seems equally certain that we know nothing not only of the true nature of the complaint nor of the chemical and physical qualities of malaria. Authors have, it appears to me, in vain endeavoured to prove that it is the result of the exhalation of decaying animal or vegetable matter.

Having been for a long period in districts prolific of the disease and an attentive observer of the growth of vegetation it would appear to be marvelous how such an idea could be entertained. During the whole of the year 1860 (with the exception of 3 weeks) HMS Highflyer was at anchor at Whampoa in the Canton River. The district around is for the most part covered with paddy fields. The paddy is planted in spring and cut in July. When cut the ground is almost immediately afterward ploughed over and a fresh crop of paddy is sown. From the cutting down of the 1st the crop until the planting of the second does not take more than a week or ten days. With regard to the other portion of the land about here it is chiefly hilly and for the most part uncultivated.

Now mark the result. During the first Quarter of the year during which time the ground lies fallow with the roots of the second crop of paddy seen here and there and that in many places in a state of decomposition there is according to my experience but little ague. In the spring and summer months after the paddy has been planted and the fields assume a smiling aspect being green with vegetation in the vigour of its growth the cases of ague become common enough and continue so until the cutting down of the second crop of paddy in the month of when Intermittent Fever begins to decline. In other words during the time that the paddy is growing and the wild plants on the hills are flourishing ague is rife so that it is when vegetation is composing not decomposing that the greater number of cases of ague occur.

The writer therefore is bound to confess that it appears to him that malaria, whatever its true nature may be, is not generated by the decomposition of organic substances [3]. Heat acting on an alluvial soil which is frequently submerged by water, whether there be vegetable matter or no, seems to be the only thing essential to the generation, accumulation and diffusion of the poison. It would appear from some experiments performed at Whampoa that the amount of ozone in the atmosphere is in direct ratio to the amount of movement of the air and that whenever the amount of ozone is diminished then intermittent and remittent fevers are more frequent. It may therefore be presumed that ozone acts in some measure as a disinfecting agent.

The two most frequent forms of ague in the South of China are the Quotidian and the Tertian [4]. There is a form of ague which has been noticed at Shanghai in few cases. The patient has every day, or on the alternate days, a slight cold stage of ague followed by the hot stage. Then the hands and feet begin to perspire most profusely, the water standing in beads on the skin, and even running off the hands when they are held down, the rest of the body being quite dry. This species of ague, with its confined local perspiration, is accompanied with intense headache, and more general discomfort and suffering than usually occurs during common ague. Quinine is as efficacious in removing this, as it is in removing other forms of intermittent fever.

The young and robust seem particularly liable to be effected by intermittent fever. The middle aged are not very susceptible to the influence of malaria unless they have visited China and suffered from ague when young. Although intermittent fever cannot be looked upon as a very serious complaint if one may judge by its immediate results, a far different view must be taken of this disease when it is of frequent occurrence in the same individual. In such cases it tends to disorder the digestive organs and impair the general health. The feeble gait, pallid sallow countenance and emaciated frame of men who have been often attacked with ague give evidence of the baneful influence it exerts upon the system.

It has been asserted by some writers that intermittent fever is very seldom associated with phthisis and that the two diseases are mutually antagonistic of each other. That such is the case I think admits of great doubt and I should rather be inclined to think that phthisis is as rarely associated with other disease as with ague. My own personal experience has afforded instance of the two complaints combined. And one thing is very certain that aguish districts are by no means exempt from consumption. The reports of the Chinese Missionary Hospital at Shanghai show that during a period of 5 years, there were 194 cases of phthisis under treatment as compared with 3070 cases of intermittent fever which seems to be nearly as large a proportion as that of any other complaint when compared with ague.

The occurrence of numerous cases of ague at sea when many miles from land is of much interest. HMS Highflyer after lying many months at Shanghai sailed to the Gulf of Tartary and for a cruise round Japan on the 17th of August 1859, and returned to Shanghai on the 29th of November. During the whole of the time she was absent on the cruise we had very numerous cases of ague. When in Vladimir's Bay in the gulf of Tartary we met HMS Action. That ship had been for several months on this part of the coast and had been for a long time free from ague. On board HMS Highflyer on the contrary such cases were even more numerous than usual at Shanghai. Again in the month of November 1860 after lying for 9 months in the Canton River the HMS Highflyer sailed for Swatow a locality very free from ague. The fresh sea breeze instead of doing good apparently did harm for ague and diarrhoea were rife. Finally the ship sailed for England in February 1861 after spending 4 years in China, the greater part of which time she was lying in river. During the entire voyage cases of ague were exceedingly common. No matter how fair the weather or how fresh the breeze ague and its companion disease diarrhoea were never absent from the ship.

According to my observation such cases are most frequent in moderately calm weather with a rather high range temperature immediately after heavy rains. The occurrence of such cases may be accounted for on the supposition that the patient had the poison of malaria before leaving the last place of anchorage; or it may be that the meteorological state of the atmosphere which causes the rain tends to condense and bring downwards towards the surface of the ocean the malaria which has been wafted from distant parts and which in fine clear weather is dispersed through the higher region of the atmosphere. It is not possible, however, to imagine that there can be any malaria in the atmosphere of the broad Indian and Atlantic oceans. At such distance from land such a supposition is out of the question. In such localities the appearance of ague can only be accounted for on the supposition that the period of incubation which may be many months is suddenly drawn to a conclusion by great atmosphere necessitude's and then the latent poison manifests its influence.

With regard to the treatment of intermittent fever the writer is of opinion that quinine is a specific. He would, however, qualify this remark by observing that although quinine has never failed in his hand nor in the hands of any qualified medical man he has frequently known it to fail when administered by incompetent persons without regard to the state of the stomach. When given indiscriminately and when the secretions are in a vibrated state it often does more harm than good. Frequently the writer has seen men belonging to gunboats apply to him for relief after the patient had been for many days drenched, by order of the Commanding Officer, with large doses of quinine.

The diagnosis of the disease has been correct but the remedy inappropriately administered. In such cases the patient has invariably laboured under great disorder of the digestive organs as evidenced by much headache and a very foul and loaded tongue. In such cases the administration of an alterative as aperient following by quinine or quinine combined with sulphate of magnesia has invariably affected a cure so many cases of intermittent fever have come under the writers notice that I have tried all the ordinary method of administering Quinine with the view of ascertaining the most efficient. On many occasions, I have had recourse to the system of giving large doses. This plan often succeeds in cutting short the complaint and when such is the case it has the advantage of being very economical as under no other system can so small a quantity of this valuable drug be given with such successful results. We must confess, however, that we have seen it fail in effecting so desirable an end, and even in some of the cases in which the exhibition of the large dose has not been followed by the recurrence of a fit, it would be unfair to suppose that this plan has the advantage over the small doses, as very frequently it happens that a similar result attends the other method of treatment.

Should the tongue be clean, the administration of a Blue Pill [5] followed by 5 gram doses of quinine three times a day will generally be found to effect a speedy cure. The writer would recommend the administration of the quinine at stated intervals without regard to the stage of the complaint having never seen the slightest ill effects from this plan of treatment. To wait till the period of intermission appears to him to be merely so much loss of time. He would also observe that he has never seen much good result from muddling interference during the different stages of this very common complaint, such as having recourse to the warm bath, the employment of dry heat, the administration of stimulants or the abstraction of blood from the arm during the cold stage and cold affusion in the hot stage etc.

In the year 1858 I have the following experiment with regard to the value of quinine wine as a prophylactic:

On the 25th of July 1858 the Provisional Battalion of Marines consisted of 6 companies and in the Table subjoined is their strength and the relative amount of sickness in each.

Table 9: State of health of the Provisional Battalion of Marines 25th January 1858

Companies	Strength	Disease							
		Fevers	Lungs	Stomach and Bowels	Phlemon and Ulcers	Eyes	Debility	Other Diseases	Total
1st Company	89	3	..	2	..	..	..	2	7
2nd Company	79	10	..	3	2	..	..	1	16
3rd Company	65	4	..	1	..	..	..	1	6
4th Company	74	5	..	1	1	..	..	..	7
5th Company	63	4	..	1	1	..	..	..	7
6th Company	79	6	..	3	..	..	..	1	9
Total	449	32	..	11	4	..	..	5	52

The result of this investigation led me to administer the quinine wine duly to the 2nd company exclusively as not only having the greater number of fever cases but also the large proportion of other diseases. The wine was given in doses to each man and the dose was administered at 6 o'clock am.

On the 25th of August 1858, exactly one month after the commencement of the trial the relative amount of disease in the respective companies stood as follows.

Table 10: State of health of the Provisional Battalion of Marines 25th August 1858

Companies	Strength	Disease							
		Fevers	Lungs	Stomach and Bowels	Phlemon and Ulcers	Eyes	Debility	Other Diseases	Total
1st Company	89	5	1	2	..	..	1	3	12
2nd Company	79	..	1	3	1	..	..	..	5
3rd Company	57	2	..	..	2	..	..	..	4
4th Company	74	6	..	..	2	1	1	..	10
5th Company	63	1	..	2	1	..	..	..	4
6th Company	79	2	..	..	1	..	3	..	3
Total	441	16	2	7	7	1	2	3	38

A comparison of the two Tables shows that the Company to which quinine wine was administered is now free from febrile complaints of all kinds whereas when I first commenced the exhibition of the medicine it furnished a larger number of fever cases than any other. I therefore think myself justified in coming to the conclusion that the daily administration of quinine is a very powerful preventive of disease and am of the opinion that its prophylactic power is very great [6].

EPHEMERAL FEVER

By ephemeral fever the writer means a simple fever of a continued type which runs its course in two or three days and then gradually subsides. The fever is sometimes ushered in with a rigor but more frequently there is no chill or it is very indistinctly marked. The complaint differs from intermittent fever in there generally being no distinct rigor the fever running higher and being more continuous, the cerebral disturbance being greater, there being no distinct stages, and there being no paroxysmal return. It is brought on by direct exposure to the sun and is more sudden in its attack than ague. The disease is best illustrated by a case.

James Paul, at 33, Private Royal Marines was placed on the sick list on the 20th of July 1858 for Ephemeral Fever.

The patient was relieved from his post as sentry where he was much exposed to the sun and was brought into hospital on a stretcher. On admission the patient was so giddy that he could scarcely stand, face much flushed, skin hot, pulse accelerated, tongue furred. A short time afterward nausea and vomiting supervened and there was slight delirium. When first admitted and before delirium came on he stated that he had not felt any sensation of chilliness. The patient was ordered to bed, Blue Pill given, followed by draughts of quinine and sulphate of magnesia. Cold lotions were applied to the head. The fever continued without much abatement for about 20 hours at the end of which time it began to subside and at the expiration of about 50 hours there was no febrile action, the patient merely complaining of lassitude and debility.

There was no return of the symptoms and the patient was discharged to duty on the 7th day after he was taken ill.

SMALLPOX

This eruptive fever is a common complaint in every part of China known to Europeans. Both at Shanghai and Canton smallpox seldom fails to make its appearance in the spring and autumn and its ravages are often very considerable among the native population. The fact that in many Chinese cities there are temples dedicated to the god of smallpox shows how prevalent the disease must be [7].

It is a debated question when and where smallpox first arose. This is a question which may perhaps never be settled. In a conversation which I held with Dr Macgowan at Shanghai, who has long been a medical missionary in China, he informed that the first notice of smallpox in any Chinese writer that he had read was in an author who flourished in the 2nd or 3rd century before or after the Christian era (this gentleman's library being at Ningpo he could not be certain of the exact date). The writer referred to states that when the Chinese army returned from waging a war with a northern power there were very many cases of smallpox among the men, and speaks of it as a new disease derived from foreigners.

Regarding smallpox vaccination, a missionary informed me that when at Hangchow he met an advertisement of a physician who devoted himself to this art; and that he once met an itinerant doctor at Ningpo who attempted to introduce the practice of vaccination among his countrymen.

Dr Pearson introduced vaccination at Canton in the year 1805 and by his instrumentality the Chinese vaccine establishment in that city was commenced. Dr Pearson wrote a tract on the subject and Sir G Staunton afterward translated it into Chinese.

Smallpox has engaged the attention of the Chinese from near the commencement of the Christian era, and inoculation has been practiced among them for a thousand years or more. The 聞人規痘疹論 *Wen ren gui dou zhen lun* is a work treating on this complaint with numerous prescriptions by 聞人規 Wen Ren Gui, which was published in 1323 and republished in 1542. The 種痘新書 *Zhong dou xin shu*, is another treatise on this subject, in 12 books, published in 1741 by 張琰遜 Zhang Yan Xun, giving ample details of the disease in its various forms, the appropriate treatment, and a variety of prescriptions. A small work on the same subject by 調元複 Tiao Yuan Fu bears the title 仙家秘傳痘科真訣 *Xian jia mi chuan dou ke zhen jue*, professing to embody supermundane secrets on the subject. This is illustrated by numerous illustrations of the disease. The 天花精 *Tian hua jing* is another work on smallpox with numerous illustrations.

37. A young Chinese patient with smallpox, (date unknown)

MEASLES

This is another eruptive fever well known in China. It is common among the Chinese and not infrequently attacks European children. During the stay of HMS Highflyer at Shanghai the children of an English merchant were affected by it.

During the autumn of 1848 measles prevailed epidemically in Ningpo. The malady did not assume a malignant form, but fatal cases were not rare. This epidemic prevailed in the maritime districts of the east coast of China, and throughout the whole Pacific coast, till it reached the Samoyed, amongst whom it was particularly fatal. A Russian Captain alluding to the epidemic writes in a journal printed at Honolulu, "we had throughout all our colonies the measles, and great numbers of the inhabitant were taken off. Some of our islands in the Alsatian chain lost most of their population. In Sitka, among a population of 600, we had in one month 80 deaths; nearly all, except the Europeans, were sick so that all the town was in sorrow from fear and dread" [8].

EPILEPSY

As this is not a climatic disease, I should not think of alluding to it here had I not had a very interesting case when on board HMS Minder at Hong Kong in the month of November 1857

The following are the particulars of the case.

Henry Mays, at 22 old who had been invalided from H.M.S Nankin for Epilepsy about 9 o'clock on the evening of the 8th of November when walking on the port side of the main deck suddenly fell down in a strong convulsive fit accompanied with dilated pupils, quick pulse, and grinding of the teeth. There were strong convulsive motions of the limbs and trunk of the body and spasms of the muscles of the face, the mouth being draw up into every variety of form. The first fit lasted with little intermission for about an hour and a half. This fit was succeeded after an interval of a 1/4 of an hour by several other fits which lasted about 10 minutes each until about 1/2 past 12 o'clock am when he gradually became quieter but the countenance soon afterwards assumed a death-like appearance and for a short time it seemed as though the patient would die. Soon afterward he rallied and after another fit of a slight character he was free from the complaint. The patient was troubled for two or three days with general debility and vertigo but by the administration of a little alleviative medicine and tonics he was gradually restored to health.

About an hour after this patient was first attacked a man named Joseph Jones, at 23; Quartermaster after looking at the other patient for a few minutes walked over to the other side of the ship and fell down in epileptic fit which was followed by others. About an hour and a half after the fits occurred in the first named patient a boy named Henry Turner who was invalided from H.M.S Calcutta for epilepsy was talking to another patient about the complaint, observing that "he had just such a fit as that" and almost immediately afterward fell down in a strong convulsive fit from which he soon recovered.

The man named Joseph Jones had evidently been drinking, but the other two patients had evidently not. These cases wonderfully illustrated the power of the mysterious agent sympathy in producing the disease.

INSANITY

Considering the phlegmatic temperament and temperate habits of Chinese, it might be anticipated that this malady is not of frequent occurrence; future inquiring will doubtless prove that insanity prevails to a much less extent in China than in Europe. It is rarely mentioned in the list of diseases treated by the medical missionaries, and on referring to the Golden Mirror of Medical Practice, a standard work in China we find a very meager description of the symptoms, cause and treatment of this disease. Idiocy is properly distinguished from lunacy, and this latter is divided into two kinds *kwang and tien*; the first (mania) belongs to the *yang* principle, with an excess of fire or excitement; the second (dementia, incoherent madness) partakes of the *yin*, with fluidity in excess, a state of depression; lunatic asylums are unknown in China [9].

COUP DE SOLEIL [SUNSTROKE]

During the time I have been in China I have had an opportunity of seeing about 15 cases of this fertile cause of loss of life in a tropical climate. While in charge of the Provisional Battalion of Marines at Canton, we had 9 such cases among the men namely 5 cases in June 1858 on the occasion of the white cloud expedition (one of which proved fatal), two cases in July, which occurred when the men were on fatigue duty. And two cases in August on the occasion of the Nam-Tow expedition. The man who died on the field exposed in a few minutes and before any treatment could be had recourse to. Of the other 8 cases only two came under my observation as the expedition on which the men were engaged was under the direction of other Medical Officers. I am told however, that all of them were comparatively trifling cases. They were sent to other Hospitals for treatment and all rapidly recovered and returned to the Battalion.

The two cases under my own charge were of a trivial nature and in both instances the men returned to duty in 5 days after admission to the Hospital. They appeared to me to be instances of high temperature acting on a disordered stomach. My treatment consisted in having the hair cut short, the application of cold lotions to the head and the administration of 5 grams of calomel followed by emetic mixture. Within a few hours the patients were free from all febrile symptoms and afterward only required quinine to restore the strength.

Although these were the only cases of the disease at Canton among my own men, I may perhaps be allowed to remark that during the absence of the proper Medical Officers I had charge for a few hours of a very marked and serious case which occurred among the men of the Royal Artillery. The patient was a powerfully made man in the prime of life, and when I first saw him which was about one half an hour after he was taken ill, he was rolling about in bed in the most restless manner. There was pungent heat of skin, intense headache and great pectoral pain. Pulse 126 full. His hair was ordered to be cut off, a strong emetic given followed by copious draughts of luke-warm water. His head was afterward held over the side of the bed for upward of an hour during which time an almost continuous stream of cold water was poured over it. At hour and a half afterwards, when his stomach had become quiet 10 grams of calomel were administered. It was ascertained that this man made a very favourable recovery.

In the summer of 1860 when belonging to HMS Highflyer at Whampoa, Canton River, I had three cases of sunstroke under treatment one belonging to my own ship and other two belonging to gunboats. As one of these cases will give a fair illustration of the disease as it occurs in a mild form it is here inserted.

Charles Beechin, at 21, able bodied seaman was brought on board HMS Highflyer on the evening of the 13th of July in a state of unconsciousness with dilated pupils not responsive to the stimulus of light. Respiration and pulse natural. Slight heat of skin. Hands and legs occasionally convulsed. Teeth spasmodically closed. Later in the evening he was still unconscious. Passed urine involuntarily. When roused or moved swears at the attention but otherwise does not speak. Eyes closed; mouth closed; great difficultly in getting him to swallow anything. Head to be shaved. To have 10 grams of calomel immediately. An enema of castor oil and spirits of turpentine

The next day the patient continued in a state of insensibility. Lies perfectly motionless and free from convulsions. Remained in much the same condition for about 40 hours, during which time no medical aid was given and no treatment adopted. At the expiration of three days the patient suddenly became sensible and remained so. On recovery he complained of nothing but slight prostration of strength and headache. A little aperient medicine and tonics were given. The patient returned to duty on the 25th of July.

Remark: To a person unaccustomed to the treatment of tropical disease, the patient might have been supposed to labour under cerebro-spinal disease brought on by gastric or intestinal irritation.

I beg to state that it is my opinion that the greater number of what have been termed sunstroke (coup de soleil) that have come under my notice have been instance of a tropical sun acting on a disordered stomach and that the deranged state of the digestive system had depended in most instance on the abuse of alcoholic drinks. In conclusion I have to observe that of the various methods of treatment that I have seen adopted in cases of sun-stroke, I decidedly give the preference to strong antiphlogistic measures. But in making this observation, I would not have it supposed that I give my sanction to venesection which has certainly appeared to me do no good and was followed by death in two instances out of three in which I have known it had recourse to.

BRONCHITIS, PLEURITIS AND PNEUMONIA

These inflammatory affections of the breathing organs are far more common at Shanghai and other parts of the north of China than they are at Canton, Hong Kong and other south parts. This statement is founded on the observations of various observers. As far as my own practice has been concerned the greater number of such cases occurred at Canton during the first few months of the allied occupation but then it must be remembered that the men were placed under circumstance very favourable for the development of chest complaints.

PHTHISIS

Pulmonary consumption is seen to be about equally common in all the ports open to Europeans. Although not so common a disease as in England my own experience and that of one on whose judgment I have much reliance seems to show that when once the complaint is developed it is apt to run a very rapid course. This remark applies with much force to the southern parts of China [10].

DYSENTERY AND CHRONIC DIARRHOEA

These two diseases are so exceedingly common in China, so closely allied, and so often unjustly separated that I here class them together instead of treating them under separated heads. The name chronic diarrhoea is apt to mislead for that disease as seen in China is the result of the same pathological changes in the large intestine as seen in dysentery. There are few diseases of a more fatal character as regard their immediate results and still fewer that entail upon recovery so great a liability to relapse for a slight error in diet, a change of clothing, or sudden vicissitude of temperature is sufficient to bring on a return of the disease in a patient apparently perfectly cured and may then prove quickly fatal.

Upon a review of the different treatises on dysentery that have come under my observation it is evident that the views of authors differ most materially with regard to its nature and causes although as respects to the treatment there is a greater uniformity of sentiment. Such being the case it may perhaps be thought excusable if I give my own opinions and the result of my own observations with regard to the disease.

It would appear that in all tropical climates extreme ranges of temperature of sudden vicissitude of weather by which perspiration is checked causing internal congestion and functional derangement of the liver and other internal organs, the use of unwholesome food or drink, intemperance and fatigue are the exciting causes of the complaint, but these are not of themselves sufficient to bring on an attack of the disease. In addition to such causes as these there must be some morbific influence of a specific nature which I think is malarious.

Malarious as proved by the greater frequency of dysentery and diarrhea in districts well known to be malarious by the very nature of the country and the occurrence of intermittent fever. Those districts where ague is most rife are undoubtedly the most subject to bowel complaints. All experience in China tends to prove this and to place it beyond the shadow of a doubt. But we need not appeal to China alone for testimony to confirm this remark. Other countries tell the same tale and we are informed by Sydenham that when dysentery was prevalent in London then ague was a common complaint in the same locality. As elsewhere remarked I have rarely seen a very severe case of dysentery or chronic diarrhoea occur in any one who had not previously suffered more or less from ague. We may also remark that dysentery so often follows attacks of intermittent fever that we may look upon the latter disease as an exciting cause of the complaint. Whether malaria arises from the decomposition of vegetable or animal matter, is the result of the exhalation of decomposing mud, or some peculiar electrical condition of the atmosphere are all questions of doubt but it would seem probable that whatever may be the cause of intermittent fever is also the cause of dysentery for as before observed when ague is common then dysentery and diarrhoea are frequent.

How malaria can exercise so deadly influence over the large intestine, as to give use to the formidable disease is of course a puzzle which few have attempted to explain, and why it should fix upon the large intestine in preference to the small intestine for manifesting its marked action is a question of great interest although involved in great obscurity. We may observe, however, that the small intestine being the part of the alimentary canal especially set apart for absorption whereas the large intestine is a receptacle for waste material. Writers have been fond of tracing this disease to the quality of the ingestion rather than the blood which in all probability contains in solution the poison which is excreted from it and deposited between the coats of the intestinal canal. The poison would appear to act through the blood which being poisoned manifest its injurious nature by its tendency to deposit its morbific matter between the coats of the large intestine. Dr Bleeker, of the Netherlands Medical Service has I think done good to the profession by the publication of his very able paper on dysentery in which he states that "dysentery is an exudation process, the effect of a not yet sufficiently known condition of the blood and manifests itself by localization of the exudation; chiefly between the mucous and muscular coats of the large intestine. The same author goes on to that the dysenteric process consists of 4 clearly defined stages and as all my experience, which has been somewhat extensive, tends to these views of the disease both as regards its symptoms during life and its pathology. I here insert this writer's description of the various stage of the complaint [Appendix 6].

Although dysentery is one of the most fatal and formidable disease that the medical man is called upon to treat and occasionally is of so severe a character as soon to pass beyond the control of human aid and skill there can be but little doubt that when seen in its earliest stage the prompt application of suitable remedies rarely fails to effect a cure, and that the complaint is as amenable to treatment as most other acute diseases.

The treatment which I have found most successful in acute dysentery has been the administration of small doses of Hhd. Creta combined with Dover's Powder or calomel and opium together with Compound chalk mixture every 3 or 4 hours. Tannic acid with Laudanum may frequently be substituted for chalk mixture; when there is much abdominal pain and scybala are passing or the stools are very scanty and passed with much straining a small dose of castor oil and laudanum will be often found of great service. If the disease is severe I have known the application of a few leeches to the abdomen and the exhibition of 1 gram of calomel with 2 grams of Dover's Powder administered every hour until the gums are slightly affected prove very beneficial, and in such case enemata laudanum with a few ounces of barley water starch or thin gruel, or acetate of lead with laudanum give much comfort and tend to allay the irritation of the intestine I have occasionally tried enemata of nitrate of silver with advantage and great temporary relief is sometimes derived from the injection of carbonic acid gas.

Opium may with advantage be combined with most remedies as it tends to allay the peristaltic action of the intestine, has an astringent action and allays the griping pain so commonly complained of. It must, however, be borne in mind that the principal benefit derived from enemata is seen in those cases in which the rectum or lower part of the colon is affected.

The disease is sometimes so intractable and of chronic a nature that it will be found necessary to ring the changes on every kind of treatment. On such cases sulphate of copper and opium, acetate of lead and opium and the mineral acids may be tried.

Ipecacuanha may frequently be used with success. In several cases of acute dysentery I have succeeded in rapidly arresting the disease by giving it in large doses. In these cases I applied a mustard cataplasm to the stomach and give 40 minims of laudanum to allay and calm the gastric irritability and about an hour afterward administered ipecacuanha soup with 30 minim or more of laudanum. It will be found, now and then, that this treatment fails in consequence of the medicine not being retained on the stomach but in the cases in which the stomach tolerates the medicine it will often be found a very efficient method of treatment although not so as valuable aid to every kind of treatment we must not neglect the application of flannel to the abdomen, we must warm the patient against subjecting himself to sudden vicissitude of temperature, and must see that there is a proper regulation of the diet, for without proper dietic rules medicine is of little avail. Amylaceous aliment, arrowroot, sugar, rice, milk or bread and milk, soft eggs, and a drink may be enumerated as constituting the best description of diet. In all severe cases there should be entire abstinence from animal food and fruit, in chronic cases beef tea or mutton broth may be allowed together with fowl or fish and a moderate allowance of port wine. Perfect rest is an essential aid to the treatment of all bad cases of dysentery and through every stage of the complaint.

CHOLERA

In its eastern march cholera reached China though the Straits in the years 1820, during the summer various portions of this great empire suffered severely. Since the year alluded to it has not prevailed epidemically although few years pass without the occurrence of sporadic cases. The name given to it by the Chinese is 腳筋 *Jiao jin* or the disease which contracts the tendons of the leg.

The first case of cholera noticed at Canton in the year 1858 during the allied occupation occurred among the marines stationed at the west gate outside of which are stagnant pools and marshy paddy fields. Many other cases occurred during the succeeding two months among both French and English and also in the native regiments. The cases which came under my notice presented all the marks of Indian cholera in a most striking manner; excessive vomiting and rice water evacuations, severe and painful cramps of abdomen and extremities, lividity of the skin, rapid prostration, low hoarse voice, sunken eyes, shrunken and shriveled appearance of the skin, pulse small: surface covered with a cold perspiration and finally collapse. The intellect in most cases remained clear and unclouded to the termination of the disease but in those cases in which secondary fever supervened delirium was frequently present and may probably be accounted for by the suppression of urine and consequent presence of urea in the blood.

Cholera has seldom been known to occur in China during the winter months upon what circumstance it appearance depends is hard to say but it does not appear irrational to conjecture that a peculiar electrical condition of the air is necessary for its development.

During the month of July 1859 when the writer was at Shanghai cholera made its appearance both on board the merchant shipping and the men of war. On the 29th of July a case occurred on board HMS Highflyer and proved fatal. Two other cases afterward arose in the same gunboat and some men belonging to the gunboat beside were attacked. Both these gunboats were sunk by the Chinese at the Peiho Forts on the 25th of June and remained under water for several days. A suspicion arose that they were in an unhealthy state and consequently the senior officer, Captain Charles Shadwell gave an order that they should be inspected with reference to their sanitary condition. The lining of the inner side of the vessels was removed when it became evident that the whole space intervening between the lining and the timbers was filled with soft semi fluid mud which in some places was of a dark black colour and emitted a very offensive odour. The weather was oppressively hot and it seemed probable that the action of the suns rays upon the side of the vessels would make matters worse. They were consequently reported unfit for the men to live in until they were subjected to great repairs and thoroughly cleansed and ventilated, the whole of the lining up the ships being required to be removed and exposed to atmospheric influence.

With regard to the treatment of cholera, I have usually followed that recommended by the most eminent authorities and consider it unnecessary to enter into any details. The morbid anatomy in the cases which have come under the writers notice has shown the mucous membrane of the small and large intestine of a pale appearance and the canal contained a moderate quantity of white fluid. Lung partially collapsed, liver generally healthy, gall-bladder full of bile. Venous system full, bladder empty and contracted. Secretion arrested.

HEPATITIS

This disease which is not infrequent among the Europeans in China would appear to be somewhat rarer among the natives which may perhaps be accounted for by the simple quality of their food and more regular habits. The disease is however seen even among the Chinese rather extensively as the numerous cases of jaundice enumerated in the reports of the missionary hospitals would seen to testify. The disease which is common during the hot weather and toward the end of the autumn when the temperature suddenly decreases appeared to be caused by the calorific rays of the sun which tend to stimulate the liver to an excessive secretion of bile and derange the normal function of that organ.

Upon consulting Dr Annesley's and Dr Muirhead's valuable works on the diseases of India it seems evident that hepatitis, even in the southern parts of China, is not nearly so common a complaint as it is in India which may perhaps be attributed to the mean temperature being lower. But although the disease in its severe form is not so common as in India it most be borne in mind that a very large number of Europeans who have resided long in China and been accustomed to good living, without being actually so unwell as to require confinement to bed or much medical treatment suffer occasionally from slight fullness and distension together with pain and uneasiness in the hepatic region. These symptoms are attended with more or less disorder of the digestive organs. The result of experience also shows that in China hepatitis seldom terminates in abscess.

The few cases of acute hepatitis that have come under my care were treated by the application of leeches, hot fomentations, mercurial preparations and saline purgative. During convalescence nitro muriatic acid has been given with benefit: all my patients recovered favourably and none required to be invalided. The spleen is very commonly affected in cases of ague but it is occasionally found diseased without the complaint being accompanied with intermittent fever although the previous history of the patient generally shows that the patient has suffered some time or other from attacks of ague. It would be wrong, however, to suppose as many have done that congestion and enlargement of the spleen are necessary attendants on attacks of ague, or that the disease of the spleen is the actual cause of the complaint. A very large proportion of patients affected with intermittent fever do not complain of pain in the spleen and pressure over the splenic region causes no uneasiness.

If the question is asked of a patient labouring under ague whether he has pain anywhere although he may state that he has much headache which he usually does, or may say that he has some abdominal pain as he occasionally does, very rarely indeed will he direct the attention of the medical practitioner to the spleen as a seat of disease. So that the question of ague being invariably connected with splenic disease appears to me have no foundation in truth, for in those cases in which this organ is affected it would rather seem that the disease is the effect and not the cause of intermittent fever.

Frequently attacks of ague tend undoubtedly to produce disease of the spleen and it must be confessed that we seldom meet with a case of acute splenitis in a patient who has not suffered more or less from aguish attacks. In those cases of acute splenitis which have come under the writers notice, the fever although ushered in with rigors has shown no tendency to intermit, but on the contrary the fever that accompanied the disease has shown on all occasions, a decidedly continued type, the pulse generally remaining for several days together about 96 or 100. In most cases there is so much pain that the patient cannot lie on his left side, the decubitus is generally dorsal. Generally there is derangement of the bowels as evidenced sometimes by constipation and at others by diarrhoea.

The treatment which I have generally found most successful has been the application of leeches or fomentation and the administration of calomel and opium or Dover's Powder, saline aperients with an occasional alterative or dose of castor oil and laudanum. When the more urgent symptoms have been relieved painting the region of the spleen with the compound, tincture of iodine has been had recourse to and with apparent benefit. I am perfectly aware that most writers agree that mercury is contraindicated in splenitis, but I have invariably employed it and never have I seen any bad results from its use, but on the contrary my cases have generally made very favourable recovery.

DISEASES OF THE EYE

Of the disease of the eye which form such an essential and important class of the maladies of the Chinese, catarrhal and chronic ophthalmic, acute conjunctivitis, granular lids, entropium, pterygium and trichiasis, seem to be the most general. These diseases usually excite a varicose state of the vessels of the conjunctiva, and a thickened vascular condition of the cornea or tares terminating in opacity, leucoma, and final loss of vision.

The oblique curvature of the upper palpebra, which is characteristic of Chinese physiognomy renders the inversion of the lid a relatively common affection, occasioning the loss of many eyes and opacity and vascularity of the cornea in a still greater number. The eyelashes turning in upon the eye produce itching and irritation and the person immediately commences rubbing the eye. This increases the inflammation till it runs into a chronic stage, and finally the blood vessels cross the cornea, opacity succeed, and ulceration and destruction of the eye is frequently the result.

It is an interesting subject of inquiry as to what may be the probable cause of the large amount of disease of the eye which exists among the people of this country. From the delicacy of the organ, and its exposure to irritating agents of various kinds, it is in all countries subject to many diseases, and these people are liable in common with others. But as may be seen from the lists of cases that have been treated by medical missionaries namely trichiasis, entropium, granular lids, catarrhal ophthalmic, pterygium, contraction of the tares and opacity of the cornea, prevail to a very great extent, much greater than is the usual proportion in other parts of the world.

It is evident this cannot arise from the formation of the eye itself for although the eyes of the eyes of the Chinese are small and the eyelids drawn inward and downward, in many cases, so as make a distinct fold at the inner angle, as is especially seen in many females. Still this is the natural condition of the eye throughout the whole nation and it is difficult to understand how the natural state of any organ can make it so very liable to disease. It is true that some individuals are born with a conformation of body, that they are more prone than others to disease. But this altogether is an abnormal condition, whereas the form of the eye in this people is, as before mentioned, perfectly natural. It would appear that, as the result of observation that the more frequent occurrence of the above named diseases arises in a great measure from two causes.

Firstly the severe inflammation of the eye which frequently comes on at the commencement of the northerly and northeasterly winds in October, November and December, and the occasionally prevalence of epidemic catarrhal ophthalmic during the south-west monsoon, the inflammation is permitted to run its course without relief being obtained. This leaves as it consequence various changes in the tissue of a more or less injurious nature according to the intensity of the primary inflammation of the eye and its appendage and the healthy or unhealthy condition of the sufferer.

Secondly the injurious effects of a practice which is commonly followed by the Chinese barber of everting the lower lid, and rubbing its inner surface gently with an iron or bamboo instrument, shaped like a small scoop, which they also pass across the inner lid and deep into the inner and outer canthi. This is called "washing the eye" and the declared intention is the removal of any portion of mucus that they may be lodged on its surface. This is a very common habit and may be seen daily in the barbers' shops. Where, after the head has been shaved, the man sits composed, as if enjoying exquisite delight, whilst the barber is thus operating on his eyes. If the persons eyes be examined after this process they will be found to be very red and in a state of considerable irritation, and in process of time chronic conjunctivitis supervenes, and this being considered as the result of the eye not being sufficiently cleansed, the practice is persisted in, and the conjunctiva of the lid becomes covered with granulations. Exposure to cold immediately after this operation has been frequently known to produce an attack of acute inflammation of this organ.

Catarrhal ophthalmia frequently prevails epidemically along the seaboard of China during the spring and summer months of the year. In the month of August 1859 when the writer was at Shanghai the complaint prevailed most extensively among the foreign residents, the native population and the shipping in the harbour. The usual symptoms were redness and swelling of the internal surface of the eyelids and of slight frontal headache and intolerance of the light. In severe cases there is a vascular fringe around the margin of the cornea, and here and there large spots of extravasated blood and attended with a thick and copious purulent discharge.

On board HMS Highflyer we had 34 cases admitted on the sick list and all the other men-of war suffered in an equal or greater degree. The flag-ship HMS Chesapeake had nearly 100 cases. The great majority of patients had slight attacks, many not requiring to be placed on the sick list and of those who were discharged to duty after 4 or 5 days treatment. In some few cases which came to my knowledge the inflammatory symptoms continued much longer, two or three weeks, and were followed by more or less weakness of sight rather severely being quite unable, for about 4 days during the height of the attack, to discern the light, and afterward had to complain of weakness of sight for about a month.

The administration of a mild aperient, the local application of cold or warm water to the eyes, via opium or solution of nitrate of silver together with seclusion from the glare of the sun were the chief remedial measures employed, and they were successful in all the cases which came to my own immediate observation. Among the Chinese these epidemic attacks of catarrhal ophthalmic are frequently attended with material injury or even destruction of both eyes the patient having been improperly treated or coming too late to the missionary hospital for relief.

RHEUMATISM

On looking over the reports of the Medical Missionary Hospital in China I find that out of 62,888 patients attended there were 4,362 cases of rheumatism. The greater numbers occur, as might be expected, at the northern ports, and I notice that the cases are more numerous at Ningpo than at Shanghai.

SCROFULA

On examining the Reports of the Medical Missionary Hospital which have come into my hands, I find that there are 629 cases of scrofula out of 64,878 patients. Scrofulous enlargements if the glands appear to be more common in the south of China than in the northern parts of the empire, my experience would seem to show that scrofula is less amenable to treatment than it is in Europe.

CUTANEOUS DISEASES

Cutaneous diseases are more frequent and severe in some of the northern parts than they are in the south of the empire. The chief cutaneous diseases are psora, psoriasis, lepra, prurigo, leprosy, elephantiasis, lichen, herpes impetigo and scabies, pustular scabies is very common among the lower orders.

A disease commonly called "Chinese Ringworm" (herpes circinnate) is also very frequently met with and proves very troublesome to Europeans. It appears to me to be a contagious disease propagated by contact with persons suffering from it or by wearing the clothes of those affected with the complaint, and seems to have no reference to the state of health of the person labouring under it. A large number of patients that I have attended have had no marked disorder of the digestive organs and in many instances were strong healthy men apparently little liable to any cutaneous disorder arising from a bad state of health. The disease is extremely difficult to cure. The local application of nitrate of silver, sulphate of copper and compound tincture of iodine are among the best remedies. The compound tincture of iodine is perhaps the most efficient. Some of the native remedies are more efficacious than our own.

Leprosy exists in China in 5 or 6 different forms. It is very common in the south where lepers' villages and houses exist throughout the provinces of Kwangtung and Kiangsi. The Rev N Lobcheid, German missionary, informs me that proud and powerful clans bury the lepers alive. The Chinese believe that the disease arises from some peculiar change of blood. No one acquainted with the complaint doubts that it is of a contagious nature. It is related by the Chinese that after the last war it was impossible for Cantonese to induce some northern men, who had been sent to fight against the English, to return home. Unable to conquer them, and knowing them to be ignorant of leprosy, they sent a number of leprous women among them, from whom they caught disease; conquered now, though, not by the sword, but by a loathsome disease, they consented to being sent home. They embarked, but when in the open sea the junks were sunk by the Cantonese and all perished. Elephantiasis, although not so common a complaint as in some other countries, is of frequent occurrence. It is said to be particularly common in the island of Chusan.

HYDROPHOBIA

This disease is somewhat rare in China. It is very little alluded to among the ancient writings of the country although sometimes among the clauses or notes which accompany the Penal Code there is mention made of the Kwing Tur or mad dog. There is a popular belief that dogs go mad from swallowing some acrid herb (蓼 *liao*) which has been chewed and vomited by venomous snakes.

The writer has only accurate information concerning 4 cases, one of which occurred in the spring of 1830, one in the winter of 1848 one in June 1859 and fourth occurred in 1858 to a second Class Boy belonging to HMS Action who was bitten by a dog belonging to Commander Ward.

These were all cases of great interest. The particulars of all of them are in my possession, but they would occupy too much space for insertion in this book. I have also several Chinese prescriptions for the cure of hydrophobia of much interest, although of doubtful value. The limited number of pages in this book also forbid their insertion.

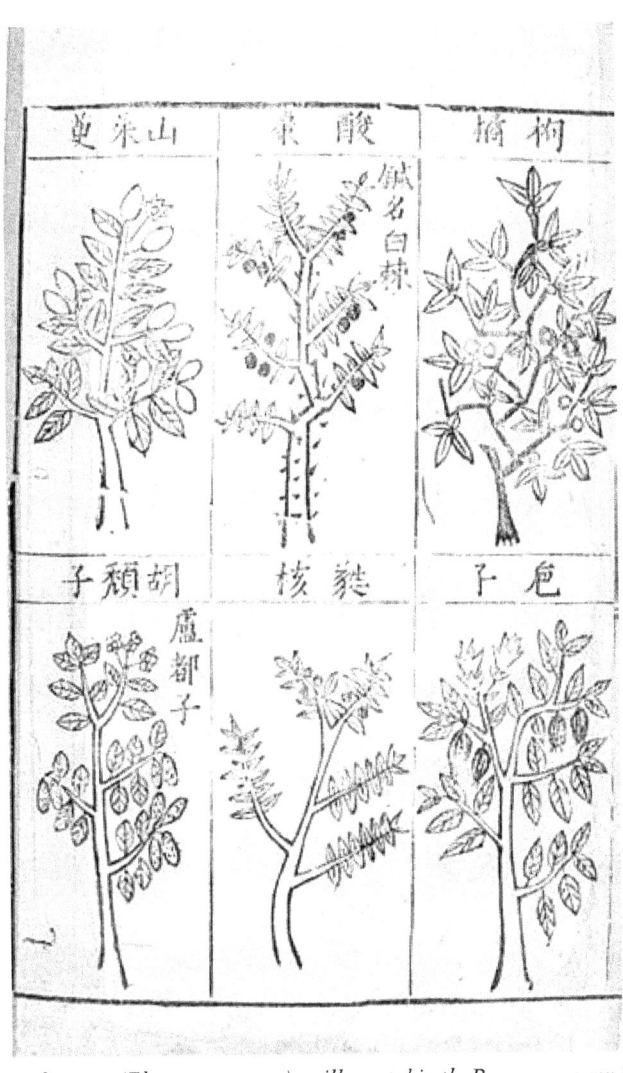

38. *Thorny Elaeagnus (Elaeagnus pungens) as illustrated in the Ben cao gang mu by Li Shi Zhen, Wellcome Library, London.*

Chapter 15 An Essay On Chinese Medical Literature

In common with every other civilized nation, the Chinese have paid considerable attention to the study of medicine. No country in the world is an exception: the most published nations of Europe possess many volumes of books in connection with the healing art.

From the earliest age writers on medicine and its hundred sciences are numerous. The medical literature seems almost inexhaustible. The best informed Chinese scholar would require to devote many years to the subject to give an accurate translation of even a very few of the most respected authors. Li Shi Zhen [1] in the 6th volume of his Materia Medica give a list of 276 medical works and monographs, a list of 440 miscellaneous works, historical and biographical, and from which he made extracts for his Materia Medica.

In looking over the library of the London Missionary Society of Shanghai, I find that the number of Chinese medical books is very considerable, although they form a small portion of the medical works to be found in China. So that the reader can appreciate the general nature of the medical literature of the country, I give a list of the works.

- *Jian yan ji zheng* 檢驗集證 The coroners guide 3 volumes
- *Xi yuan lu* 洗冤錄 On post mortem investigations.
- *Zheng ni liang fang* 拯溺良方 Plants for restoring persons in a state of asphyxia.
- *Jing yan liang fang* 經驗良方 Verified receipts
- *Ji yan liang fang* 集驗良方 Amply verified receipts 6 volumes
- *Yi fang ji jie* 醫方集解 Explanation of a collection of medial receipts
- *Niu jing da quan* 牛經大全 The cow doctors complete manual 2 volumes
- *Liao ma ji* 療馬集 Veterinary surgeons guides 4 volumes
- *Sha zheng quan shu* 痧症全書 The complete book of cholera
- *Sha zhang yu heng quan shu* 痧脹玉衡全書 Complete directory to the treatment of cholera
- *Shang han quan sheng ji* 傷寒全生集 Treatise on cold diseases 4 vols.
- *Fu you bian* 福幼編 Treatise on the diseases of infants
- *You ke bai xiao* 幼科百效 Approved method for treatment of infants
- *Meng shi you ke* 孟氏幼科 Dr Meng on the diseases of infants
- *You ke zhi nan* 幼科指南 Guide to the treatment of infants
- *You you ji cheng* 幼幼集成 Collection of methods for the treatment of young infants 6 vols
- *Mai li mi jue* 脈理祕訣 Secrets of the pulse
- *Yi xue zhen mai* 醫學診脈 The physicians guide to the pulse 2 vols.
- *Da sheng yao zhi* 大生要旨 Fundamental principles of parturition
- *Da sheng pian* 達生篇 Treatise on parturition
- *Chan ke xin fa* 產科心法 The principles of parturition

- *Xian jia mi chuan dou ke zhen jue* 仙家祕傳痘科真訣 Secret memoir on the true method of treating small-pox, handed down by the immortals
- *Zhong dou xin shu* 種痘新書 New treatise on small-pox, inoculation 6 vols
- *Nv ke mi chuan* 女科祕傳 Secret method on female disease
- *Ji yin gang mu* 濟陰綱目 Leading principles in the medical treatment of females
- *Nu ke jing lun* 女科經綸 A arrangement of female complaints 6 vols
- *Fu ren liang fang* 婦人良方 Receipts for female complaints, 12 vols.
- *Zheng zhi hui bu* 證治匯補 Supplementary collection of accredited plans of medical treatment, 4 vols
- *Zun sheng ba jian* 遵生八牋 8 chapters on the preservation of life 10 vols
- *Wei sheng hong bao* 衛生鴻寶 The treasure for the preservation of life 4 vols
- *Song ya zun sheng quan shu* 嵩崖尊生全書 Song Ya's complete guide to the preservation of life 6 vols
- *Shou shi bian* 壽世編 Treatise on the method of attaining old age
- *Dong yi bao jian* 東醫寶鑑 Mirror of medical practice in the east 8 vols
- *Ji jiu guang sheng ji* 急救廣生集 Collection of methods for saving life in extreme cases
- *Tai yi yuan ji jiu liang fang zhai yao* 太醫院急救良方摘要 Selected receipts of the Imperial Medical Institute for saving life in extreme cases
- *Wai ke jing yao* 外科精要 Important rules for the treatment of external complaints
- *Wai ke shi fa* 外科十法 Ten methods for the treatment of surgical cases
- *Wai ke zheng zong* 外科正宗 Treatment by surgery
- *Jin jian wai ke* 金鑑外科 Mirror of surgery 11 vols
- *Lei jing* 類經 Medical encyclopedia 32 vols
- *Cuo shuo* 痤說 Remarks on skin eruptions
- *Chuang yang jing yan* 瘡瘍經驗 Chuang Yang verified treatise on eruptions
- *Shen shi yao han* 審視搖函 Treatise on diseases of the eyes 6 vols
- *Yan ke da quan* 眼科大全 Complete treatise on diseases of the eye 6 vols
- *Nei ke zhi yao* 內科知要 Important facts respecting internal complaint
- *Yang ke* 瘍科 Selected instances of infectious complaints 7 vols
- *Yang yi da quan* 瘍醫大全 Treatise on the medical treatment of infectious complaints
- *Huang di su wen ling shu* 黃帝素聞靈樞 Ancient medical thesaurus by hwang-te
- *Su wen ling shu lei zuan yue zhu* 素聞靈樞類纂約註 Classification of the contents medical thesaurus
- *Yi xue xin yu* 醫學心語 Considerations respecting the study of medical 4vols
- *Tui na guang yi ji* 推拿廣意集 Treatise on the treatment of disease by manipulation
- *Yi zong bi du* 醫宗必讀 The physician handbook
- *Ben cao bei yao* 本草備要 Essence of the universal herbal 4 vols

- *Ben cao gang mu* 本草綱目 Universal herbal 40 vols
- *Ye shi ben cao jing jie* 葉氏本草經解 Explanations of the text of the universal herbal 4 vols
- *Wan san gao dan zuo fa* 丸散膏丹做法 Manufacture of pills, powders ointments and boluses
- *Shen ti bing yao zi dian* 身體病藥字典 Materia medica
- *Shu xin zhao pai za ce* 書信招牌雜冊 Collection of medical placards
- *Qin ding si ku yi shu mu lu* 欽定四庫藝書目錄 Catalogue of medical books in the Imperial Library
- *Tai yi yuan mu lu* 太醫院目錄 Dictionary of terms used in the Imperial Medical Institute
- *Zhong de tang wan san gao dan hua lu mu lu* 種德堂丸散膏丹花露目錄 Catalogue of pills, powders, ointment and medicaments, sold at the chung-tih tang apothecary's establishments
- *Wu fu ji* 五福集 Collection of receipts, for the attainment of happiness of various kinds
- *Jin ling jiu sheng ju* 金陵救生局 Report of the Nankin Human Society

The great majority of the volumes which have been published may not justify the labour of translating, yet there are some important matters to awaken the strongest curiosity and to enlighten us even in this enlightened age. The subject has never been thoroughly investigated by medical men acquainted with the language; a language which is, I confess, one of the most difficult of all languages. The complete examination of the subject would require much devoted research, a profound knowledge of the language and of technical terms used by Chinese authors. But if the path be difficult, and requires hard work, the rewards will be in proportion and worthwhile including the high honour of pursuing the study.

As far as antiquity is concerned the Chinese system of medicine has high claims to our consideration for it is superior in this respect to the works of Pythagoras and Hippocrates. From the obscurity, however, which hangs over the first period of Chinese history it is difficult to understand the great antiquity assigned to the earliest medical writers. For instance, it is said that Shen Nong composed a Materia Medica 3100 years BC the emperor Huang Di wrote the *Su wen* or *Plain questions*, about the year 2630 BC [2].

Although the dates may be uncertain, the fact certainly proves that considerable attention was paid to medicine at a very early period. The *Nei jing* a very ancient and celebrated work, which still exists, was written during the Zhou dynasty about 1050 years BC. The famous work on the doctrine of the pulse, by Wang Shen He (epitomized by Dr Halse) was written during the reign of Che Huang Di, the book burner, about the year 510 BC and its author frequently speaks of more ancient works.

An Essay on Chinese Medical Literature

Since the Christian era began 2000 years ago, a great many medical works have been published, especially during the Tang and Sung dynasties. About the year 229 AD, Dr Chong Kai Bin composed the first regular work containing prescriptions in addition to the theoretical part of medicine. About 750 AD, Dr Wang Bing published a new edition of the *Plain questions* by the emperor Huang Di and added a commentary by himself to the original work. The great Materia Medica, or *Ben cao gang mu* was written by Li Shi Zhen and published by his son about 1600 AD, during the reign of Wan Lian. The *Yi zong jin jian*, a *Golden Mirror of Medical Authors* was published in 1743 AD, the 7th of *Jian lun*, which is a one of the largest Chinese medical works, occupying 32 active volumes and containing upward of 400 wood-cuts. It was compiled by imperial authority from the best works of previous writers, but more especially from the *Nei jing* and the writings of Dr Chong Kai Bin.

Medical science as understood by the Chinese is a combination of anatomical facts and some really valuable practical observations within a mixture of astrology and superstition. In many respects, it is very similar to what was practiced in Europe during the 16th-17th centuries. Their philosophers admit the existence of five elements (*wu xing* 五行), as fire ,earth, metal, wood and water and believe that the human body is made up of these in various proportions, each element, however, has its own peculiar position in one or more of the internal organs, from which store-house or reservoir, it is distributed throughout the body by means of the all-pervading principles *yin* 陰 and *yang* 陽. Fire is said to reside in the heart, air in liver, water in the kidneys, metals in the lung, and earth in the spleen and stomach. Whatever may be thought of such a philosophy it compares with that of Nicholas Culpeper [3], gentleman student in physick and astrology, living in London, who in his day, the middle of the 17th century AD, was a most renowned medical practitioner. He tells us "what diseases each planet " signifies "what diseases are under every sign of the Zodiack, what parts and numbers of the body every planet rules, what parts of the body are under every sign of the Zodiack", and who believed in the wonderful harmony of the disease with the motions of the heavens.

There are a great number of Chinese medical authors, and the historical interest attaching to Chinese medical practice is documented through 20 centuries or more. The mature traditions which ascribe the earliest writings in the medical art to Shen Nong and Huang Di are as above. It appears natural, and even probable, that some advance had been made towards a comprehensive medical system several centuries before the Christian era. In the *Han shu* we have a catalogue of 36 works on therapeutics , divided into 11 classes, the first called *Yi jing* 醫經 are devoted to a examination of the internal structure of the human frame, with the peculiar functions of the several members, and pronounce upon the causes of symptoms of disorder ; the second called *Jing fang* 經方 takes up the question of the suitable remedies to be applied; the

113

third called *Fang zhong* 房中 on the regulation of sexual intercourse; and the fourth called *Shen xian* 神僊 are occupied with a visionary theory, by which the subject is supposed to avoid illness by properly regulated discipline. These two last branches of medicine have in modern times become united, and are now discarded by medical authors. The practice of medicine has been divided into a number of branches from very early times, defined with greater or less precision at various periods. During the Ming dynasty, the faculty was definitely fixed by the government as consisting of thirteen branches. At the commencement of the present Ching dynasty, eleven branches of medical practice were recognized by the imperial medical college but the number was afterward reduced to nine. These are named, great blood vessel complaints, lesser blood-vessel complaints, fevers, smallpox, female complaints, cutaneous complaints, cases of acupuncture, eye complaints, throat mouth and teeth complaints, and bone complaints.

These distinctions however, are not accurately presented by most writers. There appears to have been little variation in the line of practice adopted by successive practitioners until about the 12th century, when we find several innovations introduced into the ancient theory, and the medical art became divided into several schools. From the very great detail given in Chinese medical works regarding the structure of the human body, it was thought that dissection must have been practiced in ancient times. However we have no record of the fact, and, if it was so, it has been discontinued for many centuries while there is little evidence of any widespread practice of human dissection having taken place in recent times. The diseases of animals have been included as a subsidiary branch of the medical profession from the earliest times.

The oldest medical treatise that exists is probably the *Huang di su wen* 黃帝素問 which, there is reason to believe, was written several centuries before Christ. It contains a summary of the traditional knowledge of medicine handed down from the most remote times. The oldest commentary on the work that exists was written by Wang Bing 王冰 in the 8th century, in 24 books. Another work ascribed to Huang Di, the *Ling shu jing* 靈樞經 deals with internal maladies and the practice of acupuncture. This latter work is not actually confirmed to have appeared earlier than the 11th century, and it is thought to be the production of Wang Bing mentioned above, but it is probable that it contains a great part of a more ancient work. It was formerly published in 24 books but in the later editions they are reduced to 12. The contents of these two treatises were rearranged and classified under nine headings by Wang Ang 汪昂 in 1689 with the title *Su wen ling shu lei zuan yue zhu* 素問靈樞類纂約註. The *Nei jing zhi yao* 內經知要 is a selection of passages from the *Su wen* and *Ling shu*, with a commentary by Li Nian E 李念莪. This was revised and published by Xue Sheng Bai 薛生白 in 1764.

Even earlier, a small treatise was written, in the 3rd century BC, termed the

Nei jing 難經, containing a solution to 81 questions. Eleven commentaries had been written on this previous to the Ming dynasty, the only one of which now existing is the *Nei jing ben yi* 難經本義 by Hua Shou 滑壽 who wrote about the close of the Yuan dynasty. In the early part of the 16th century Zhang Shi Xian 張世賢, a famous physician, published an edition illustrated by a diagram and notes to each of the 81 questions with the title *Yuan zhu nan jing* 原註難經. A compilation from various books was also drawn up during the Ming dynasty by Wang Jiu Si 王九思, Shi You Liang 石友諒, Wang Ding Xiang 王鼎象, and Wang Wei 王惟, with the title *Nei jing ji zhu* 難經集注.

The *Yin hai jing wei* 銀海精微 is a small treatise on eye complaints which professes to be written by Sun Si Miao 孫思邈 of the Tang dynasty but the evidence seems to indicate that it is a production subsequent to the Sung dynasty. It is held in high esteem, however, for the method in which it treats the subject.

The *Su shen liang fang* 蘇沈良方, in 8 books, is a collection of famous prescriptions by Shen Kuo 沈括 of the Sung dynasty with some additional material by Su Shi 蘇軾, also known as Su Dong Po the poet. Therefore the two names (Su and Shen) are united together in the title. Neither of these was practicing physicians, but having a general knowledge of the theory of medicine, they were able to investigate the medical properties of various substances and have given the result of their experience in a series of prescriptions.

Toward the end of the 3rd century a celebrated treatise on the pulse entitled *Mai jing* 脈經, in 10 books, was written by Wang Quan He 王權和 the court physician during the Western Tang dynasty. This contains a summary of the methods and knowledge of the subject which had been handed down previous to that period. The manuscript of this was revised and published in the year 1068 under superintendence of Lin Yi 林億. It was reprinted in 1094 and again in 1164. Two editions were issued during the Ming dynasty and a new issue has appeared as *Song jiang* within the last 30 years, a production composed during the Song dynasty appears to have been long received as the genuine treatise of Wang Shu He.

The book *Mai jing* consists of a series of rhymes on the functions of the pulse and the simple style in which it is written has insured its popularity. Shang Shi Jian of the Ming dynasty, who had not sufficient critical penetration to discover the facts, added a commentary and diagrams, in which it is stated the book has been in wide circulation for centuries until the present time, with the title *Huan zhu mai jue bian zhen* 圖註脈訣辨真. The principal part of this book was translated by the missionary Hervieu under the impression that it was the work of Wang Shun He. His translation has been published in Duhalde's "Description of China". There is a small book on the pulse issued by the Peking Medical College entitled *Mai li mi jue* 脈理祕訣 . Another small treatise on the same subject is styled the *Yi xue zhen mai* 醫學診脈 "Physicians guide to the pulse."

The *Shang han zong bing lun* 傷寒總病論 is a treatise on fevers in 6 books written by Pang An Shi 龐安時 in the 11th century. At the end is a chapter explanatory of the sounds and meaning of the characters used in the work and another on the composition of medicines, both drawn up by Pang's pupil Dong Bing 董柄 , according to the instructions received from his teacher.

The *Fu ren da quan liang fang* 婦人大全良方 , in 24 books, is a treatise on female complaints written by Chen Zi Ming 陳自明 , about the year 1239. It consists of more than 260 articles, categorized under 8 headings. Each article is followed by prescriptions suitable to the ailment in question. This was revised, abridged and commented by Xue Ji 薛己 of the Ming dynasty, who added a number of actual examples, illustrative of the particular cases.

The *Yi lei yuan rong* 醫壘元戎 , in 12 books, is a treatise on the art of medicine, by Wang Hao Gu 王好古 , written previous to the year 1241. The arrangement of the work is accordance with the theory of the twelve larger blood vessels, commencing with fevers, and having an appendix on miscellaneous diseases. It was republished in 1543 and again in 1593 and has become considerably changed from the original in the course of several editions. The *Ci shi nan zhi* 此事難知 is a nearly identical production of the same author, the object of which is to make known the system of Li Gao 李杲 for treating fevers. The original work of this book is now lost, however this little treatise of Wang Hao Gu contains the only remains of it that are preserved. It was completed in 1308. A treatise on medicaments by the same author, is named the *Tang ye ben cao* 湯液本草 . The first book concerns the method of the using several medicines at the same time, while the second and third books point out the application of every kind of medicine to the various complaints respectively connected with the twelve blood-vessels, according to an artificial system in which the several agents are designated prince, ministers, assistants, etc.

The *Rui zhu tang jing yan fang* 瑞竹堂經驗方 is a collection of verified prescriptions, written during the Yuan dynasty by Sha Tu Mu Su 沙圖穆蘇 , apparently a Mongolian, though there is no biographical notice of him that exists. The original has long been lost and the edition now in use contains less than half the work that was originally written by the author.

The *Shi yi de xiao fang* 世醫得效方 , in 20 books, is a collection of prescriptions from the hand of Wei Yi Lin 危亦林 being the combined experience of himself and ancestors including five generations. The author began the work in 1328 and finished it in 1337. It is divided into the following seven headings: great blood-vessel complaints, lesser blood vessel complaints, nervous complaints, child-bearing and general female complaints, eye complaints, mouth teeth and throat complaints, and setting bones and cure of arrow-wounds. The last book consists of the hygienic precepts of Sun Shi Mo of the Tang dynasty. The cases in which acupuncture may be applied are distributed through the several divisions.

The *Wai ke jing yi* 外科精義, by Qi Zhi 齊之 of the Yuan dynasty, is a small treatise on cutaneous complaints. In the first part he discusses the cause and character of eruptions and in the last prescribes the requisite remedies, consisting of poisonous compounds to destroy the foreign material and restorative application to heal the wounds.

The *Yi jing su hui ji* 醫經溯洄集 by Wang Lv 王履, who lived at the close of the Yuan dynasty, is a small treatise on fevers, containing a revision of 397 precepts delivered by Zhang Ji 張機 of the Han dynasty. Most of these are repetitions and others are added which are missing in Chang Ge's work, leaving the number 397 as before. He has also a very detailed discussion of internal and external diseases, apoplexy, and internal heat.

The *Pu ji fang* 普濟方 in 168 books is a guide to therapeutics, by Zhu Su 朱橚, one of the imperial princes, at the commencement of the Ming dynasty. Being the most complete work of the kind that has ever been written, it contains in all 1960 treatises on 2175 different subjects, with 778 rules, 21,739 prescriptions, and 239 diagrams.

The *Zheng zhi zhun sheng* 證治準繩, in 120 books, by Wang Ken Tang 王肯堂, is a collection of medical treatises, written at different times. The treatise on the treatment of miscellaneous complaints and that on classified prescriptions were both written during the years 1537 and 1538. That on fevers, and the one on sores, were completed in 1544 and those on infantile and female diseases were finished in 1547. He has extracted extensively from preceding authors and the work is considered one of the most complete of its kind. It was published in 1602 and again in 1791.

The *Ji yin gang mu* 濟陰綱目, in 14 books, is a general treatise on the treatment of female complaints, written by Wu Zi Wang 武子望 in 1728, and contains the substance of Wang Ken Tang treatise on female diseases.

The great Materia Medica known as the *Ben cao gang mu* 本草綱目, in 52 books, was compiled by Li Shi Zhen 李時珍 of the Ming dynasty who spent 30 years on the work, having made extracts from upward of eight hundred preceding authors from whom he selected 1518 different medicaments, added 374 new ones, making in all 1892. These are arranged in 62 classes, and the 16 divisions; water, fire, earth, minerals, herbs, grain, vegetables, fruit, trees, garments, and utensils, insects, fishes, crustacea, birds, beasts, and man. Under each substance the correct name is given which is followed by an explanation of the name. After this there are explanatory remarks and correction of errors to which is added the smell, taste, and applications, with the prescriptions in which it is used. There are three books of illustrations at the beginning with 2 books of directions and books forming an index to the various medicines, classified according to the complaints for which they are used.

Some idea may be formed of the care the author took with the work from the fact that he wrote out the manuscript three times before he was satisfied it was completed. It was first printed in the Wan Lian period, and was presented to the emperor by Li Jian Yuan, the son of the author. It was revised and printed in the time of the first emperor of the present Ching dynasty, and several editions have appeared since that time. The nucleus of all the writings on this subject is a small work, which tradition ascribes to the ancient Shen Nong. Since the time of Li Shi Zhen there have been numerous treatise criticizing and elucidating this great work but it still stands unrivalled. The *Ben cao bei yao* 本草備要 is a brief epitome of the *Ben cao gang mu*, compiled by Wang Gang, mentioned above, in 1694, it is illustrated by wide pictures interspersed with the text. The *Ben cao jing jie yao* 本草經解要 is a summary of the most important parts of Li Shi Zhen's work, written in 1724 by Ye Tian Shi 葉天士, a famous physician of Soochow.

The earliest work devoted to the practice of acupuncture is the *Tong ren zhen jiu jing* 銅人針灸經, in 7 books. In 1027, by command of the emperor, Wang Wei De 王惟得 made two brass anatomical figures of the human frame by which he illustrated the above art and that exist wrote a treatise on it with the title *Tong ren shu xue* 銅人腧穴. The earliest editions that exist are of the time of the Ming dynasty, and illustrated by a number of very wide pictures. The *Ming tang jiu jing* 明堂灸經, in 8 books, is of uncertain date, the author being named as Xi Fang Zi 西方子 "Western scholar". The expression *Ming tang* in the title is the name of an apartment in the palace of the ancient Huang Di, where he delivered his views on the venous and muscular system hence it has became a general designation for acupuncture in all its forms and consequences.

The *Lei jing* 類經, in 32 books, is the production of Zhang Jie Bao 張介寶, a celebrated physician. The theme of the work is the text of the two ancient books *Su wen* and *Ling shu* and the chapters were rearranged under the 12 headings; sanitary consideration, masculine and feminine principles, form of the intestines, pulse and appearance, sinews and nerves, radical and ultimate conditions, breach and taste, medical treatment, disease and sickness, acupuncture, circulation of air, and pervading principles. These disquisitions which embody the views of the author, are followed by 11 books of diagrams, and auxiliary remarks, which with 4 additional books of remarks conclude the work; this was finished 1624, being the result of three years labour.

One of the best works of modern times for general medical information, *Yu zuan yi zong ji jian* 御纂醫宗金鑑, in 90 books, was composed in compliance with an imperial order issued in the year 1739. The first 25 books contain the *Shang han lun* 傷寒論 and *Jin gui yao lue* 金匱要畧, two works by Chang Ge of the Han dynasty, with a commentary. This is the earliest medical writer who gives prescriptions in addition to theory. The following 8 books give a revised edition of the prescriptions of the most celebrated physicians. The next book contains important rules regarding the circulation of air in the body. After this there are 94 books or rules regarding several classes of complaints, and 4 books of rules for setting bones. The work is illustrated by diagrams and plates throughout; and parts of it are sometimes published separately.

The *Chuang yang jing yan quan shu* 瘡瘍經驗全書, in 13 books, is a work on the treatment of cutaneous complaints, the efficacy of which, it professes to have been proved is ascribed to Dou Han Qing 竇漢卿, the court physician during the 11ᵗʰ century, while his descendant Dou Meng Lin 竇夢麟 is said to have revised and prepared it for publication. It is believed, however, that the greater part is the production of the latter, who borrowed his ancestors' fame to give currency to the book. It is illustrated by a human figure, exhibiting varieties of cutaneous eruptions; a new edition was published in 1717.

The *Yi zong bi du* 醫宗必讀, in 10 books, is a brief summary of medical practice, by Li Zhong Zi 李中梓, published toward the close of the Ming dynasty.

The *Zheng zhi hui bu* 證治匯補 is a general medical treatise written by Li Xing An 李惺庵 in 1691, intended to be supplementary to the various works of the same characters already published.

The *Yi xue xin yu* 醫學心語 is a particular disquisition on the practice of medicine in all its branches, written by Cheng Guo Peng 程國彭, in 1723.

The *Yi gang ti yao* 醫綱提要, in 8 books, is a general compilation on medicine in all its branches by Li Zong Yuan 李宗源. It is divided according to the 8 following headings: masculine and feminine, internal and external, exterior and interior, cold and hot, vacant and full, dry and moist, ascending and descending, free passage and stoppage. It was published about the year 1831.

There is a large work termed, the *Dong yi bao jian* 東醫寶鑑, apparently of Korean origin, which has been several times published in China. This embraces all disciplines of medicine and differs in some aspects from other publications.

The *Shang han quan sheng ji* 傷寒全生集 is a treatise on fevers, written by Tao Jie An 陶節庵 in 1445. This was revised and published by Ye Tian Si in

1782; The *Shang han lun yi* 傷寒論議 is another short work on fevers, written by Ke Qin 柯琴, in 1674.

The *Sha chang yu heng quan shu* 痧腸玉衡全書 is a treatise on cholera with the method of treatment, and a large collection of prescriptions written by Guo Zhi Sui 郭志邃 in 1675. The *Sha zheng quan shu* 痧症全書, is another work on cholera, written by Wang Kai 王凱, in 1686, who professes to hand down the instructions of his teacher Lin Sen 林森, a recognized expert in the medical profession. This was revised and published in 1798 and again in 1826. Smallpox has engaged the attention of the Chinese from near the commencement of the Christian era, and inoculation has been practiced among them for a thousand years or more. The *Wen ren shi dou zhen lun* 聞人氏痘疹論 is a work treating this complaint, with numerous prescriptions by Wen Ren Gui 聞人規, which was published in 1323 and republished in 1542. The *Zong dou xin shu* 種痘新書 is another treatise on the subject, in 12 books, published in 1741 by Zhang Yan Xun 張琰遜, giving ample details of the disease in its various forms, the appropriate treatment and a variety of prescriptions. A small work on the same subject by Tiao Yuan Fu 調元復, bears the title *Xian jia dou ke mi chuan zhen jue* 仙家痘科秘傳真訣, professing to embody secrets on the subject. This is illustrated by numerous drawings of the disease. The *Tian hua jing* 天花精 is another work on smallpox, with numerous illustrations. The *Wai ke jing yao* 外科精要 is a treatise on the most important points in the character and cure of external maladies, by Chen Zi Ming.

The *Wai ke shi fa* 外科十法 is ten rules for the treatment of external complaints, written by Ching Kuo Pang, in 1733. The *Wai ke zheng zong* 外科正宗, in 12 books, which treats at length all external complaints, was written by Chen Shi Gong 陳實功, in the early part of the present Ching dynasty. It was revised and republished by Zhang Jing Yi 張驚翼; in 1785. The third book has illustrations of eruptions of various kinds. The *Dong tian ao zhi* 洞天奧旨, in 16 books, is another work of the same description. This was written by Chen Shi Duo 陳士鐸 in 1698 and revised and published again in 1790. It has 14 illustrations of the disease. One of the most recent works on this subject is the *Wai ke zheng zhi* 外科證治, written by Xue ke chang 許科昌 and Bi Fa 畢法, and published in 1831. The *Yang ke xuan cui* 瘍科選粹, in 8 books, is a work on sores of every description by Chen Wen Zhi 陳文治 published in 1628. The *Yang yi da quan* 瘍醫大全, in 20 books, is a treatise on sores with their remedies and prescriptions by Gu Shi Cheng 顧世澄, published in 1773. It has many illustrations.

The *Nv ke jing lun* 女科經綸, in 8 books, is a treatise on diseases peculiar to females written by Xiao Xun 蕭塤 in 1864. The *Chan ke xin fa* 產科心法 is a small work on the maladies attendant in child-bearing, by Wang Zhe 汪喆 in 1780, and published in 1834.

The *Qian shi xiao er yao cheng zhen jue* 錢氏小兒藥澄真訣 is a treatise on children's complaints written by Qian Yi 錢乙, the Court physician in 1093, and published by his pupil Yan Xiao Zhong 閻孝忠, in 1119. This was rearranged and a commentary added to it, by Xiong Zong Li 熊宗立, in 1440 when it was published with the title *Lei zheng zhu shi qian shi xiao fang jue* 類證註釋錢氏小方訣 in 10 books. The *You you ji cheng* 幼幼集成 in 6 books, is an extensive discussion of the maladies to which children are liable, written by Chen Fu Zheng 陳復正, in 1750. The *Fu you bian* 福幼邊 is a short discourse on the diseases of children, with prescriptions and certified cases, by Zhuang Yi Kui 莊一夔, published in 1777. The *You ke zhi nan jia chuan mi fang* 幼科指南家傳秘方 is a collection of rules and prescriptions for the treatment of the young, written by Wan Quan 萬全, a modern author, and republished in 1829. There is also a treatise on the same subject by Meng He 孟河, a Nankin physician, entitled, *Meng shi you ke* 孟氏幼科. The *Cuo shuo* 痤說 is a small treatise on a form of infantile cutaneous eruptions, by Jin Wei 金位, a physician of Hangchow.

One of the most popular treatises on diseases of the eye is the *Shen shi yao han* 審視搖函, in 6 books, by Fu Ren Yu 傅仁宇, published in 1647. Another essay on the same subject is entitled *Cao ting mu ke quan shu* 草亭目科全書, written by a physician named Deng Yuan 鄧苑. A great part of the book is occupied with prescriptions for eye diseases.

The *Ji jiu guang sheng ji* 急救廣生集 is a collection of illustrations and prescriptions for saving life in cases of extreme peril, such as attempted suicides, unforeseen calamities and method of prolonging life under dramatic circumstances of uncommon occurrence

The *Da sheng yao zhi* 大生要旨 is a treatise on child birth, written by Tang Qian Qing 唐千頃 in the early part of the present dynasty and has been several times republished. The *Shou shi bian* 壽世編 is a short disquisition on child birth and the rearing of children, with a variety of prescriptions, published about the year 1772.

The *Song fang ji jie* 嵩方集解 is a collection of medical prescriptions, with elucidations, written by Wang Gang, in the year 1682. The *Cheng shi yi jian li lun* 程氏易簡力論, in 6 books, is a similar collection by Cheng Lv Xin 程履新, which dates about 1693. It has extensive discussions on the properties of the medicines employed. In 1707 another was published by Yu Yi 羽儀, with prescriptions for almost every complaint, under the title *Jing yan liang fang* 經驗良方. The *Ji yan liang fang* 集驗良方 is an extensive collection of prescriptions, in 6 books, embracing the whole range of pathology compiled by Nian Xi Yao 年希堯, about the year 1724. The *Jing yan guang ji* 經驗廣集 is another famous collection, made about the year 1754, by Li Wen Bing 李文炳. The *Wei sheng hong bao* 衛生鴻寶 is a comprehensive general collection in 6 books, with a commentary, published in 1844. The *Ning kun mi ji* 寧坤秘笈 is a book of prescriptions for female complaints, published by one Li Tang 礪堂, in 1786. The *Zhi gu xin fang* 治蠱新方 is a treatise on antihelminthics, written by Liao Fu Zhao 繚福照, in 1835. The *Tai yi yuan ji jiu liang fang zhai yao* 太醫院急救良方摘要 is a selection of prescriptions employed by the Imperial Medical College for saving life in cases of extreme peril.

The *Zun sheng ba jian* 遵生八牋 is a discourse in hygiene, in 20 books, written by Gao Lian Shen 高濂深 in 1591. It is divided into 8 parts, namely seasonable regimens, rest and pleasure, prevention of disease in the future, eating drinking and clothing, amusements, retirement, efficacious medicines, and examples of living a virtuous life.

An old treatise on the ailments of the buffalo, entitled *Shui niu jing* 水牛經, professes to be written by Zao Fu 造父, during the 7th century, but it is probably of much more recent authorship. The *Liao ma ji* 療馬集 is a simple treatise on the veterinary art, composed by Yu Ren 喻仁 and Yu Jie 喻傑 in 1598. The concluding part is on the treatment of camels.

The *Nu jing da quan* 牛經大全 is a small work on the medical treatment of oxen and buffaloes by the same authors as the preceding.

Some few contributions were made to medical science and anatomy by the European missionaries who came to China during the 17th century, but the books they wrote are merely preserved as literary curiosities and do not appear to have made any impact on Chinese medical practice. Recently Dr Hobson (Note 22, Introduction) has done good service by his several publications in this department and there is reason to believe that the principles of the science may be accepted. A book on physiology, the *Quan ti xin lun* 全體新論 which was published in 1850, has been very favourably received. He has more recently issued the *Xi yi lue lun* 西醫畧論 on the principles and practice of surgery, the *Fu ying xin shuo* 婦嬰新説 on midwifery and the diseases of children, and the *Nei ke xin shuo* 內科新説 on the practice of medicine and materia medica. They are accompanied by a vocabulary of medical terms in English and Chinese.

Regarding Chinese physiology, for the sake of convenience of descriptions, the body is divided in various ways. The most usual way is into exterior and interior. The whole exterior surface is marked out into regions and a different name is given to almost every inch of skin. These divisions may be useful in determining the locality of any particular disease whether internal or external. In the anatomical illustrations is a series of rings connected by lines, which are in various directions. These rings are intended to point out the position of a large number of cavities (*xue* 穴) which are supposed to exist beneath the surface, and through which it is believed the blood flows in the course of its circulation. It has, however, been imagined that these rings must have originally been intended to represent the valves of veins.

The notions of Chinese physiology are so intimately related with astrology and philosophy that some knowledge on these subjects is necessary for the proper understanding of the Chinese system of medicine.

The two subtle fluids or active principles *yin* and *yang* are represented as acting reciprocally upon each other in opposition, maintaining the harmony of nature by their proper equilibrium but immediately destroying it whenever the balance is lost. In the human body, therefore, any excess or deficiency of either of them leads to serious results and becomes a rich source of disease. These opposing forces only become known to our senses when either of them is in excess. When the equilibrium is maintained we are not cognizant of their existence. They have inappropriately been compared to the terms positive and negative in electricity. There is, however, no evidence to prove that the ancient Chinese were in any way acquainted with the science of electricity. The Chinese represent *yin* and *yang* by a variety of diagrams. The most common one is formed by describing a semicircle on the opposite side of each half of the diameter of a circle so as to divide the circle into two equal proportions each having the form of a comma. One is then painted black and the other red or white. The dark portion represents *yin* or female (negative) which is considered the inferior or grosser of the two and which in its uncombined state constitutes animal spirits residing in the lungs. The white portion of the circle is appropriated to *yang* or male (positive) which is the pure, subtle, invisible matter and which when uncombined constitutes hun or human soul, and is believed by the Chinese to reside in the liver. Other diagrams are more simple, e.g. a black circle surrounded by a red or white zone.

After the *yin* and *yang*, the *qi* or air is next in importance. The word *ke* usually implies air, vapour, breath or the animal spirits and is not be confounded with feng, the external air or atmosphere. It is through the medium of the *ke* that various watery secretions are formed, and it is said to circulate along with the blood, not however mixed with it, but occupying the outer part of the interior of the blood-vessels, the blood itself being in the center of the tube and immediately surrounded by a covering of the *qi*.

With regard to the constituent elements of the blood, the Chinese have very little information of the existence of blood corpuscles, nor of the changes which the venous blood undergoes in its passage through the lungs. The knowledge of such things was reserved for the days of modern chemistry and discovery of the microscope. That the Chinese have been for ages acquainted with the fact that the blood is a circulating fluid there can be no manner of doubt from the very numerous references to the fact scattered throughout their works, although it is certain that they have not very correct knowledge of the anatomy of the heart nor the very important part it plays with regard to this important function.

Whether there is the distinction between the arteries and veins seems unclear. As there are various terms used in describing the blood vessels this subject may be considered a fair subject for controversy. Although a variety of terms are employed, it is uncertain whether such distinctions are intended to convey any idea of difference in the quality of the blood circulating in the blood vessels.

The following account of the blood by Dr Liu Cong is an example of the most correct interpretation of the Chinese physicians' theories concerning the blood. "The blood," he says, "is the essence of the food and its changes are produced in the spleen and it all passes through the heart. The *tsung* receives it from the liver, after which it proceeds to the lungs, and the watery portions flow out at the kidneys. It flows throughout the whole body." Another account of the circulation of the blood translated from a set of anatomical plates is also worthy of perusal, " The commencement of the circulation is from the *zhong jiao* 中焦 (or middle region), to the *tai yin* and *yang ming* blood vessel of the hand; from the *yang ming* of the hand it proceeds to the *yang ming* and *tai yin* of the foot; from the *tai yin* of the foot to the *shao yin* and *tai yang* of the hand past *tai yang* of the hand to the *tai yang* and *shao yin* of the foot to the *shao yang* in the middle of the hand; and from the *shao yang* of the hand to the shao yang and *jue yin* of the foot, from which it returns again to the *tai yin* of the hand. The united length of these blood vessels in 162 cubits. At one expiration and inspiration together make one breath; and during the breath the blood moves six inches.

During one day and night a man breathes altogether 13,500 times, and the blood moves 50 times around the body, or a distance of 8100 cubits, performed during 100 *kih* of the *clepsydra*. The *yang* is incessantly moving at the rate of 25 revolutions, or a distance of 4050 cubits, and the *yin* also makes 25 revolutions, during the same period of time every half hour. Therefore the blood flows once round the body, in a length of 162 cubits." The doctrine is also taught that the blood when it exudes from the body becomes the perspiration.

The total number of principal blood vessels is said to be 4 allowing 3 *yin* and 3 *yang* in each of the four limbs and which after entering the thorax, unite together in pairs, and by the union form the 12 *jing* 經 or "noble organs," in other words the viscera.

The *yin* and *yang* vessels respectively receive the same names both in the upper and lower extremities, the three *yin* being called *tai yin* 太陰 , *shao yin* 少陰 and *jue yin* 厥陰 which are situated on the inner side of the each limb; whilst the three *yang*, viz the *tai yang* 太陽 , *shao yang* 少陽 , and *yang ming* 陽

明 are to be found on the outer or posterior aspect. The three *yin* of the hand are to go from the *zang* 臟 viscera (heart, liver, spleen, lungs and kidneys) to the hands and the three *yang* from the hands to the head; the three *yang* of the feet, go from the head to feet and the three *yin* proceeding from the feet, enter the abdomen. The following are the names of blood-vessels

>*tai yin* or blood-vessel of the lungs
>*shao yin* or blood-vessel of the heart
>*jue yin* or blood-vessel of the pericardium
>*tai yang* or blood-vessel of the small intestines
>*shao yang* or blood-vessel of the *san jiao*
>*yang ming* or blood-vessel of the great intestines
>*tai yin* or blood-vessel of the spleen
>*shao yin* or blood-vessel of the kidney
>*jue yin* or blood-vessel of the liver
>*tai yang* or blood-vessel of the urinary bladder
>*shao yang* or blood-vessel of the gall bladder
>*yang ming* or blood-vessel of the stomach

Such being the Chinese theory concerning the course and rate of the circulation and distribution of the blood vessels taken in connection with the supposition that each internal organ has a *yin* and a *yang* blood vessel assigned to it's own use and connected with corresponding vessels in the surface of the body, renders it no difficult matter to understand how it is believed. It's possible therefore to ascertain the condition of an internal organ by the indications of the pulse. This accounts for the very great attention the Chinese physicians have paid to the study of the pulse and the numerous works they have written on the subject.

Before giving a decided opinion on any serious internal complaint, the Chinese physicians feel the pulse attentively in each wrist and in each wrist the pulse is felt at three different points. The following exhibits the connection of the three points with various viscera, when examined by the physicians with different degrees of pressure. The season of the year is also taken into account. The different seasons being supposed to exert a marked influence over the pulse.

Left Wrist

>*inch* when lightly pressured, indicates the state of the small intestines
>*inch* when heavily pressured, indicates the state of the heart
>*bar* when lightly pressured, indicates the state of the gall-bladder
>*bar* when heavily pressured, indicates the state of the liver
>*cubit* when lightly pressured, indicates the state of the urinary-bladder
>*cubit* when lightly pressured, indicates the state of the kidneys

Right Wrist

inch when lightly pressured, indicates the state of the large intestines
inch when heavily pressured, indicates the state of the lungs
bar when lightly pressured, indicates the state of the gall-stomach
bar when heavily pressured, indicates the state of the spleen
cubit when lightly pressured, indicates the state of the *san jiao*
cubit when lightly pressured, indicates the state of the *ming men*

This also shows the sympathy which is supposed to exist between the several organs, as between the small intestines and heart, between the liver and the gall bladder, between the urinary bladder and kidneys, between the large intestines and the lungs, between the stomach and the spleen, and between the *san jiao* and the *ming mun*. To ascertain the state of the heart or liver the pulse of the left wrist requires minute examination, whereas knowledge of the condition of the lungs or stomach is to be obtained by feeling the pulse of the right wrist. The hand selected for ascertaining the state of the kidneys depends upon whether the right or left kidney is supposed to be diseased.

The Chinese have a great variety of terms to indicate the different kinds of pulse corresponding as near a possible with our terms: weak, slow, sharp, sluggish, slippery, full, long tremulous, short tremulous, overflowing, small, weak, long, short, variable, embarrassed, empty, hurrying, hard, flying, low, deep, slender, soft and bubbling. Every organ is supposed to have its own peculiar pulse, which differs somewhat in each sex and as before stated even the seasons of the year are supposed to exert an influence over the circulation and modify the pulse.

An ancient writer gives seven cautions to a physician about to feel the pulse:-
1st He must be in a calm disposition of mind.
2nd He must be as attentive as possible, laying aside even the smallest disorder or absence of the mind.
3rd With respect to his body, he should be in a state of tranquility, and his expiration ought to be free and regular.
4th He should, after he has laid his finger softly and touched lightly the skin at the proper places, examine that which regards the six seats of vital heating, the small intestines, gall-bladder, large intestines, etc.
5th This done, let him lay on his fingers more hard, moderately pressuring the flesh, to examine how the pulse is which is called the pulse of the stomach.
6th Then let him press so hard as to feel the bone, and let him examine what relates to the seats of radical moisture, the heart, liver, stomach, lung and kidneys.
7th Let him examine the quickness and slowness of the pulse, to see if the number of beats is more or less than it ought to be in the space of one respiration.

It will readily be perceived that the system of examining the pulse is exceedingly complicated, and one which would require long and persistent study to master.

Barrow, in his "Travels in China" relates that being attacked with cholera he visited the Governor of the city and enquired for some opium and rhubarb. The Governor sent him instead one of his physicians "with a serious appearance similar to the serious expressions of physicians in London or Edinburgh. The physician fixed his eyes on the ceiling while he held my hand, beginning at the wrist and proceeding toward the bend of the elbow, pressing sometimes my hand with one finger, and then lightly with another, as if he were running over the keys of a harpsichord. This performance continued for about 10 minutes, when he pronounced my complaint to have arisen from eating something that disagreed with the stomach".

With regard to the information of the ancient Chinese physicians concerning the circulation of the blood it becomes of the greatest interest to ascertain what was the real amount of knowledge they possessed in reference to the anatomy of the heart. Here I would like to be understood that it is worthwhile to enquire how far the Chinese physicians have understood the theory of the circulation as it was understood and thought by the immortal Harvey. Now in the first place the chief guides on which most rely for information are diagrams and written descriptions of the heart.

The heart is described as situated below the windpipe and above the diaphragm and is attached to the 5th vertebra. The shape is pyramidal and circular, and it has the appearance of the unopened bud of the water-lily. There are no orifices below, but has seven orifices above, opening upwards toward the tongue and by four of these apertures tubes pass out to the remaining 4 *zang* viz; lungs, liver, spleen, and kidneys. Within its cavity are several hairs *san mao* 三毛 (musculi pectinate) and externally it is surrounded by red and yellow fat which forms the pericardium. The *Nei jing* says that the heart weights 12 *taels*, and is capable of containing 3 *ko*. It is an organ containing little air and little blood.

This description should be paraphrased so as to show that the heart must have been inspected to be so accurately described. With regard to the expression that the heart contains but little air and little blood no doubt is to be deduced for it is evidently a reference to its empty state. The same author states that "the stomach is an organ containing much air and little blood". The author who thus describes the heart probably had the knowledge of its proper function. The writer observes in another part of his work that "The heart regulates the blood-vessels and beautifies the complexion. The subjoined diagram is taken from the Chinese anatomical plate appended to this journal.

The third diagram is taken from a small amulet or chasm made in the shape of the human heart which was found inside an idol in one of the temples of Canton soon after capture of that city. The subdivisions are indicated on the surface of the organ.

The Chinese character or symbol for the word heart was originally designed to represent the organ. Chinese literature abounds in sentences which would seem to imply that the heart is the foundation of existence. One author makes use of the expression, "the heart is the fountain of life," a phrase which reminds me of the words of Solomon " out of the heart are the issues of life". The phrase for palpitation of the heart is the *tan te*志丕 literally translated means heart ascending, heart descending, so that it includes the idea of the physical action

We would further notice that the word fear *pa*怕 is composed of two characters signifying "heart" and "white" seeming to have some reference to the state of mental depression constituting fear and to its effect on the circulating fluid as indicated by the pale face.

It would therefore appear from an impartial consideration of the subject that before the 14th century of the Christian era there was no nation upon earth that could boast of a better knowledge of the blood and its varied uses in the economy than the Chinese for a careful examination of their medical works gives convincing evidence that they have been from the earliest times acquainted with the fact that the blood was a circulating fluid, that they were aware that the blood starting as it were from a given point , made the circuit of he body returning to the same point, that they even calculated the time it took to perform this circuit and calculated the relative frequency of the pulse as compared with the respirations

After this review of the matter I think we may take it for granted that the Chinese have understood the true uses of the blood in the animal anatomy far better than any ancient Greek or Roman writer and that the knowledge of Hippocrates and Galen was very weak and imperfect as compared with the knowledge of the Chinese authors quoted. In fact until we come to the time of Serveto, Columbo and Arantius, who all seem to have been acquainted with the course of the blood through the lungs although they possessed no accurate understanding of the greater circulation, a discovery which was reserved for the immortal Harvey. We shall find nothing at all either in ancient or modern writers that will bear comparison with the information the Chinese have possessed.

This therefore is no attempt to decry the merits of an illustrious countryman Harvey who seems at once to have mastered every point connected with the subject with the single exception that he was not aware of the true nature of the communication between the arteries and veins. This is for the simple reason that the art of injecting the blood-vessels had not been discovered and the microscope had not become an important instrument of science. Some may have endeavoured to reduce the glory of Harvey but their attempts have only served to establish it. Harvey was the first man in all the world to publish an account describing in unmistakable language the heart as the center of the circulation and was the first to describe the true course of the blood.

Chinese authors have, as I think proved that the blood was in circulation and has described a course in which they supposed it to flow but the path of the blood as described by them is of course very different indeed from that promulgated by Harvey and so amply verified by our present anatomical knowledge. Our description of the course of the blood teaches that the right auricle receives the venous blood from the vena cava and coronary veins and discharges it in to the right ventricle. This propels the blood into the pulmonary artery and thence into the lungs. The blood is here oxidized, and is conveyed back by the pulmonary veins into the auricle, this propels the blood into the left ventricle; and this, by means of the aorta and its numerous branches diffuses it over the whole body, whence it is returned by the veins. This account differs remarkably from the Chinese, which describes the blood as passing from the heart, liver, spleen, lungs and kidneys to the extremities of the hands; from the extremities of hands to the head; from the head to the feet and from the feet to the abdomen.

The bones are, as might be expected, are well described by Chinese authors. Each bone is named and described including the phalanges of the fingers and toes.

The brain is called the "marrow of the head", but appears to hold a very subordinate rank in the opinion of the Chinese authors. The only use of the brain appears to be that it has something to do with the elaboration of the seminal fluid and communication with the kidney by means of the spinal cord. In the translation attached to one of the anatomical maps the interior of the skull it is alluded to as "an exceedingly mysterious region and directly communicating with the extremity of the 'spinal column'. The spinal cord is described as an elongation from the brain and branches (nerves) are said by some authors to proceed from each side of it. One of the abdominal viscera is supposed to be the seat of thought, the ideas corresponding to the ancient expression "bowels of compassion." The muscular part of the body is described by the general term *rou* 肉 (flesh). There is no description that muscles are capable of contraction and relaxation.

The lymphatic vessels are not described in Chinese literature; however Chinese medical books abound in lengthy descriptions of all the great internal organs of the body. For example the *Nei jing* says that the lungs have a white

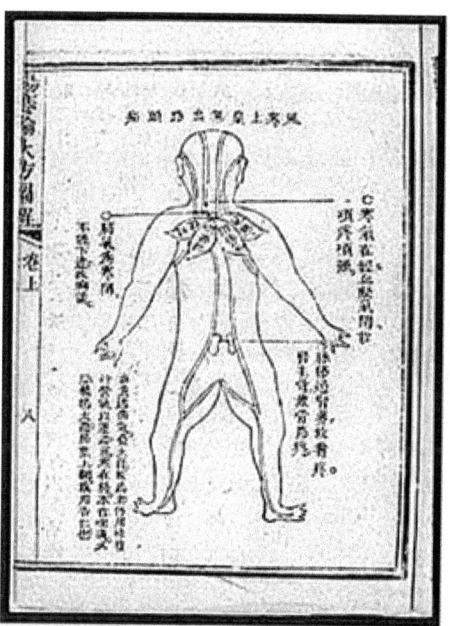

39. *Effects of Ma huang to enhance the flow of blood and qi*, Ming dynasty, Wellcome Library, London

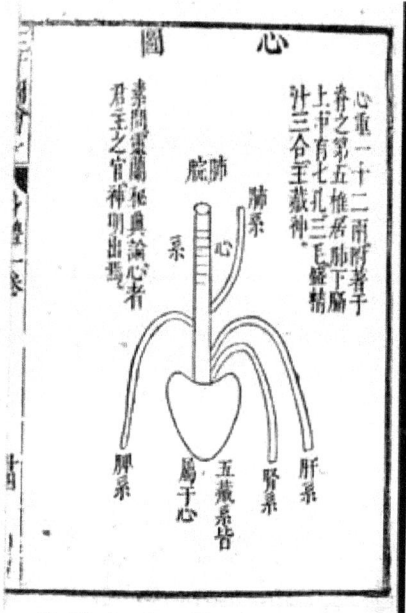

40. *Woodcut from Shenti sancai tuhui* by Wang Siyi, Ming dynasty, Wellcome Library, London

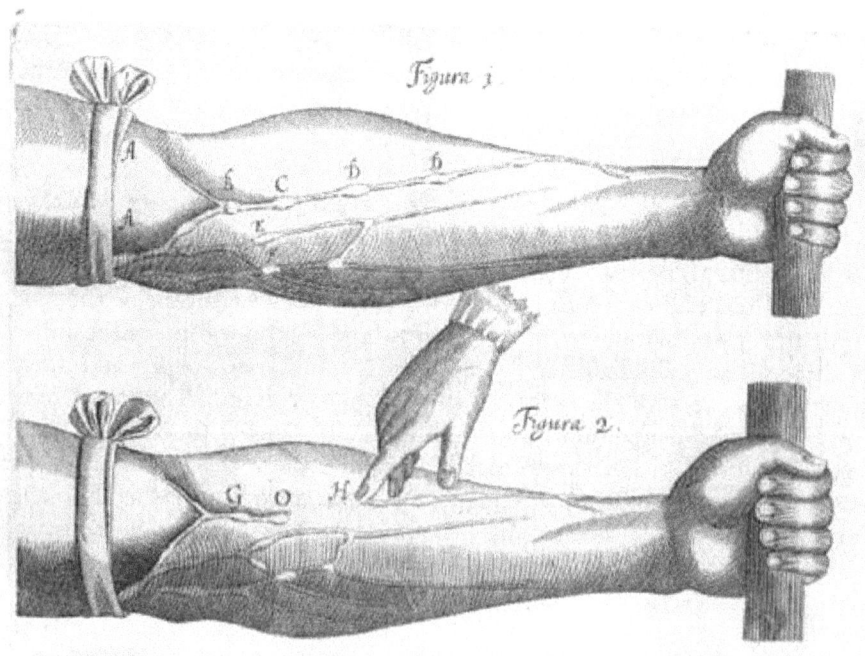

41. *Illustration from William Harvey's Exercitatio Anatomica de Motu Cordis et Sanguinins in Animalibus, 1628*

and glistening aspect and are hollow within the honey comb with six lobes or leaves and two ears. Dr Chong Kai Bin says that "the lungs have a white a glistening aspect and are hollow within like honey-comb but have no opening below, and states that during inspiration they are full of air but during expiration they are empty and are mans airbag containing much air and little blood." In reading this description of the lungs we cannot help believing that Chinese knowledge of the great respiratory organ is very close to the truth. In Chinese texts "the truth is often mystified by remarks as the following, it is stated to lungs are the ministers from whom laws and government arise."

The Chinese divide the internal organs into two classes viz. *zang* and *fu* which together make up the 12 *jing* or noble organs. The *zang* are the solid organs viz. the lungs, heart, liver, spleen, kidneys and the *xin bao* (pericardium). The *fu* are the hollow organs viz. the large intestines, small intestines, stomach, gall-bladder, urinary bladder and *san jiao*, an imaginary organ. The solid organs are represented to be under the dominion of *yin* or radical moisture and the hollow organs under the dominion of *yang* or vital heat. As might be expected no allusion is made in Chinese books to the chemico-vital processes of secretion. They believe that the secretions are produced by filtration or by the condensation of some vapour. This idea of the process of digestion is that the food, after mastication, enters the stomach along with the fluids and having been subjected to the triturated action of the spleen and the application of the animal heat, the spirit and essence again pass through the cardiac orifice which they term *fu men*, bubbling door, and ascend to the spleen and lungs thence to be diffused through the various blood vessels of the body. The more solid matters and the water pass downward until they arrive at the ilio-caecal valve, which they term the *lan men* or "obstructed door". The following extract, from a work entitled *Chang sheng* or 'The art of procuring health and long life' is a near approach to modern medical science and seems worthy of insertion in this place. "It is in the stomach that the concoction and digestion of the food are made; it is the first cause of the blood, of the vital spirits, of the juices, and the humours, which are dispersed into the different part of the body to keep them in their natural vigour."

Having referred to the heart the lungs and the stomach and given an accurate account of the Chinese theories concerning the anatomy and physiology of these organs it only remains to make a few remarks concerning some of the other organs. The best Chinese anatomists always give the weight and dimensions if the organ is a hollow organ such as the bladder, stomach or gall-bladder and a statement is made of the quantity of fluid it is capable of containing. When this fact is taken into consideration, and we reflect upon the appropriate character of some of the names employed in describing particular parts, such as *lan men* or obstructed door-way to the ilio-caecal value and *you men*, or hidden door, to the pylorus and when we come to read of the kidneys being described as resembling kidney beans we conclude that the Chinese had a thorough knowledge of anatomy in an early period of history. Indeed I believe there is evidence enough to prove that post mortem examinations were carried on in the Han dynasty a period corresponding to the 3rd century of the Christian era.

The knowledge of the liver and spleen are limited regarding their true physiology. Modern medical science, however, has little to boast as only within a very recent period is there any accurate understanding of the physiology of the liver and even at the present day the function of the spleen is a much disputed subject.

The liver is represented as situated below the diaphragm and its upper surface is attached to the lower edge of the ninth vertebra. It communicates above with the heart and lungs but has no opening below. It contains much blood and little air. The *Nei jing* says that the liver weighs two catties and 4 taels: on the left side it has 3 lobes and right side 4; altogether 7 lobes. The hun, or soul, resides in it.

The spleen has the form of a sickle, and is connected with the same membrane as the stomach, to the left extremity of which it is attached above, but below to the 11th vertebra. It contains much air and little blood. In the *Nei jing* we are informed that the spleen weighs 2 *catties* and 3 *taels*, that it is 5 inches in length, and 3 inches wide, and has about half a catty of fat scattered over it in masses.

Kidneys. They are attached to the lower part of the 14th vertebra; they are two in number, and together weigh 1*catty* and 2 *taels*. They contain little blood and much air. Dr Chong Kai Bin says that they have the form of kidney beans placed side by side corresponding with each other and that they are attached to each side of the spine, at a distance of about an inch and a half from its center. Externally they are completely covered with yellow fat, and two tubes pass out each of them, the upper tube going to the heart and to the lower to the great bone of the spine which it joins at a point a little more than half a hand breath from its commencement. In the center of each kidney there are two sinuses or cavities, out of which the vessel proceeds to the spine and through it to the brain. According to Chinese physiology, they are responsible for producing power and skill; ingenuity proceeds from them, and the subtle or generative fluid is eliminated by them; above to the brain and below to the sacral extremity they are the rulers. The urine is not supposed to be produced by them. The right kidney is represented as under the domination of *yang* and the left are under *yin*.

The gall-bladder in placed below the liver and projects upward into it. It has the responsibility of judgment; determination and decision proceed from it and when people are angry it rises up or expands. It is described in the *Nei jing* as being situated in the middle of the small lobe of the Liver. It weighs 3 *taels*, 3 *zhu*, and is 3 inches in length, when full, 3 *he* of gall. It has much blood and little air.

The small intestines, *xiao chang* 小腸, are attached posteriorly to the spine and in front to a point a little above the umbilicus. They are repeatedly folded toward the left side, having in all 16 contortions; they are 32 feet in length and two and one half inches in circumference, rather more than 8/10 of an inch in diameter, and capable of containing 2 *tow*, 4 *sheng* of rice, with rather more than 6 *sheng*, three and one half *he* of water. The upper opening of the small intestines is the lower opening of the stomach, and is situated about 2 inches above the umbilicus, and near the spine: At about an inch below this they become attached externally to the umbilicus near the spine; at about one more inch below this they become attached externally to the umbilicus near the *shui fun* sinus; where the lower opening is situated, opening into the upper orifice of the large intestines by the *lan men* 闌門 or "obstructed doorway"(the ilio-caecal value). They contain much blood and little air and weigh 2 *catties* 14 *taels*.

The large intestines *da chang* 大腸 have 16 folds on the left side of the umbilicus, and this contorted portion is 21 feet in length and 4 inches in circumference, or rather less than an inch and a half in diameter, and is capable of containing 1 *tow* of rice or seven and one half *sheng* of water. At the termination of this part, they are attached to the spine, and here become 8 inches in circumference, rather more than of eight and one half inches in dimensions, which diameter is retained throughout a length of 2 feet 8 inches, so that this portion is large enough to hold 9 *sheng* and three and one eighth *ko* of rice. According to the *Nei jing*, the large intestines contain much air and little blood, they weigh 2 *catties* and 12 *taels*, and the weight of the anus alone equals 12 *taels*. Dr Chong Kai Bin observes that the wide part is great in proportion, as there are more contortions in the remainder; he also says, that the "straight gut", *zhi chang* 直腸 is the last portion of the large intestine and terminates below at the anus. The urinary bladder, *pang guang* 膀胱, is situated at the 19th vertebra below the kidneys and in front of the large intestines. It has no opening above, but below it has an orifice two and one half inches in circumference. It contains much blood and little air. In the *Nei jing* its weight is said to be 9 *rules* and 2 *zhu*, with a diameter of 9 inches, and capable of holding when full 9 *sheng* and 9 *ko* of water.

Independently of the various organs here described two other organs are spoken of in the Chinese anatomical works. These organs are called the *san jiao* 三焦 and *ming men* 命門. English physicians and other foreigners have looked upon these as purely imaginary organs which do not exist in nature. They have not, however, been so described by Dr Harland, one of the very few who has examined the subject and published a small treatise on Chinese anatomy.

For my own part, I have no doubt that Dr Harland's view of the question is the correct one. I think the *san jiao* is simply the term employed for several divisions of the trunk denominated thorax, abdomen and pelvis. The following is a translation of a paragraph in The Golden Mirror.

"The upper *jiao* terminates at the superior orifice of the stomach and governs the ingestion of food but not the excretion. The middle one commences at the upper curvature of the stomach; it regulates the fermentation and digestion of the food, and propels the milk and watery secretions in the form of vapour, transforming them into the lighter and more subtle fluids which flow upward to the lungs, there to be converted into blood, by which the animal frame is supported. The lower one commences below the ilio-caecal valve, it governs the excretion but not the ingestion".

In The Golden Mirror we also find the following: "The classics say that the upper *jiao* is like vapour, the middle one like a sponge and the lower one like a flowing stream. They are the regulators of the flowing stream or watery secretions, and are organs which contain little blood and much air." The above description hinted to the thorax, abdomen, and pelvis and to the functions performed in each region. In this way the upper region containing the lungs may be compared to a vapour; the middle region continuing the principal solid organs besides the greater proportion of the small intestines, whence the lacteals suck up or absorb the nutritious portions of the food, so far resemble a sponge; and the lower region whence the urinary and seminal secretions and the above evacuations escape from the body, may indeed be compared to a flowing stream.

The *ming men* 命門 or gate of life is also an organ which has been considered purely imaginary, but from a careful review of what has been written on the subject I have little hesitation in asserting that the term has reference to the process of generation. It appears to be a term applied the right kidney of the male and the uterus of the female. The Chinese ascribe to the kidney the responsibility of storing up the subtle fluid. The function of the uterus is of course understood. A Chinese author says "when the mind is moved the *ming men* (near the kidneys) is moved and the upper, middle and lower divisions of the human body are affected and then seminal evacuations proceed from there."

The physicians of China have no particular privileges and are not required to pass any examinations for anyone who has read a few medical books and has confidence in himself may practice medicine. Physicians are often unsuccessful literary candidates or poor scholars. The result is that the medical profession is not held in very high regard, for the degree of reputation and the fame of a Chinese doctor is entirely dependent on his own energy and skill. There are no medical schools in the country, but at Peking there has been established a great medical college, and persons most thoroughly acquainted with medicine and possessing an unblemished character are after examination selected to enter the college and to fill its office and to practice there.

The great medical college has one principal director, and also one of a secondary, and another of a subordinate rank who superintend and examine the treatment of all the nine classifications of disease and who is entrusted with the business of the institution. The result of such a state of things is that a great majority of the Chinese physicians have very little idea of the true anatomical structure of the human body, having no clear understanding of the arrangement or relative position or functions of the different organs of the body. This will continue so long as the present fear of dissecting dead bodies continues.

Physicians are however not allowed to escape unpunished if their patients die from gross ignorance. The penal code in referring to injuring or killing persons by unskillful practitioners status "whenever an unskillful practitioner, in the administering medicines or using puncturing needle, proceeds contrary to established medical practice and thereby causes the death of a patient, the magistrate shall call in other practitioners to examine the medicine or the wound and if it appears that the injury done was unintentional, the practitioner shall then be treated according to the statute for accidental homicide and shall not be allowed any longer to practice medicine. But if he ignores established practice and deceives in his attempts to cure the illness, in order to obtain property, then according to its amount he shall be treated as a thief. If death shall be caused from his malpractice, then for having used medicine with intent to kill, he shall be beheaded."

In the 6th volume of the work *Ben cao gang mu* it is stated that diseases may prove fatal in the five following ways.

1st by its not being examined
2nd by its not being acknowledged
3rd by its being neglected
4th by the bad choice of a physician
5th by his not understanding the disease

Considering the great multitude of physicians, and the numerous treatments they possess, it is clear that centuries of experience have taught them many useful and effective methods of healing disease. The high estimation in which physicians are often held and the great quantity of medicine consumed, are evidence that this is true. The proverb says, "A good physician is a public benefactor," and an eminent physician is called the "arm of his country". The trade in medicines is one of the most important and profitable branches of business. In the large cities, streets are taken up with drug stores neatly arranged with draws and jars labeled in the most approved manner. A very noticeable point of difference from our own drug-shops is the absence of glass bottles. Porcelain jars and demijohns are used instead.

The study of medicinal agents used by the Chinese and their application of them to the cure of disease open very wide fields of investigation to those who have the opportunity to study them. The Materia Medica of the Chinese contains a greater variety of medicines than any other nation. Everything in the vegetable, animal or mineral kingdom that they imagine can be of any use has been adopted as a medicine. The writer has been in many pharmacies in which the number of articles of Materia Medica has amounted to upward of 1000. In one shop at Shanghai the number told him by the pharmacist was 1360 and inspection of the shop proved that the number was accurate or nearly so. The greater portion of the drugs is derived from the vegetable kingdom, and there is scarcely a leaf stem or root that has not enjoyed more or less fame as remedy for disease. In some of the Chinese medical books it is taught that the top of a plant is the most appropriate remedy for head affections, the stem for disease of the middle portion of the human body, and the root for the lower extremities.

Many of the articles they use are officinal with us, but the Chinese pharmacopeia stands alone in recognizing the following, which are given as specimens of what are peculiar to themselves namely paws of the bear and monkey, tiger bones, dried crabs and lizards, liver, heart, and marrow of the horse and mule, various parts of the pig and dog, placenta of several animals, dried silk-worms, bears gall, elephants skin etc. The Chinese have long been familiar with the powers of arsenic as an antiperiodic, and they treat syphilis with a preparation made by subliming together mercury and arsenic.

The best work in Materia Medica is the Materia Medica of Li Shi Zhen, comprised in 40 octavo volumes, divided into 52 chapters. The 1st and 2nd chapters consist of introductory matter, filling 7 volumes. The 3rd and 4th contain lists of medicines for the cure of all diseases, which fill 3 volumes and a 1/2. The 5th chapter discusses waters; the 6th of fires; the 7th of earths, in chapters 5,9,10, and 11 metals and rocks are described. Chapters 12 to 37 inclusive are devoted to the vegetable kingdom. The 38th discusses garments and domestic utensils. The remaining chapters from 39 to 52 discuss the various tribes in the animal kingdom. The preceding chapter fills 39 volumes; the 40th is filled with dissertations and notices respecting the pulse. The properties of the articles discussed are considered in a very methodical manner, so that the student can immediately turn to a plant or mineral and ascertain its virtues in a moment's inspection. Thus the properties of the various parts of a horse are treated of fewer than 24 heads; in which the qualities and efficacy of the viscera, hair, and hoof are described. Of the 365 kinds of medicine forming the system of the celebrated *Ben cao gang mu* 71 are to be used alone, 12 are to be used with each other, 90 are employed as agents, 78 stand in awe of each other, 60 are repulsive or hate each other, 18 are opposites, and 36 neutralise each other.

The 365 medicines of this notable arrangement are divided into three classes. Of the 1st class of medicines there are 120 kinds which are considered above all others, and the chief supporters of human life, thereby resembling heaven. They are not poisonous and however freely and constantly used they are harmless. If you want to stimulate the body and improve health, and retard the approach of age, use this first class of medicines.

Of the 2nd class are 120 kinds which are ministering servants, and the chief supporters of human nature, thereby resembling man. Some are poisonous and some not, and they ought to be used with caution if you wish to stop the progress of disease and restore those who are thin and emaciated, use the second class of medicines.

Of the 3rd class there are 125 kinds which are assistants and agents, curing diseases, thereby resembling earth. They are poisonous and ought not to be used often. If you wish to remove cold or heat, correct bad breath, or break up congestion, or cure disease use the medicines composed in this class. These three kinds being united make 365, corresponding in number to the 365 degrees into which the Zodiac is divided, one degree answering to one day and so completing a year.

The articles mineral, animal and vegetable composed in the Materia Medica of Li Shi Zhen are described in the following order. Taking, for example, *da huang* 大黃 or rhubarb, which is the 1st article in the 4th family of the 1st order of vegetable productions, in vol. 44 chap. 17, it is described under 8 distinct headings. The whole description occupying seven leaves, or 14 octavo pages, under the 1st heading, *shi min*, the Chinese scientific name and the synonyms by which it is known are explained. Under the 2nd *ji jie*, there is a collection of explanations, comprising the history and botanical description of the plant. Under the 3rd *zheng wu*, are corrections of errors, and instructions for preventing the improper use of the article as a medicine. Under the 4th *xiu zhi* the mode of preparing it for use is described. Under 5th, *qi wei*, its taste, smell etc are noticed. Under the 6th *zhu zi*, its masterly operations, namely its specific virtues as a medicine are enumerated. Under the 7th *fa ming*, is given a clear exposition of its uses, in other words, its rationale. Under the 8th and last heading *fu fang*, there is a list of recipes with the names of the maladies for which it is a remedy. There is some variety in the mode of describing different articles. Thus the roots, branches, flowers, secretions and fruit of a tree, if each is to be used separately as a medicine will have the same description. So in describing animal, the various organs and secretions are treated under separate headings enabling the student to immediately refer to any part he wishes to examine. Mostly however, the above order is preserved throughout the book.

The reader, however, will have a better idea of the Chinese treatments by the following translation of the description of *liu qiu zi*. Tradition relates that the Imperial Officer Guo, in treating the complaints of children, made use of this medicine for most patients, hence succeeding physicians gave it the name *shi jun zi*. It grows in Hangchow and Canton, and resembles the *zhi zi* 梔子 in form. It has deep angular furrows, is conical at both ends and Li Shi Zhen says it is like the *ke li le* 訶梨勒, but lighter."

"The Officers Berry" Li Shi Zhen says "I find in the *Ji botany of the South*, it is called *liu qiu zi*, and it said to be employed for the complaints of infants". Hence it has been used from the time of the jin and wei dynasties, only under a different name.

Su Sung says it is now found everywhere in the south of the *mei ling* hills growing on the hill and waste lands, and by the waters edge. The stalk grows like cane, about a finger thickness; the leaf resembles two fingers and is two inches long. In the 3rd month it produces blossoms of a pale red colour which afterward change to dark red and have five petals. In the seventh and eighth month the fruit is formed about the size of the thumb, an inch or more long very similar to the *zhi zi* with five angles. The shell is of a bluish black colour and there is a white seed inside. It is plucked in the seventh month.

Li Shi Zhen says it was originally brought from Sichuan. Now it is cultivated at Shao wu in Fu jian, and Mei zhou in Sichuan, if it is grows without care the tendrils twining round trees like *mu* 苜 plant. The leaves are bright green like those of the *wu jia* 五加. It blossoms in the 5th month, one stalk bearing from ten to twenty flowers of a red colour, light and graceful like the *hai tang* 海棠. The fruit is more than an inch in length, formed in a 5 angular divisions. The fruit is half yellow, but when old it becomes purplish black. There are seeds inside which look like plum seeds. After a time it becomes bright and black and it is unfit for use. Its flavour is sweet and warm without any poisonous properties.

It is employed for dyspepsia in children, also when the urine of children is white and thick and also for killing worms and for the cure of dysentery. It is employed to strengthen the stomach and dispel lassitude: It is used in the treatment of all kinds of children's complaints and also for cutaneous eruptions

Li Shi Zhen writes that the medicines used for killing worms are in general bitter and pungent but *shi jun zi* and the seed of the *Taxus nucifera* are exceptions, these being sweet to the taste and used for the same purpose. Adults or children who are troubled with worm complaints have merely to eat a few of the *shi jun zi* seeds early in the morning upon an empty stomach, during the first decade of each month, or boil down the shells and drink the liquor, then the worms will all be killed, and ejected on the following day. Some say it is a good plan to eat seven raw and seven roasted. If hot tea is taken immediately after, the counter acting effect produces diarrhoea. This remedy is sweet to the taste, mild in it is nature, and is good for killing worms and beneficial to the stomach. It concentrates the internal heat and stops diarrhoea and is an important medicine in all infantile diseases.

Many doctors say that "if the worms are all killed, food will not digest". This is not correct, Is it good or bad to have insects in a tree, to have ants in a house or to have robbers in a country? He that would attain to a state of immortality must first expel the three cadaverous elements". Therefore please understand the principle.

Remedy for stoppage in the stomach of children: take equal quantities of *shi jun zi* and bitter aloes which reduce to powder and take one tenth of an ounce at a time, in rice water.

Excrescence on the inside of children; when the abdomen gets large, the body becomes thin, the face yellow and the stomach gradually gets blocked, take 3/10 of an ounce of the *shi jun zi* seed, ½ an ounce of the seed of the *mu bie* 木鱉 fruit; reduce them to powder, and make them up with water into a bolus about the size of the dimocarpus fruit. Break a hole in the end of a hen's egg and insert the bolus; then steam it in a pot of rice, till the egg is cooked, and eat it on a hungry stomach. For tape-worm in children when saliva runs out of the mouth, reduce the seed of *shi jun zi* to powder, mix it with rice water and take 1/10 of an ounce at about 3 or 4 o'clock in the morning.

Swelling of children. When the head, face and testicle membrane become flabby use one ounce of *shi jun zi* without the shell and 1/2 an ounce of honey and when sufficiently roasted, reduce to power and after meals take 1/10 ounce in rice water.

Scabby head and eruption on face, take a small quantity of fragrant oil, in which soak the seeds of the *shi jun zi* (*Quisqualis indica*). Take three to five of these at bed time, chew them well and swallow them with the fragrant oil. The complaint will be cured in the course of time.

Pain in the tooth, boil down the *shi jun zi* fruit, and frequently rinse the mouth with liquor.

It is a curious fact that the practice of surgery is almost entirely unknown to the Chinese. It seems difficult to explain how this could be in a nation where physicians have always been so numerous and so honorable and when the experience of centuries has been handed down from generation to generation in learned treatises. Whatever may be the reason it certainly is a fact that in all the empire of China, there are no Chinese surgeons (except a few educated by foreigners) capable of performing extensive operations requiring the use of the knife. They possess no surgical instruments. The treatment of fractures and dislocations is very little understood. Most disease and injuries requiring surgical interference are beyond the reach of many doctors. Foreign physicians have cured cataract, removed tumors, performed lithotomy and amputated limbs.

The *Yi zhong jin jian* speaks of eight surgical operations as follows.

The 1st is called feeling: feeling is the very careful use of both hands, in rubbing them on the parts which are injured, in order to ascertain whether bones are broken, or are splintered into small pieces, whether they are in and out of place or whether they have become too weak or too hard. Whether the tendons are too stiff or too loose, whether they have been broken or distorted, enlarged, reversed or affected with cold or heat. Also whether the injuries are deep or superficial, minor or serous, likewise whether the injury is recent or long standing.

The 2nd is the reduction of fractures
The 3rd is the reduction of dislocations
The 4th is the elevation of depressed bones
The 5th is the depression of the elevations
The 6th is trituration which may be defined a gradual moving and rubbing of the hands
The 7th is protrusion. This may be defined a pushing outward with the hands, so as to cause any part out place to be restored.
The 8th is grasping or tension. This may be defined as the taking hold with one hand or both hands of the injured parts and then with due regard to the condition of the wound gradually reduce them to their former situation. The surgical instruments appear limited. Ten surgical aids, mentioned and described in the Golden Mirror, seem to constitute the whole of their surgical apparatus. These ten aids are bandages, beaters, blood supporters, climbing cords, piled bricks, brick splints, suspensory bandages, pine compresses, and knee caps with nine needles.

Two of the great remedies of the Chinese and also the Japanese surgeons are acupuncture and burning with the moxa. The practice of acupuncture has been resorted to from early times and many treatises have been written on the subject. The Golden Mirror speaks of nine descriptions of needles namely, the arrow-headed, blunt, puncturing, open, pointed, ensiform, round, capillary, long and great many of these needles are nearly as fine as hair. They are generally made of silver but sometimes of gold and occasionally of steel. The bony parts, nerves and blood vessels are carefully avoided, and while they are passed through the skin and muscle they are twisted about in a peculiar manner.

The following is a translation of an article on acupuncture given to me by a Japanese physician of Yedo: "The needle ought to be made thin, bright and sharp pointed on the top provided with a little handle to be twined round with some strength between the thumb and fore-finger, in order to prick through the skin and flesh. The needles are of various lengths depending on the different parts of the human body to which they are to apply. More than one needle should never be used on one diseased spot. If the disease is near the lungs keep the needle slanting, and do not insert it too deep. In other parts of the body like the feet and hands, there is no danger in pricking deep even although the point of the needle might appear on the opposite side. To make the pricking easy the needle is sharpened in purposed quicksilver the little particles of which will fill the pores of the metal. Each needle is kept in a small copper pipe to prevent it being bent."

It should be known that the needle is used to cure spasmodic and painful diseases. By the prick of the needle the virilibility is excited and after that the part operated on will be stunned and the pain eased. The use of needles proves fruitful in all febrile disorders.

Another favorite remedy is burning with moxa. The substance used is the woolly part of the young leaves of the *Artemisia*. It is procured by rubbing and beating the leaves till the green part separates and nothing remains but the wool which is sorted into two kinds. When applied, it is made up into little cones, which being placed on the part selected for the operation are set fire to from the top. They burn very slowly leaving a scar or blister on the skin, which, some time after, breaks and discharges.

In the practice of midwifery among the Chinese, the functions are always performed by women, and usually by those who from experience and success in the art have acquired celebrity. The practice of Chinese midwives is very different from Europe. When labour comes on, the midwife is sent for and the patient sits on a little stool which is placed inside a low tub. They think it astonishing that any woman can be so unclean as to remain in bed. An assistant supports the patient's back and she is always delivered sitting up. It is only in very severe cases that the patient is allowed to lie down. Sometimes they walk about to ease the pain. Medicines are given to expedite delivery and nearly every woman takes a "hastening pill" at the commencement of labour. The umbilical cord is cut with scissors or a piece of broken porcelain, and is then bound up in rice flour. The placenta is allowed to come away of itself. As soon as the child is born it is wiped with soft paper and wrapped up in old clothes of any kind but it is not washed until the third morning. It is fed with soft boiled rice immediately after birth and continues to have two meals of this per day.

There is a popular superstition in some parts of China that when a woman dies in childbirth she descends into a pool of blood. When death occurs under such circumstances it is usual to make an image of the woman and child and to place them under a large bell, which is tolled for three or four days in order to raise her from the place of misery to which she has gone to a place of greater happiness.

The Chinese have as might be expected many superstitious notions concerning disease and death. A divinity named Po Niang 婆娘 the old lady who is the patroness of sick children is often worshipped. No image is used only a vase with incense sticks placed before the worshipper. A superstitious rite is also performed called *Zhuan yun* 轉運 "to give a turn to destiny", by priests of the Tam sect for persons dangerously ill.

Another ceremony is called *Yao shai ji* 搖篩箕 "to shake the sieve". The sieve is filled with fruit and rice is placed at the door of the house before the idol at the gate in cases where children are dangerously ill. The contents of the sieve are afterward thrown into the street.

The *Rang xing li dou* 穰星禮斗 is the name of a superstitious service to the stars performed in the sick man's room by the priest of the Tam sect, a ceremony called the *Nam wei* or "The recall" is one frequently performed in cases of illness: when any person, father, mother, sister, brother, child, or other relative, is attacked by sickness. The Chinese believe that the patient's soul has been frightened away and that if they do not succeed in bringing it back, the patient must inevitably die and the soul enter into another body. This ceremony is often performed at great expense because the sick engage (besides a number of old women) a band of musicians who play all night whilst a conjuror, heading the old women, takes a long stroll to a river or other solitary place and blows on a buffalo's horn which is relieved by the doleful cries of the old women.

The latter are generally provided with a basket of rice and other offerings besides a pair of trousers belonging to the sick and a bundle of straw over which the trousers are wound whilst the other women recall the soul. When one burns the incense another woman scatters the rice about calling out the same time: "spirits from the east, spirits from the south, spirits from the west, and from north, come quickly and partake of my rice' soul. I call you hastily to return home there is wine, meat, gold, silver, rice, and grain for redeeming. Recall your three souls and seven animal spirits and to bring them home again. Ah! It's his soul, do return home now, whether you have been frightened at the beginning or end of a road, or in a cross road, whether in the morning or at evening whether by a spider, a chicken, a serpent, a rat, worms, ants, birds, animals, a hog, a cow, a hen, a dog, by acquaintances or strangers, by parents, sister, brother, uncles or aunts whether by the living or dead by a squirrel or a frog if any of them have caused your spirits to depart, do now return at our entreaties! Oh! Return, return! Venerable Pak Hei, and venerable mother of the ninth heaven, bring his soul back to his home, that he may be near his father and mother and follow his ancestors that he may grow up, long enjoy happiness, and be blessed with longevity! Oh! May your soul return, return home. May hereafter no disease trouble you! May nothing, either good or bad, prevent you from eating, drinking, and sound sleep during the night, and may you awake refreshed and cheerful in the morning! Oh! Your soul, do return, return, to the person that he need not fear, but have courage as great as heaven. Oh! Bring back his spirits to his own person, that he may look as before, may have strength, sleep soundly, awake cheerfully, and that it may be his fortune to enjoy bodily health and happiness."

After this they roll the trousers together and return home, believing that the rice and the promises have induced the soul to return to the sick person. If the person gets well; then their means have been effective, for it was by them that the person got well. If the patient dies then the soul is born again in another body and this latter event is specially believed by them when a child happens to be born in the neighbourhood, or in a neighbouring village, at the same time of the patient is deceased.

Chapter 16   Translation Of The Chinese Anatomical Maps

Zang Fu Ming Tang Tu
Explanatory Map Of The Contents Of The Human Body

An ancient classical work says:" *Xin* the heart is chief among the five rulers of the body, it is that from which the intellectual faculty proceeds. The *fei* or lungs are assistant-rulers and govern affairs; or government comes from the lungs. The liver (*gan*) is the ruler or general, and contrivance comes from it for the liver is contriver general. The *dan* or gall is central ruler of propriety and correctness and decisions proceed from it. The *shan zhong* or pericardium is ruler of servants, and joy proceeds from it. The *pi* or spleen is united with the *wei* or stomach, is the storekeeper and the five tasks or flavours proceed there from. The *da chang* or great intestines are the general circulators and digestion proceeds there from. The *xiao chang* or small intestines are general receivers and transformation proceeds there from. The *shen* or kidneys are rulers over hardness or hard substance and cunning proceeds there from.

The *shan jiao*, or upper central and lower cavities are current regulators and water courses proceed from them. The *pang guang* or bladder is departmental and parochial ruler, and is a store house for watery secretions and other fluids after undergoing the necessary transformations so the fluids proceed from it.

These 12 divisions must always be clearly discriminated and never confusedly blended.

2 The heart *xin* is the marrow sea. All the marrows belong to the brain. The *shen* or kidneys rule all this, from the brain in the top even to the coccyx.

3 The *shan zhong* or pericardium is the seat of breath; situated just between the breasts is the fountain of breath of life which can brood over the feminine and masculine principles and cause them to become the fountain of creation and transformation; It can't sustain any violence (or all violent contact must be avoided).

4th The *ge mo*, or diaphragm, is a membrane below the heart and lungs, which, with the spinal joints and the ribs and belly forms a tent-like covering which keeps down effluvia and prevents all foul air from coming up.

5th Liquids go into the *pang guang* or bladder, solids and dregs run into the great intestines.

6th Mans 5 *zang* (heart, liver, spleen, lungs and kidneys) and 6 *fu* (stomach, gall, pericardium, great intestines, small intestines and bladder), 9 apertures, veins, muscles, are relatively connected, each being united to the other, without interruption: there they are coarsely delineated in general manner in order to be easily investigated.

7th At the 7th joint from the base of the backbone is the little heart or *xiao xin*, which is connected with the seat of life. At the 14th joint is the duct from the kidneys (into the heart). The hearts duct is at the 6th joint reckoning from the top.

8th The urethra is the tube through which the urine flows.

9th The seminal duct.

10th When the mind is moved then the life door, near the kidneys, is moved and the upper central and lower divisions of the human body are affected thereby and seminal evacuations proceed there from.

11th The brain sea is an exceedingly mysterious region, and directly communicates with the extremity of the spinal column.

CE REN MING TANG TU – SIDE VIEW MAP OF THE HUMAN BODY

The *Nei jing* or Physicians classic says " the source of the lungs is in the *tai yuan* or great water; the source of the heart is in the *da ling* or great hill, the source of the liver is in the *tai chong*; the source of the *pi* or spleen is in the *tai bai* or great white; the source of the kidneys is in the *tai xi* or great stream; the hearts source is in the *dui gu* or western bone, which is the spirits door; the galls source is in the *qiu xu*, or the mound; the stomach source is in the *chong yang* or working toward the masculine principles; the source of the three cavities is in the *yang chi* or masculine pool; the source of the bladder is in the *jing gu* or capital bone; the great intestines source is in the *he gu*, or united valley (the place where the thumb and forefinger meet); the small intestine source is the *wan gu*, or hand bone, one must not be ignorant of the 12 things enumerated above."

ZHENG REN MING TANG TU - FRONT VIEW MAP OF THE HUMAN BODY

In every mans two hands and two feet there are three masculine (*yang*) and three feminine (*yin*) pulses, and these united make twelve circulating courses. The three feminine pulses of the hand travel from the viscera to the hand; the three masculine pulses of the hand travel from the hand to the head. The three masculine pulses of the foot travel downward from the head to the feet. The three feminine pulses of the feet travel from the feet into the abdomen.

The circulation of the pulse in its onward course never ceases, therefore the courses of the pulse carry the blood and breath through the masculine and feminine principles in order to nourish and invigorate the body. In its beginning of process from the central region of the body to the great feminine principle of the hand or lungs, and to the clear masculine principle of the hand or large intestines; from the large intestines it proceeds to the clear masculine principle of the foot, or stomach and the great feminine principle of the foot or spleen, from the spleen to the hand's little feminine principle or heart and from the hand's great masculine principle or small intestines: from the small intestine to the foot's great masculine principle or bladder, and the foot's little feminine principle or kidneys; from the kidneys to the *sue sines* or *jing luo*, that is the pericardium and the hand's little masculine principle, that is the *san jiao*, or upper central and lower cavities; from the three cavities to the foot's little masculine principle or gall, and the foot's *jue yin* or liver; from the liver it returns to the *sou tai yin* or hand's great feminine principle , that is the lungs.

From the dawn to the evening and from evening to morning this circulation proceeds uninterruptedly, like the constant dripping of the hydrochronometer; or the interminable circulation of the heavens in one unvarying round.

Fu Ren Ming Tang Tu - Back View Map of The Human Body

In every man the pulse travels along the 12 courses and through the eight circuits. According to the *Nei jing* or Physicians classic the length of its course is 162 Chinese feet. When a man makes an expiration of the breath the pulse or circulation travels three inches and when he takes an inspiration it travels three inches. Thus a breath travel 6 inches. In a day and a night a man draws 13500 breaths, and thus his pulse travels 50 degrees. Through his body the united travel is 8100 feet. By the dropping of the hydrochronomenter in a day and $4/96^{th}$, in the inside and outside of the veins the masculine principle travels 25 degrees and the feminine also travels 25 degrees: in two ninety-sixth of a day it thus travels the round of the body.

In the *shou yang ming*, or large intestines, the pulse begins in the *shang yang xue* index finger and ends in the *ying xiang xue* at the end of the nose: the *shou shao yang* is three cavities; the pulse begins in the *guan chong xue* in the finger next to the little one, and ends in the *si zhu kong* in the ear.

The *shou tai yang* or the pulse of the small intestine begins in the *shao ze* at the end of the little finger and ends at the *ting gong xue* in the cheek. The *zu yang ming* or stomachs pulse begins in the *cheng qi xue*. just above the jaw, and ends in the *li dui xue* between the great and second toes.

The *zu shao yang* is the gall: its pulse begins in the *tong zi liao* near the outer extremity of the eye, and ends in the *qiao yin xue* in the end of the 4th toe.

The *zu tai yang* is the bladder: its pulse begins in the *jing ming xue* at the interior corner of the eye, and ends in the *zhi yin xue* at the extremity of the either toe.

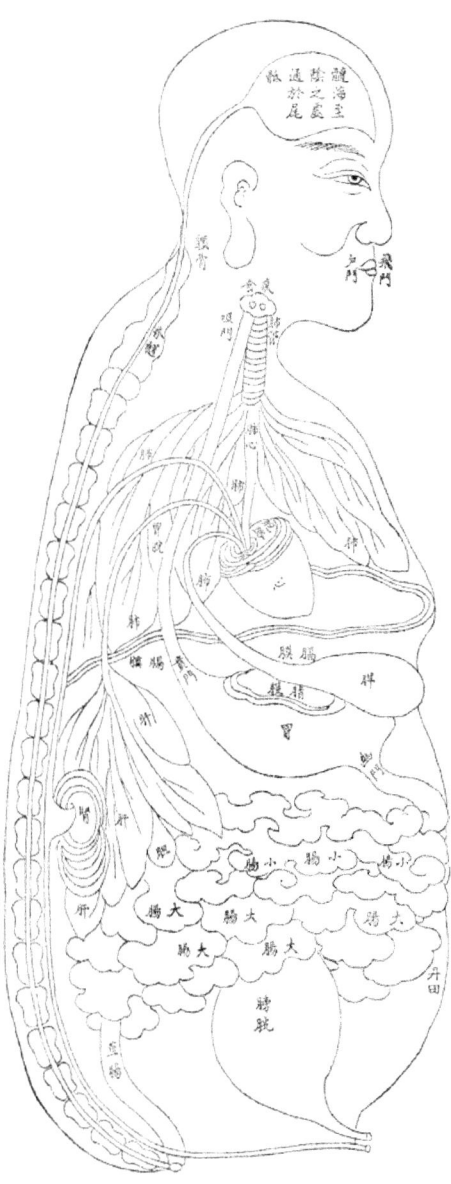

42. *Zang Fu Ming Tang Tu. Explantory map of the contents of the human body*

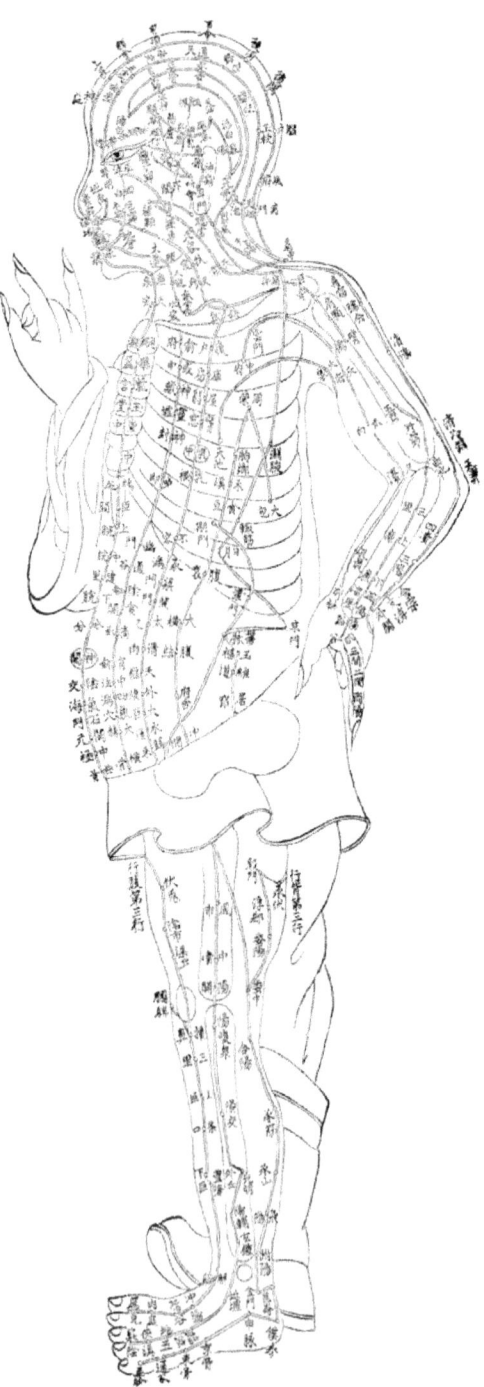

43. Ce Ren Ming Tang Tu. Side view map of the human body

Translation of the Chinese Anatomical Maps

正人明堂圖

44. *Zheng Ren Ming Tang Tu. Front view map of the human body*

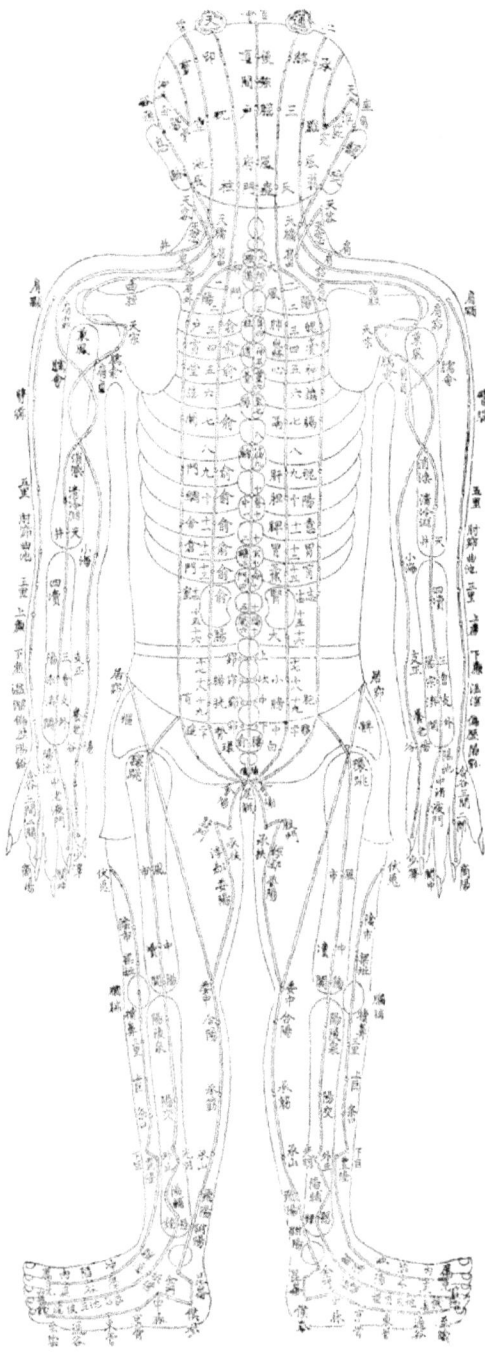

45. *Fu Ren Ming Tang Tu. Back view map of the human body*

CHAPTER 17 **AN ESSAY ON THE SMALL FEET OF CHINESE WOMEN**

ORIGIN OF THE CUSTOM AND ITS EFFECTS UPON THE HEALTH

The custom of the crippling the feet of Chinese women and reducing them to the smallest possible dimensions seems to be involved in much obscurity for there are several different explanations, and different motives are assigned for the practice. The fact that none of the Chinese classics allude to the subject is presumptive evidence that the practice did not exist so early as the days of Confucius. One account states that it owes its existence to the whim of a prince of Keang Nan, whose court was at Nankin. He ruled from 961 to 976 A.D. and was subdued and finally poisoned by the founders of the Sung dynasty.

Another account is that the origin of the practice is to be attributed to an infamous Empress 1100 BC who was born with club feet. She is represented as having great influence over the emperor whom she induced to issue an imperial edict, adopting her feet as the model of beauty and requiring the compression of the infant females' feet so as to conform to the imperial model. This account is necessarily traditional as it dates from a period long prior to the universal destruction of Chinese books in the Qin dynasty 300 BC.

There is also a third story that the Emperor Yang of the Sung dynasty 605 AD ordered his concubine to bandage her feet, and in the sole of her feet was placed a stamp of the lotus flower. Hence the saying that her steps produced the golden lotus, and to the present day men compliment little girls with small compressed feet, by designating them the golden lotus.

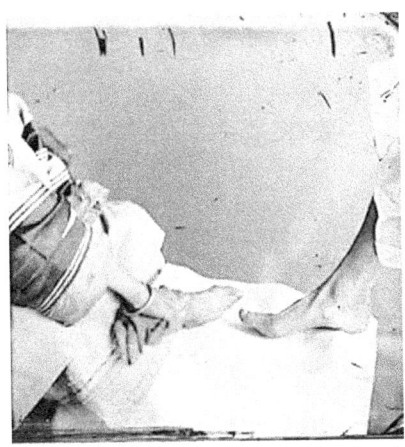

46. First ever photograph of the result of foot binding {left} by John Thomson 1865-1868, Wellcome Library, London

How so great a deformity should have ever come to be considered as great beauty is remarkably strange, and difficult to be explained. The custom thus prevails universally among the higher classes, but is by no means confined to them, for it is common particularly in some parts of China even among the lower classes. The prevalence among the lower classes is ascribed to the fact that a woman has no chance of marrying well and thereby rising in life unless she has diminutive feet, for none of the Lords of creation would condescend to marry a female with feet of the ordinary size. In cases of marriage the parties not being able to see each other it is customary to sent the exact dimensions of the lady's foot to her intended, instead of sending him her portrait, as we do in Europe.

It seems somewhat strange that the custom of deforming the feet should never have found favour among the Japanese, a people in many respects similar to the Chinese in regard to their manners and customs. The married women of Japan have, however, a practice which is equally disfiguring and unnatural. I allude to the custom of blacking their teeth with a mixture which is said to be composed of iron filings and sake.

In consequence of the horror which the Chinese have of dissection or of disturbance of the dead, it is no easy matter to get the skeleton of a foot. Dr Adams RN obtained the foot of a woman who was killed at the bombardment of Canton in 1857, and by his kindness I am enabled to give its different measurements, which are as follows:-

Extreme length of foot from tuberosity of os calcis to the extremity of the ungual phalanx of great toe .... 5 ½ inches
Length of tarsus .... 2 ¾"
Extreme breadth of tarsus .... 1 $^{8}/_{10}$"
Extreme breadth of toes... 2 $^{1}/_{10}$"
Extreme height from highest part of the dorsum of the
  foot to the pad of the heel .... 2 $^{8}/_{10}$"

To produce this artificial deformity the foot is tightly bandaged in early life, the tarsus or insteps being bent on itself, the os calcis or heel bone is thrown out of the horizontal position, and what ought to be the posterior surface is brought to the ground, so that the ankle is, as it were, forced tighter up that it ought to be, producing in fact artifical talipes calcaneus. The four smaller toes are pressed down under the instep and checked in their growth, till at adult age all that has to go into the shoe is the end of the os calcis and the whole of the great toe.

As the os calcis is nearly vertical there may be said to be no heel projecting backwards for the posterior extremity of the astragalus projects nearly as far behind as the os calcis. The bones of the tarsus though much compressed are not ossified together for distinct ligaments and synovial membranes intervene. The tuberosity of the scaphoid bone generally appears very prominent. This practice of course, destroys the symmetry of the foot and renders the gait of the women uncertain and painful. Few of the Chinese women can walk far or walk quickly and running is quite out of the question, for the foot, instead of being broad and large in proportion to the size of the body so that it may form a firm basis of support, is reduced to the smallest possible dimensions, and instead of the bones of the tarsus being freely moveable on each other, so as to break shocks and increase elasticity, they are all squeezed together so that the spring of the foot is entirely lost. Beneath the two chief points of support, namely the heel and ball of the great toe are thick callosities of cellular tissue. The muscles of the calves of the legs are much atrophied and loose their natural power.

In healthy constitutions this constriction of the foot may be carried on without any very serious consequences and it must be confessed that the amount of actual disease is small. In scrofulous constitutions, however, the scaphoid bones and the internal cuneiform bone which supports the great toe are very liable, from the constant pressure and irritation to which they are exposed, to become diseased, and many cases have been seen where caries, softening, and even death of the bone have taken place, accompanied with much suppuration and great consequent suffering. Cases have occurred where children have lost both feet at the ankle from the strong compression used, gangrene having commenced from the excessive suffering to which the children have been subjected. Chinese women are very subject to corns. By the confinement it occasions this custom must as a matter of course in nearly all cases necessarily detract from physical health and vigor, and it may be injurious to health in other respects, as there is the most intimate sympathy between the several parts of the body.

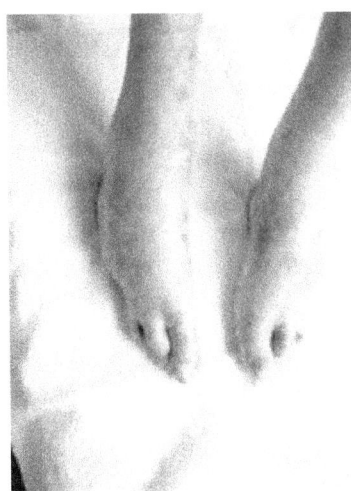

47. Result of foot binding, Hong Kong, 1980's (Editor's collection)

Chapter 18 An Essay On Opium Smoking

Opium has of late years been so extensively introduced into China and is now consumed by so many millions of that vast empire that who attempts to write on a subject connected with the country would scarcely be excused should he omit to touch upon the opium question. There are few subjects connected with the modern history of the nation that has attracted so much attention as the trade in opium. It was not only the immediate cause of England's first war with China in 1839, but commercially politically and morally it is a question of surpassing interest and importance.

Although the greater part of the opium consumed in China is introduced from abroad, the poppy is now cultivated in several parts of the empire for its narcotic juice. Dr Macgowan who has throughout investigated the history of Chinese opium in a note read before the China Branch of the Royal Asiatic Society says "There are many species of the genus *Papaver* found in China, including the *P. Sanentate* and *P. Somniferum*, and both varieties of the latter, *P.S. Album* and *P.S. Nigruria*. They are found throughout the hilly districts from Shing king to Kwang he, from the Himalayas to the Pacific. In Chinese, *Papaver* is called *ying su*, deriving its name from the form of its capsule, which resembles a *ying* or jar, and from its seeds, which on account of their nutritive properties are classed with *sun* or *su*. The literal signification of *ying su* or *Papaver* is rice jar, thus the plant which has proven the bane of the Chinese race bears the name of their staff of life. Its synonyms, too are all indicative of its edible character, *mi yu* [imperial rice], *mi nang* [rice sack], *mi ku* [rice grain] and *xiang mi* [elephant rice]. In like manner we derive the name from pap, "infants' food". It appears that as early as 1068-85 AD, poppy seeds were extolled by the brothers Su for the nutritious gruel they afford. The pharmacologist Wang writing in the beginning of the Sung dynasty, between 960 and 979 AD, says "Opium comes from Arabia and is procured by incising the capsule of the red Poppy". This is the first notice of opium to be found in Chinese books. The *Pun tsau* a materia medica published in 1550 treats opium as a novelty at Pekin where it was used as an aphrodisiac. The earliest dictionaries and encyclopedias make no mention of the poppy from which it may be inferred that the plant is not indigenous. It appears to have been first cultivated for its farinaceous seeds and two centuries ago is treated by writers as an article proper to resort to for sustenance in times of scarcity being classed with barley and other nutritious grains. There is no evidence of its cultivation in China for the sake of the inspissated juice of its capsules before the commencement of the present century.

Opium does not appear to have become an article of commerce of any importance before the middle of the 17th century the date assigned by some for the commencement of opium smoking. The practice, however, probably commenced at a still earlier date for Barbour writing at the beginning of the 16th century uses the word Ameiam, and in his account of Malacca, enumerates it among the articles brought by the Moorish and Gentile merchants of western India, to exchange for the cargoes of the Chinese junks, and such we know is in some degree the course of trade even in the present day.

Opium Chests Imported to China

1790	4,054
1800	4,570
1810	4,968
1820	4,006
1830	16,877
1840	20,619
1850	52,925
1857	76,000

The East India Company made its first experiment in the opium trade in the year 1773 and the seductive nature of the practice and the rapid extension of opium smoking may be at once appreciated by a glance at the subjoined table.

Of the various causes which have led to the habit of opium smoking among the Chinese is their social and luxurious disposition. In China every person in easy circumstance has a saloon to his house elegantly filled up for the reception of his friends with pipes for opium tobacco. All are invited to smoke and many are thus induced to commence the practice from curiosity or politeness and few are afterward able to discontinue the practice. A belief it is said founded on experience that the practice heightens and prolongs venereal pleasure is another inducement to commence the practice. It is, however, admitted by all that opium smokers become impotent at a much earlier period of life than others, the drug apparently having the power of emasculating those addicted to its use. In painful and incurable disease, in all kinds of mental and corporal sufferings, in mercantile misfortunes and in other reverses of fortune the opium shop is resorted to as an asylum where, for a time at least the unfortunate may drown the recollection of his cares and troubles in an indescribably pleasurable feeling or indifference to all around. But although there may be reckoned among the chief causes which induce so large a number of the people of China to resort to opium smoking we must never forget that opium is a drug of priceless value as a medicine and that when taken in small quantities it allays pain and hunger and tends to soothe the vascular and corporeal system, diffusing in a mysterious manner a transient feeling of health pleasure and vigor though the system.

John Hunter, [1], one of the most celebrated men of his day was often heard repeating to himself as he passed along the ward of his hospital, "thank god for opium" referring to its extreme value in the treatment of disease. That a medicine of such undoubted utility should be much abused and applied to improper purposes is natural enough considering the frailty of human nature. Opium is a narcotic stimulant and when under the influence of which what may be termed a moderate dose a man may for a time gain an accession of nervous energy and be able to perform a greater amount of labour than usual, just as a tired horse may go, if well whipped, fasten for a short time. Reaction of course follows and the man's last state becomes worse than his first.

48. *Opium warehouse, Patna, India, Wellcome Library, London*

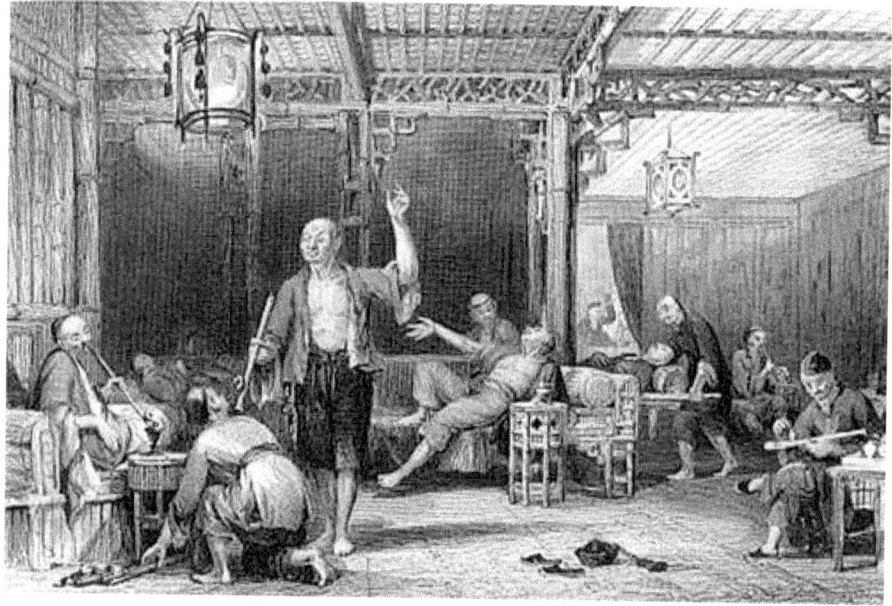

49. *Engraving of an opium den by Thomas Allom, 1843 - 1847*

The opium smoking shops are, as a general rule, somewhat miserable looking places. They are kept open from early in the morning until late at night. The smoking room is furnished with several wooden couches constructed of bamboo and covered with mats. At the head of each is a narrow pillow or bolster for the head to rest upon. In the centre of each shop there is a small lamp which while serving to light the pipes diffuses a cheerless light through the gloomy abode. The pipe is composed of a shank and a headpiece. It is bored through the centre from the mouthpiece to the head where there is a cup to collect the opium. The smokers generally go in pairs and recline on the couches with the head resting on the pillow. The mode of proceeding is as follows. One of the pair takes a small portion of opium on the point of a small metallic rod, and lighting it at the lamp applies it to the small aperture resembling the touch-hole of a gun and which is not larger than a pin's head in the bowl of the pipe. After inhaling a few whiffs he hands the pipe to his friend, who lights another piece of opium at the lamp, and thus they go on alternately smoking till they have had sufficient.

The fume is always expelled through the nose and old smokers even draw into lungs before it is expired. This process generally lasts about half an hour. One or two whiffs are the utmost that can be inhaled from a single pipe. During the smoking time they are at first exceedingly loquacious and the conversation highly animated, but, as the opium takes effect, the conversation drops, they frequently burst out into loud laughter from the most trifling reasons or without any apparent cause at all, unless it be from the train of thought through their excited imaginations. The next phase presents a vacancy of countenance with pallor and shrinking of the features, so that they resemble people convalescent from fever. A dead silence precedes a deep sleep which continues from half an hour to three or four hours, in which state the pulse becomes much slower, softer and smaller than before the debauch.

The apparatus for smoking is spread out, not unlike a small tea service. A little cup contains the delectable liquor, nearly of the consistence and colour of tar. There are also on the table, a small glass lamp and a silver capped pipe and a few other articles as brushes, needles, etc. for cleaning and trimming the pipe. The opium pipe is generally 20 inches in length, and is generally made of some reed variously ornamented having at one end an ivory or bone mouthpiece. The substance which is smoked is not the pure opium as sold in our druggists shops, it is a watery extract prepared by powdering the opium and then boiling it. After a certain quantity of the fluid is evaporated the remainder is strained with Chinese blotting, which is an exceedingly good description of the article, and what is collected is the substance used for smoking. The object of the boiling and straining is to remove all the feculent and extraneous matter from the opium. In many parts of China, the opium is only submitted to one evaporation and the extract is then collected and considered ready for use. In other parts of the country it is submitted to three evaporations and is three times strained. What is collected at each straining is used for smoking, but the product of the third evaporation is considered the best article, is said to be least injurious to health, and is sold at the highest price. The product of the first straining may be termed the poor man's opium, the product of the second straining the opium of the middle classes, and the product of the third straining is the rich mans opium. The total amount of solid extract collected from the three strainings may be estimated at 4 1/2 ounces for each pound of opium used.

Of this quantity 1 ounce is collected at the first evaporation and 1 ounce at the second, and 2 1/2 ounces at the third evaporation. The baneful effects of opium smoking on the human constitution are conspicuously displayed in the confirmed opium smoker by stupor and unconquerable drowsiness, forgetfulness, general deterioration of all the mental faculties, emaciation, debility, sallow and somewhat shining complexion; lividity of lips, languor, lack lustre of the eye, appetite either destroyed or impaired, irritability of stomach and a morbid state of the secretions.

Those sad indications of the pains and penalties attached to opium smoking may be observed by one who chooses to visit the opium smoking shops of China. No language that can be used is strong enough to convey an idea of the sad effect of the inordinate use of opium. Misery, degradation and woe follow almost for a certainty. But although it is the unbiased conviction of the writer that the habitual use of opium is generally injurious to the health and happiness of those addicted to the practice and although the daily use of such a drug as a narcotic stimulant is an abuse , in the same manner as the habitual use of small quantities of prussic acid or any other poison would be a misappropriation of its use, there can be but little doubt that thousands consume it in small quantities without any apparently deleterious effect. It certainly does not necessarily follow, as has been represented, that he who begins the practice of taking small quantities of opium, will soon fall into the habit of smoking it in excessive quantities and will necessarily die an early death. Pernicious as the habit is, it must be allowed that many persons have attained to be the age of 60, 70 or more who have been well known as habitual opium smokers for more than 20 or even 30 years of their lives.

As compared with spirituous liquors, opium smoking is more seductive but although its excessive use is more physically injurious than excessive drinking it is not so ignoble and brutalizing a vice. Many eminent authorities have of late years borne testimony to the effect that of the two forms of vice the immoderate indulgence in spirituous liquor is if anything the worse. The Colonial Surgeon of Hong Kong, a few years ago, gave evidence as the result of his experience and the table of mortality that more disease and a greater mortality resulted in Hong Kong from the abuse of spirituous liquors among the 600 European residents, than from the use of opium among the 60,000 Chinese.

Dr Galwete, a man of great ability gives it as his deliberate opinion that "Proofs are still wanting to show that the moderate use of opium produces more pernicious effects upon the constitution than the moderate use of spirituous liquors; while it is certain that the consequences of the abuse of the former are less appalling in their effects upon the system, and less disastrous to society at large than the consequence of the abuse of the latter".

Dr Oley, a physician and naturalist of eminence, and who had a longer experience than most men gives the following opinion; "The inordinate use, or rather abuse of the drug most decidedly does bring on early decrepitude, loss of appetite, and a morbid state of the secretions, but I have seen a man who had used the drug for 50 years in moderation, without any evil effects; and one man I recollect in Malacca who had so used it for upwards of eighty. Several in the habit of smoking it have assured me, that, in moderation, it neither impaired the functions nor shortened life; at the same time he fully admitted the deleterious effects of too much."

Even in England we have had of late one notable example to the effect that opium may be taken habitually for many years without necessarily bringing on premature old age or blunting the intellectual faculties. The writer alludes to Mr Thomas De Quincey, the author of; "Confessions of an opium eater" who died on the 8th of December 1859 aged 75. Till near the hour of his death his pure and high intellect shone clear and serene as when in its zenith. Almost till the very last his perceptions were as vivid, his interest in knowledge and affairs as keen as ever; and while his bodily frame, wasted by suffering and disease, day by day faded and shrunk, his mind retained unimpaired its characteristic capaciousness, activity and acuteness.

The Christian philanthropist may deplore the misery and wretchedness that result from the extensive consumption of opium in China but as the evil is beyond the control of any government we all must rejoice that the trade in this article is now legalized and that the old system of imperial prohibition and local connivance has been abolished. Nothing but evil could result from such a state of things, for it has always been beyond the power of the government of China to prevent the introduction of opium into territories and the rigorous prohibition of the cultivation of the poppy in India would inevitably lead to its cultivation in neighbouring states, and a further extension of its cultivation in China. As long as the demand exists we may depend upon it that so long will there be a supply.

By moral means and moral means alone can we hope to induce the people of China to abandon this seductive unhealthy and demoralizing habit. The government of China has in times gone by, ostensibly done all in its power to check the introduction of opium into the country. Imprisonment, fine and death have been the reward of those who have attempted to buy or sell opium so that one would imagine that the regulations had been sufficiently severe to ensure the entire exclusion of the article. It may well, however, be doubted whether the government, or at all event its officials have ever been very sincere in their endeavours.

For opium shops have for many years been numerous in most of the towns of China and more especially in the maritime districts. No secret is made of the business. Were the authorities anxious for the suppression of the traffic much more might certainly be done than is now attempted. But whatever doubt may exist regarding the honesty and sincerity of the intentions of the government and its officials there can be but little doubt that a vast number of people in the Empire who see clearly the bad effects of opium smoking, deplore the extreme prevalence of the vice. Opium is regarded by them as a great evil and the introduction of it by foreigners is certainly one cause of hostility against them. Their objections are of a moral nature being founded on the belief that it is a deleterious drug the use of which deteriorates the morals and undermines the health of the people.

Considering the vast amount of injury that opium smoking produces there can scarcely be any wonder that the good and virtuous should deplore the spread of the custom. Of late years this pernicious habit has frequently been a cause of much embarrassment to the very rulers who connive at the practice. It is related that as far back as 1832 of a thousand men sent by the governor of Canton to act against the rebels, the commanding officer sent back 200, rendered totally unfit for active service by the habit of opium smoking.

Chinese physicians prescribe opium in various diseases and recommend the opium pipe in cases of obstinate ague or rheumatism, and doubtless as a temporary measure it may afford relief, although the cure may often prove worse than the disease by inducing the patient to commence a practice of using an article which he afterwards finds himself unable to refrain from.

The general plan pursued for the cure of the habit of opium smoking is as follows. The first thing to be done is to get the use of the opium pipe discontinued, supplying its place at first by opium and camphor in pills, or small doses of Dover's Powder, [2], giving at the same time astringents as pomegranate, etc to check the wasting diarrhoea that almost always follows as a sequence of abstinence from the habitual use of opium. Tonics are also administered such as suffusion of quassia with Gilles tincture of any kind and any of the essential oils with camphor mixture. Wine, ammonia and quinine and other tonics are also given when required. A generous diet is recommended. After continuing the opiates for a few days, they are gradually reduced in quantity till they are left off altogether, and the tonic is then given alone till the case is complete. When the confirmed opium smoker commences the plan of treatment here alluded to, he generally suffers much from debility, loss of appetite, diarrhoea, abdominal pain, and soreness in all the bones, but if the patient has resolution enough to persevere he may in the course of one or two months be reclaimed from the vice and again become a happy and useful member of society.

NOTES

INTRODUCTION

1. There are many journals of naval surgeons kept in The National Archives, Kew, London in the files catalogued as ADM 101.

2. These journals are from Captain Robert Young who was surgeon on HMS Ardent at the battle of Camperdown in 1797. It is one of the most graphic accounts of the conditions that a naval surgeon was required to work under during a naval battle. The battle of Camperdown was part of the French Revolutionary Wars and took place on the 11th October 1797 when a British fleet engaged the Dutch navy. The Ardent engaged the Dutch flagship Vrijheid. It was a fierce battle and on the HMS Ardent there were finally 40 dead and 96 wounded [Appendix 2].

3. Qualifications required for the post of Assistant Surgeon in the Royal Navy, Victualling Office, The Admiralty. 1826. Archives of St Thomas's Hospital Medical School TH/FP12/1.

4. The father of Charles Courtney, Abraham Courtney managed his own hydrotherapy clinic after retirement from the Royal Navy and is mentioned in research papers of hydrotherapy [Bradley J, Dupree M. Opportunity of the Edge of Orthodoxy. Medically Qualified hydrotherapists in the Era of Reform 1840-60. Social History of Medicine (2001), 14(3). 417-437.] He also published scientific papers on the subject [Courtney A, Hydrotherapy defended by facts, 1844, London] and also wrote papers on temperance [The moderate use of intoxicating drinks, being the substance of a lecture delivered at a meeting of the Isle of Thanet Temperance Society. The New British and Foreign Temperance Society (1840), London].

5. Service Record of Charles Courtney ADM104/18 p77.

6. C. Pemberton Hodgson published an account of his experiences in Japan entitled 'A Residence at Nagasaki and Hakodate in 1859 and 1860'. Republished by Elibron Classics, London 2005.

7. The battle for the Taku Forts at the mouth of the Peiho River was precipitated by the desire of the British to install envoys in Tianjin which

required passage up the Peiho River. However the river was obstructed by booms made of heavy spars of wood cross-lashed with cables and presented formidable obstructions. There were forts on both sides of the river mouth, the size, fortifications and armaments were difficult to discern. After passing through one boom ships became caught and then the shore batteries opened fire and the battle begun. Marines were landed to attack the forts on foot but quickly became hampered by the muddy shoreline and intensive gunfire and eventually withdrew to the ships. The British lost five ships, two sank due to the accurate fire of the shore batteries and three were fast in the mud. Altogether there were 89 killed and 345 wounded in the engagement before the fleet withdrew in defeat.

8. Malaria was a serious problem in Hong Kong and it was known that a particular area of high risk was the swampy area to the east of Victoria harbour that was known [to this day] as Happy Valley. It is lore that the name derived from the delirium of fever that often accompanies malaria. The swampy area was drained and filled in and is now the site of the racecourse of the Jockey Club of Hong Kong.

9. The term Hong Kong Fever was initially called West Point Fever as that was where the disease was most commonly reported and most vicious. However as it became clear that the fever could be contracted at several locations, including Stanley on the south coast of Hong Kong island, the name Hong Kong Fever was adopted. [Barton G K. Observations on the Causes, Nature and Treatment of Hong Kong Fever. Dublin Journal of Medical Sciences 1851].

10. The Cree Journals are an account by Dr Edward Cree who served as Surgeon on board HMS Rattlesnake along the China coast. His diary is wonderfully illustrated with the coloured drawings by Cree himself. He was in Hong Kong in 1840 and 1841.

11. Miasma is defined as 'Infectious or noxious exhalations from putrescent organic matter; poisonous particles or germs floating in and polluting the atmosphere; noxious emanations, esp. malaria.' Oxford English Dictionary 1989.

12. This is taken from the Medical Letters of a certain Dr Edwards quoted by Dr G K Barton [9, above].

13. Typhus fever [not to be confused with typhoid which is unrelated] is a febrile illness cause by a small organism known as *Rickettsiae*. The organism is carried by lice which commonly infest humans and rats, hence is associated with poor hygiene and overcrowding. In sixteenth century England the illness was referred to as 'gaol fever' as it was particularly

common in prisons due to severe overcrowding and poor hygiene. It caused many deaths amongst prisoners and also was responsible for illness and deaths in court officials who were infected by inmates during court proceedings. Hence the observation by Courtney that the disease appeared more common in policemen on duty in crowded slums, is a pertinent one. The illness starts with high fever and prominent symptoms include muscle aches, headaches cough and delirium and can be fatal.

14. Typhoid fever [not to be confused with typhus which is unrelated] is caused by a *Salmonella* bacterium and infects humans by the ingestion of food or water that is contaminated with the faeces of an infected person and as such is associated with unclean water supplies and poor hygiene in food handlers. It is a gastrointestinal infection with symptoms of fever and gastroenteritis, diarrhoea and profuse sweating. As the disease progresses other tissues may be infected including the liver, brain and bones. In the pre-antibiotic era the disease often progressed to death by the fourth week. Charles Darwin contracted typhoid fever on the HMS Beagle in 1835 during a voyage to Chile.

15. This account is documented in the Atlas of Materia Medica or the *Ben cao tu jing* of the 11th Century compiled by Song Su [1020-1101] who was an expert in medicine and natural sciences. It was first published in 1061 and was one of the earliest pharmacopoeia organized by the Chinese government. Zhijun Shang. *Ben cao tu jing*. Anhui Science and Technology Press (1994).

16. Dr James Lind was a surgeon's apprentice at the age of 15 and subsequently earned a medical degree from Edinburgh University. He wrote two important books, 'A Treatise on the Scurvy in Three Parts containing An Enquiry into the Nature, Causes and Cure of that Disease together with A Critical and Chronological View of what has been published on the subject. London, 1772. He also wrote 'An Essay on Diseases Incidental to Europeans in Hot Climates'. London 1771.

17. John 'China' Thomson [1837 – 1921] was a geographer and photographer who traveled extensively through Asia and China in the 1860's and 1870's creating a comprehensive and unique collection of photographs. His pictures included important structures, palaces and the Great Wall and also people, from beggars and farmers to rather more formal portraits of noble families and Mandarins. He spent three months travelling on the Yangtse River. The China collection of his photographs is housed at the Wellcome Library, London.

18. Joseph Needham [1900-1995] was originally a biochemist who changed discipline and became one of the most accomplished sinologists writing

the *Science and Civilization in China* series that has now reached 27 volumes are others are still in preparation by scholars at the Needham Institute, Cambridge. The opus included a treatise on early medicine in China which offers invaluable insights into Chinese medical theory, medical education in China, forensic medicine and on numerous maladies including smallpox. His life-long collaborator was Dr Lu Gwei-Djen, a biochemist from Nanjing, who went to Cambridge to work in Needham's laboratory in 1937. Needham was Master of Gonville and Caius College, Cambridge and a Fellow of the Royal Society.

19. This is one of many highly significant observations that were made by Needham and Lu Gwei-Djen in the *Science and Civilization in China* series. There is one volume dedicated to the history and philosophy of medicine in China, detailing many aspects that were both unique and advanced in the entirety of world medical knowledge. Science and Civilization in China, Volume II:6, published in 1970.

20. William Harvey [1578 – 1657] was an English physician who was the first to accurately describe the circulation of the blood, in particular describing the central role of the heart. He published his findings in *Exercitatio Anatomica de Motu Cordis et Sanguinins in Animalibus* in 1628, one of the greatest landmarks in human physiology.

21. Dr W A Harland moved to Hong Kong in 1846 to escape an unwise marriage, abandoning his wife. He was a physician and a natural scientist, learned Chinese and studied Traditional Chinese Medicine. He worked at the Seaman's Hospital in Hong Kong and compiled the Colonial Surgeon's Reports for 1848 to 1850. Harland was also a founder member of the China Medico-Chirurgical Society [which became the China Branch of the Royal Asiatic Society in Hong Kong] and published a number of papers including 'The Chinese system of human anatomy and physiology' in the Transactions of the China Branch of the Royal Asiatic Society 1847. He died of a fever in Hong Kong in 1858 aged 39 years. In his will he left most of his possessions to his Chinese housekeeper and his natural history collection was bequeathed to the Scarborough Philosophical Society in Yorkshire, England. His memorial in the Colonial Cemetery, Happy Valley, Hong Kong reads "Admired for his scientific enquiries, trusted for his abilities as a physician and loved for his qualities as a man". It is one of the largest monuments in the cemetery.

22. Dr Benjamin Hobson [1816 - 1873] a much respected medical missionary worked in China from 1839 to 1859 mostly in Macao, Hong Kong, Guangzhou and finally Shanghai. In Hong Kong he was a founder member and the first appointed secretary of the China Medico-Chirurgical Society which later became the China Branch of the Royal Asiatic Society. He was

an influential promoter of western medicine and science in China. During the 1850's he wrote five books on medical science which were translated into Chinese, four of which were concerned with anatomy and physiology, surgery, midwifery and childhood illnesses, medical practice and materia medica. His book, *Bowu xinbian* (Natural philosophy and natural history) which was published in 1855 provided a general introduction to chemistry, physics, astronomy, geography and zoology. The translations into Chinese for oxygen, hydrogen and nitrogen namely *yangqi* (nourishing gas), *qingqi* (light gas) and *danqi* (diluting gas) are still in use today. It is likely from the texts in the Courtney journal that Hobson met with Courtney in 1858/1859 in Shanghai.

23. Dr Patrick Manson [1844-1922] graduated from Aberdeen University, passed his medical examinations at the age of 20 and then travelled to work in Formosa [Taiwan] at the age of 22 to be Medical Officer for the China Imperial Maritime Customs Service. After 5 years he moved to Amoy [Xiamen] where he worked for 13 years. During that time he conducted many experiments including feeding mosquitoes on the blood of his manservant who suffered from filariasis and then visualizing the filariae in the stomachs of the mosquitoes under a microscope. He published extensive reports of his research and other medical observations in the Medical Reports of the China Imperial Maritime Customs Service.

24. Surgeons of the Opium War: The Navy on the China Coast, 1840-42. McLean, David. English Historical Review, Vol CXXXI [491], 487-504.

25. www.badc.nerc.ac.uk.

Notes

Chapter 1

1. Graywacke is a variety of sandstone characterized by its hardness, dark color, and poorly-sorted angular grains of quartz, feldspar small rock fragments or lithic fragments in a compact, clay-fine matrix.

2. Intermittent fever is a fever that recurs in cycles of paroxysms and remissions, such as in malaria. In this case probably most cases of intermittent fever were caused by malaria which was common in South China at that time but has now been eradicated from Hong Kong and Guangdong.

3. The symptoms of malaria were described in ancient Chinese medical writings. In 2700 BC, several characteristic symptoms of what would later be named malaria were described in the *Nei jing*, (The Canon of Medicine). The *Nei Jing* was edited by Emperor Huang Ti during the second century BC. The Qinghao plant Artemisia Annua was described in the medical treatise, 52 Remedies, found in the Mawangdui Tomb. In 340 BC, The anti-fever properties of Qinghao were first described by Ge Hong of the East Yin dynasty. The active ingredient of Qinghao was isolated by Chinese scientists in 1971. Known as artemisinin, it is today a very potent and effective antimalarial drug, especially in combination with other medicines.

4. A Joss house or Miu is a place for worshiping a variety of indigenous Chinese deities, saints and supernatural beings from Taoism, Buddhism, Confucianism and Chinese folk religion. Here "Joss" is a corrupted version of the Portuguese word for "God". Joss house is usually translated as temple, although the phrase was in common use in English in western North America during frontier times, when joss houses were a common feature of places with Chinatowns. Joss houses are distinct from Taoist temples and Buddhist monasteries in that they are established by nearby villagers or fishermen to pray for good luck; only few or none of monks, nuns or priests study religion or stay in joss houses. Joss houses are usually small houses decorated with traditional figures on their roofs although some evolve into significant structures.

5. Yamun, an official residence provided for Chinese officials.

6. The stinkpot is an earthenware vessel filled with sulphur and gunpowder. Each junk had cages at the mast-head, which in action were occupied by one or more men, whose duty it was to throw these stinkpots on to the decks of the enemy or into boats attempting to board. There were also men

at the foot of each mast to haul up the baskets containing the stinkpots by means of a pulley. Each basket contained ten or more stinkpots, and these were hoisted up the mast-head. The stinkpot would be lit and then thrown at the enemy immediately, causing dreadful injuries and burns.

7. Quinine came to attention of western physicians after Spanish Jesuit missionaries in South America learned of a medicinal bark from indigenous Indian tribes. It is said that the Countess of Chinchón, the wife of the Viceroy of Peru, was cured of her fever. The bark from the tree was then called Peruvian Bark and the tree was named Cinchona after the countess. There is some doubt concerning the authenticity of this history, even so the legend prevails.

Chapter 2

1. Quartz is the bedrock for much of Hong Kong and Kowloon. Deep drilling into the rock is required to sustain the high-rise buildings. Over the years many construction workers suffered from silicosis, an occupational lung disease from working deep in foundation wells drilling into the dense quartz.

2. Hong Kong Fever was reported as a distinct entity by a number of physicians, most notably by Dr Barry in the Dublin Journal of Medical Sciences [Bibliography]. However there was controversy around this term as alluded to by Courtney as certainly there was more than one cause of fever and the symptoms could be variable.

3. The census shows that in 1859 there were nearly 87,000 people living on Hong Kong island. Currently there are approximately 7 million inhabitants in Hong Kong, Kowloon and the New Territories.

Chapter 3

1. Camoens (1524 – 1580) is considered Portugal's and the Portuguese language's greatest poet. He is best known for his epic work The Lusiads.

2. George Chinnery (1774 – 1852) was an English painter who spent much of his life in Asia, arriving in South China in 1825. He travelled extensively around the Pearl River Delta between Macao and Canton and was in Hong Kong in the early 1840's. His paintings are rare as he was one of the very few western painters in South China in the early and mid 19th century. He presented the everyday life of common people and landscapes of the Pearl River Delta at that period. He died in Macao in 1852 and is buried in the Old Protestant Cemetery.

Chapter 4

1. These observations concerning typhoons were quite prophetic as in 1922 a devastating typhoon swept through Shantou, the storm front causing waves of two metres above normal. It is estimated that at last 60,000 people died making the storm one of the deadliest typhoons on record.

Chapter 5

1. Sporadic outbreaks of cholera did occur and naval surgeons were aware that cholera was a water borne disease. Confirmation came from the work of John Snow on his observations of the outbreaks related to water pumps in London. Snow was a skeptic of the then-dominant miasma theory that stated that diseases such as cholera, and the Black Death (Plague) were caused by pollution or a noxious form of "bad air". The germ theory was not widely accepted by this time, so Snow was unaware of the mechanism by which the disease was transmitted, but evidence led him to believe that it was not due to breathing foul air. He first publicized his theory in an essay *On the Mode of Communication of Cholera* in 1849. In 1855 a second edition was published, with a detailed map showing the relationship of the cholera cases to the water-supply [the Broad Street water pump] in the London epidemic.

Chapter 6

1. Hot springs are still active in Fujian and have not changed since visited by Courtney. Particularly in the Gutian mountains the sulphur springs are said to be the purest with hot clear water that posses medicinal properties.

Chapter 7

1. Dr Macgowan (Daniel Jerome Macgowan) was an American Baptist medical missionary who went to Ningbo in 1843. In 1851 he published the Philosophical Almanac in Chinese *{Bowu tongshu}* mostly concerning electricity, electrotherapy and magnetism. A copy of the almanac was subsequently translated into Japanese by a publisher in Tokyo. He used coloured models imported from Europe to teach anatomy to his students. He subsequently served as American Vice-Consul.

Chapter 8

1. Containing relatively large isolated crystals in a mass of fine texture.

2. Elephantiasis is endemic in parts of south China and is caused by the parasite *Wuchereria bancrofti*. This is the parasite that Manson was to study

Notes

in Xiamen some 20 years later, his conclusions being a critical turning point in medicine, leading to new thinking in the pathogenesis of infectious diseases.

CHAPTER 9

1. Karl Gutzlaff [1803-1851] was a protestant missionary who traveled extensively in the 1830's writing three books of his travels and then was later resident in Hong Kong and Shanghai. He mastered the Chinese language and contributed to the translation of the Bible into Chinese and also assisted in the negotiations during the First Opium War of 1840-1842. He died in Hong Kong in 1851 and is interred in the Hong Kong Cemetery.

2. The clinical features in this patient's history together with the marked fever, headache, and faint red rash and then purple spots and fatality point towards the diagnosis of meningococcal meningitis. Courtney names this illness as a 'fatal form of petechial fever that occurs occasionally.' Clearly he recognized the illness as being distinct from the other more common fevers that he described.

3. The goddess of cutaneous diseases [mostly smallpox] is named Dou Shen Niang Niang and was widely worshiped in China to ward off smallpox or to hasten a cure for those that had contracted the disease. With the control of the disease the number of temples dedicated to the goddess or larger temples that housed the deity, has declined significantly.

4. Almost certainly epidemic conjunctivitis, caused by a virus or bacterium.

5. See Note 22, Introduction.

CHAPTER 10

1. Tartar is an alternative term of the name Mongol which formerly extended to nearly all Central Asian, Turkic and Mongol ethnic groups.

2. Tung Chow is the former name for modern day Tongzhou, situated about 20 kilometres directly east from the centre of modern-day Beijing. In ancient times it was a very important starting point for the Grand Canal of China, the earliest parts of which were built in the 5th century AD. The canal stretches from Tongzhou to Hangzhou, a distance of 1,776 kilometres and passes through the important cities of Tianjin, Xuzhou, Yangzhou and Suzhou. Most of the incoming ships and barges to Beijing would moor at Tongzhou and discharge their cargoes and passengers there as the canal was too narrow for most vessels to navigate from there to the capital.

3. There is an indoor museum dedicated to the various battles for the Peiho River and the Taku forts situated in Tang Gu city. Parts of the old forts by the river have been restored and are open to the public.

CHAPTER 11

1. Deshima Island. In 1636 the Shogun had ordered the construction of the tiny artificial island of Deshima. It was originally planned to host the Portuguese merchants and isolate them from the Japanese population. But when the construction works had been finished, the Portuguese were removed and the Dutch moved from Hirado to Deshima. Usually two Dutch ships arrived in Nagasaki harbor per year. The arrival was a big event for everybody and especially for the Dutch residents in Deshima. The permanent staff comprised a Director of the Dutch East India Company and about ten employees. The Dutch ships imported mainly silk from China and goods from Southeast Asia and Europe and exported Japanese porcelain. Arita, Imari and other Japanese ceramics were very popular in the Netherlands and in other European countries. The Japanese artisans catered for their European clients with Dutch motifs. When demand could not be met by imports, the Dutch copied Japanese porcelain in large quantities. In 1823 Philip F von Siebold, a physician, arrived at the Deshima trading post. He used his stay for an intensive study of Japan. After his return to Europe he published his knowledge in 1832 in a book entitled 'Nippon'. His presence had an important impact on Japan by bringing western medicine to the country.

CHAPTER 12

1. Straddling a canal that demarks the business from the government districts was the Nippon Bas or Bridge of Japan, from whence distances were computed throughout Japan. The bridge was rebuilt several times following a series of accidents. On one occasion the bridge collapsed due the weight of Tokyo residents fleeing a fire.

2. The feudal system in Japan of relatively small castles inhabited by war lords and their retinue and troops was in contrast to the system in China where whole towns and cities were surrounded by fortified walls.

3. Courtney clearly met Townsend Harris, described by Courtney as 'Mr Harris, the American Minister.' In 1856 Townsend Harris arrived in Japan as the first American Consul General. He opened a temporary Consulate in Gyokusenji Temple in Kakizaki, Shimoda.

4. The Japanese government and Harris signed the 'Treaty of Amity and Commerce between the United States and Japan'. The Treaty stipulated

that "Japan accept the posting of a an American diplomatic envoy in Yedo and the opening of four ports, Kanagawa, Niigata, Hyogo, and Nagasaki, in addition to Hakodadi. (The port of Shimoda is closed.)." Harris was elevated to Minister Resident on January 19th 1859. In July, he moved from Shimoda to Yedo, and opened a legation in Zempukuji Temple in Azabu, a facility on loan from the Japanese government. The American Consulate opened in Hongakuji Temple in Yokohama on July 4, 1859.

Chapter 13

1. In 1859, C Pemberton Hodgson started a tour of duty as British Consul at Hakodate in southern Hokkaido and he clearly took a wider interest in the country than his official duties might suggest. An extensive account of the observations of Hodgson, the first British Consul in Japan, can be found in 'A residence at Nagasaki and Hakodate in 1859 and 1860 with an account of Japan generally with a series of letters on Japan by his wife' reprinted by Elibron Classics 1992. This is an often entertaining account of a family settling into a completely alien environment and conveys the richness of the experience together with the frustrations.

   He also was a keen amateur botanist and sent many specimens to the Botanical Gardens at Kew in London. In the main, he sent back dried specimens, studied by Sir WJ Hooker and subsequently listed in his 1861 Catalogue of Japan Plants. Hodgson also sent back some living material, notably the handsome *Ligularia hodgsonii*, figured in Curtis's Botanical Magazine for 1863. Hodgson's specimens were also written up by the first Curator of the Kew Herbarium, Allan A Black.

2. The temple offered to Hodgson as the British Consulate and residence was the Shimyoji Temple, a Buddhist temple with numerous outbuildings which could serve as offices and also family accommodation. A temple stands on the same ground today however there have been a succession of new temples erected since Hodgson's time due to the frequent fires that commonly destroyed large areas of property.

3. Beche de Mer or sea cucumber is popular in Japan and also in China where it is known as the 'Ginseng of the sea'. Hokodate remains a busy fishing port and is an important centre of the squid industry in Japan.

4. *Capsella bursa-pastoris* known by its common name 'shepherd's purse' because of its triangular purse-like pods is a member of the mustard family. It is native to eastern Europe and the near East and is considered a common weed in many parts of the world including Britain. It is also found in China. This is one of the first accounts of the plant being found in Japan.

5. Courtney also met Dr Michael Albrecht during his visit to Hakodate. Albrecht was a Russian Medical Officer to the Russian Consulate and is memorialized in the plant known as *Rhodedendron albrechtii* or commonly known as Albrecht's Azelea. Albrecht discovered this azalea growing near Hakodate in 1860. Albrecht opened a hospital in Hakodate and treated Japanese patients using western techniques which caused some controversy at the time. An account of the overland journey from Tokyo to Hakodate was written by Albrecht's wife. [*Morskoi sbornik,* 54:7 (1861), 73–74 .]

CHAPTER 14

1. There has been much speculation as to the root cause of the fevers seen in Hong Kong. It is likely to be actually a mixed picture that includes malaria, relapsing fever, typhoid and typhus. There have been specific treatise aimed to elucidate the fever, one of the earliest attempted to characterize the fever under one entity 'Hong Kong Fever' even though there were many variations in the presentation. Hong Kong Fever. See Note 9, Introduction.

2. Medical Notes on China, 1846, Dr J Wilson. Churchill [London].

3. This is an important scientific finding based on careful observation. The cause of malaria could not be attributed to rotting vegetation in paddy fields. Courtney states 'malaria, whatever it's true nature may be' alludes to the fact that the root cause was unknown but was clearly moving away from the notion that it was related to miasma.

4. The observation of Quotidian and Tertian fevers, makes a distinction between the fever patterns of two types of malaria, the Quotidian which may have febrile episodes every day [often caused by *Plasmodium falciparum*] and Tertian malaria where the fever is every 2nd or 3rd day [often caused by *Plasmodium vivax}*.

5. Blue Pill [also known as pilula hydrargyri] was a remedy prescribed for constipation and other ailments. It contained 1/3 elemental mercury by weight, mixed with honey of rose, liquorice, glycerin and inert ingredients to form pills of about 48 grains in weight. It was used frequently as the diet at sea often contained little fibre and constipation was a common consequence.

6. This experiment is a very important contribution concerning the use of quinine. Although quinine had been found to be useful in preventing fevers by ships in West African waters in the 1840's, the use of quinine had not been investigated with such scientific rigor.

Notes

7. Dou Shen Niang Niang is the Chinese Goddess of smallpox and there were many temples dedicated to her when smallpox was common. There were also deities for measles and pock marks in general [See Notes, Chapter 9].

8. Measles is generally regarded as a mild disease but can be fatal for both adults and children. Mortality has been reduced significantly with the widespread introduction of childhood vaccination.

9. An observation on the infrequency of mental illness in China at that time. Later writers have described mental disturbance as being a common problem and suicide a frequent occurrence. [An Australian in China. Being the narrative account of a quiet journey across China to Burma. G.E. Morrison 1895. Reprinted. Earnshaw Books 2010. Shanghai].

10. This is an unusual observation as it is likely that 'Phthisis' [tuberculosis] would be equally as common in China as in Europe.

CHAPTER 15

1. Li Shi Zhen [1518 – 1593] was the greatest Chinese herbologists in Chinese history. His major contribution to medicine was his forty-year opus in the making, the *Ben cao gang mu* or "Compendium of Materia Medica". The book has details of more than 1,800 drugs including 1,100 illustrations and 11,000 prescriptions. It also describes the type, form, flavor, nature and application in disease treatments of 1,094 herbs. The book remains the premier reference work for herbal medicine. The book was reprinted frequently and five of the original editions still exist. In addition, Li wrote eleven other books, including *Binhu maixue* "A Study of the Pulse" and *Qijing bamai kao* "An Examination of the Eight Extra Meridians".

2. The *Huangdi Nei jing* also known as The Inner Canon of Huangdi or Yellow Emperor's Inner Canon, is an ancient Chinese medical text that has been treated as the fundamental doctrine for Chinese medicine for more than two thousand years. The work is composed of two texts each of eighty-one chapters or treatises in a question-and-answer format between the mythical *Huangdi* [Yellow Emperor] and six of his equally legendary ministers. The first text, the *Su wen* is also known as the Basic Questions and covers the theoretical foundation of Chinese Medicine and its diagnostic methods. The second, the *Ling shu* discusses acupuncture. These two texts are known as the *Nei jing* or *Huangdi Nei jing*. Usually the title *Nei jing* refers only to the *Su wen*. Two other texts also carried the prefix *Huangdi Nei jing* in their titles: the *Ming tang* and the *Tai su* ["Grand Basis"], both of which have survived only partially.

3. Nicholas Culpeper (1616 – 1664) was an English botanist, herbalist, physician, and astrologer. Culpeper spent the greater part of his life in the English outdoors cataloguing hundreds of medicinal herbs. Culpeper devoted himself to using herbs to treat the illnesses of his patients and published two famous books, The English Physitian (1652) and The Complete Herbal (1653), both of which contain a rich store of pharmaceutical and herbal knowledge. He published these as cheaply as possible so that more physicians could have access to his writing.

CHAPTER 16

In the third century AD, during the Jin dynasty in China, acupuncturist Huangfu Mi edited the book *Acupuncture jia yijing*, literally meaning *The system of acupuncture*. It incorporates the acupuncture theories of *Su wen* and *Ling shu* with the book *Ming tang essentials of points*. It is a complete edition of acupuncture. The essence of the earlier acupuncture classic *Ming tang essentials of points* has been preserved in the *Jia yijing*.

The *Jia yijing* is the earliest extant comprehensive book on the science of acupuncture and moxibustion. Its first part deals with the viscera, channels and collaterals, acupuncture points and diagnosis. The second part is about diseases and the therapy of acupuncture and moxibustion. It is a summary of China's achievements on the science of acupuncture and moxibustion before the Jin dynasty.

Although Courtney highlights 12 divisions, only divisions 2-11 are described in the journal.

CHAPTER 17

See Note 17, Introduction. The first ever photographs of the small feet of Chinese women were taken by John Thomson (1837-1921) who travelled extensively in territories now known as Malaysia, Singapore, Thailand, Vietnam, Laos, Taiwan ROC and the People's Republic of China. There are 700 photographs preserved in the Wellcome Library in their original format: negatives on sheets of glass, coated with the chemical collodion (nitrocellulose).

In China he photographed members of the Chinese imperial family and government, street traders, fisherfolk, miners, lepers, women of leisure and orphans in many areas of China including cities such as Hong Kong and Beijing. He also travelled throughout Hubei and Hunan provinces in central China, where he was probably one of the first, if not the very first, to take photographs.

On a visit by Thomson in 1920 to the first public exhibition of Henry Wellcome's historical collection in Wigmore Street, London which had opened in 1913, Thomson saw the corridor lined with photographs already in Wellcome's possession. It was a small display and had much about Africa but nothing about China. Hence Thomson negotiated to transfer 700 photographs to the Wellcome Library which included not only photographs of China but of many territories visited during his travels.

CHAPTER 18

1. John Hunter (1724 – 1793) originally trained as an army surgeon and his career developed in the fields of research and teaching. He was recognized as one of the leading proponents and teachers of scientific surgery and teachers of surgery of his time. His scientific work was rewarded in 1767 when he was elected Fellow of the Royal Society.

2. Dover's Powder was a traditional medicine against cold and fever, which is no longer in use in modern medicine. It is named after Dr Thomas Dover, an eighteenth century English physician, who first prepared it. The powder was a preparation of ipecacuanha, opium and potassium sulphate, largely used in domestic practice to induce sweating and to defeat the advance of a 'cold' at the beginning of any attack of fever. It was also known by the name *Pulvis ipecacuanhae et opii*. It enjoyed widespread use in naval medicine especially in tropical climes where fever was common.

Bibliography

Primary Sources

ADM 101/163 General Remarks. An Appendix to the Journals of the Provisional Battalion of Royal Marines serving at Canton and to the Journals of HMS Highflyer. The National Archives London. 1858 – 1860.

ADM 125/81 The National Archives, London. 1858.

Secondary References

Barton, G.K., Observation of the causes, nature and treatment of Hong Kong fever. Dublin Quarterly Journal of Medical Science 1851; 12(2):335-365.

Bradley, J, Dupree M., Opportunity on the edge of orthodoxy: Medically qualified hydropathists in the era of reform, 1840-1860. Social History of Medicine 2000;14 (3): 417-437.

Bulhan, H. A., Franz Fanon and the psychology of oppression. London: Springer, 1985.

Choa, G.H.,"Heal the Sick" was their motto: The Protestant medical missionaries in China. Hong Kong: Chinese University Press,1985.

Choa, G.H.,The life and times of Sir Kai Ho Kai.Hong Kong: Chinese University Press,1981.

Cordier, M.H.H., Life and labours of Alexander Wylie - A Memoir.London: Royal Asiatic Society,1987.

Ebrey, P., China, An illustrated History. Cambridge University Press:1996.

Eitel, E. J., Europe in China: The history of Hong Kong from the beginning to the year 1882. Hong Kong: Kelly and Walsh, 1895.

Gordon, A., A modern history of Japan. Oxford University Press: 2009.

Grant, J., Wang Ji and the Stone Mountain medical case histories. London: Routledge and Curzon, 2003.

Harland, W.A., Chinese anatomy and physiology. Transactions, China Branch of the Royal Asiatic Society. Hong Kong: 1847.

Harland, W.A., Colonial Surgeon's Reports for 1848 and 1849, Hong Kong.

Harland, K., The Royal Navy in Hong Kong. Maritime Books, Liskeard: Maritime Books, 1981.

Hodgson, C.P., A residence at Nagasaki and Hakodate in 1859 – 1860 with an account of Japan generally. London: Richard Bentley, 1861.

Hsu, E., (Ed) Innovation in Chinese Medicine. Cambridge University Press: 2001.

Levien, M., (Ed)., The Cree Journals 1837-1856. Exeter: Webb & Bower, 1981.

Lo, V., Cullen, C., (Eds), Medieval Chinese Medicine. London: Routledge and Curzon, 2005.

Lu, Gwei-Djen., China's greatest naturalist. A brief biography of Li Shih-Chen. 1976: 209-218.

Mason, R.H.P., and Caiger, J.G., A history of Japan. Tokyo: Tuttle, 1997.

McLean, D., Surgeons of the Opium War: The Navy on the China Coast, 1840-42. English Historical Review 2006; CXXI (491):487-504.

Needham, J., China and the origins of immunology. Eastern Horizon 1980; 19(1):6-12.

Needham, J., and Lu, Gwei-Djen., Hygiene and Preventive Medicine in Ancient China. J Hist Med Allied Sci 1962; 17:429.

Needham, J., and Lu, Gwei-Djen., Science and Civilization in China: Biology and Biological Technology: Volume VI: 6. Medicine. Cambridge University Press, 1970.

Pottinger, H., Letter to Lord Stanley. Colonial Office (CO) Records 1843; (25):369-376. The National Archives. London.

Rydings, H. A., Transactions of the China Medico-Chirurgical Society 1845, 1846. Journal of the Hong Kong Branch of the Royal Asiatic Society 1973; 13: 13-27.

Takeshi, K., The British Consulate in Hakodate, 1863. Chronological study on its design, works and destruction by fire. Trans Arch Inst Japan 1984; (341): 135-141.

Wylie, A., Notes on Chinese literature. London: Shanghai Presbyterian Mission Press, 1867.

Appendix 1

Details of Service Record Charles FA Courtney

20 Dec	1847	Member Royal College of Surgeons
20 July	1848	Acting Asst Surgeon HMS Victory
10 May	1849	Asst Surgeon HMS Encounter
10 May	1852	Confirmed as Naval Surgeon
13 Sept	1852	Mr Abraham Courtney, Surgeon RN, requested his son might be appointed to a harbour ship and enable him to observe professional duties
20 Nov	1852	Asst Surgeon HMS Sidow
6 Feb	1854	Enclosed certificates of service
10 Feb	1855	Enclosed certificates of Mr Dalton Surgeon of the Sidow, stating Mr Courtney served most indefatigably in his attendance to the sick both day and night during the situation of cholera on board.
1 Mar	1856	Certificate for the year 1855
10 May	1856	1856 Promoted as Acting Officer, Surgeon
15 Aug	1856	1856 Requesting to be placed on half-pay sick leave from the 30th July 1856 the date he was paid off from the Sidow
9 Jan	1857	1856 Served with the Provisional battalions during the operations at Cacataco. Mentioned favourably by Col. Holloway for services rendered during operations at Cacataco in his report to Admiral Seymour.
18 Mar	1857	Surgeon HMS Calcutta
13 Dec	1857	Royal Marine Brigade [until 4th October 1858].
5 Oct	1857	Appointed Surgeon HMS Highflyer
22 Oct	1858	Stating that after leaving the Provisional Battalion, Royal Marines at Canton in the month of October [1858] he did duty for about 3 weeks aboard the HMS Tribune during the illness of the Surgeon of that ship. That on the 5th October 1858 he was appointed to HMS Highflyer and joined her on 3rd December 1858.
Aug	1859	Was suffering from ophthalmia and could not see. Enclosed Certificates of HMS Highflyer
20 Jan	1860	Capt G F A Shadwell, Captain of Highflyer certified very favourably of him and stated that he was under great personal obligation to Mr Courtney for his attentions during the six months he had him under his hands with his foot wounded after the affair of the Peiho on 25th June 1859. Certificate attached.
31 May	1861	Completed assignment HMS Highflyer
14 Sept	1861	Capt CFA Shadwell spoke highly of him and recommended him for an appointment either at shore or afloat.
3 Dec	1861	Surgeon HMS Defiance until June 1866

Appendix

15 Jan	1866	Capt Shadwell recommended a new appointment for him. Plymouth or Portsmouth preferred
3 June	1866	Capt Phillimore applied to Lord John Hay for a Home Ship for Courtney
21 July	1866	Would prefer HMS Boscaview when vacant
5 Feb	1867	Surgeon HMS Donegal [until 30 June 1869]
14 Jan	1869	Applied to be appointed to Indian troop ships to be stationed on Med side
7 May	1869	Capt J A Pointer of HMS Donegal states that "he conducted himself with sobriety and performed his duties as Medical Officer to my entire satisfaction as an able officer".
1 July	1869	Surgeon HMS Resistance [until 17 Feb 1870]
31 Dec	1869	Capt Cdr Lusmoor of HMS Donegal stating that he has conducted himself entirely to his satisfaction.
25 Oct	1869	Complied with the DG's request forwarding his scheme for the entry of boys into the Navy
17 Feb	1870	Capt Lusmoor of HMS Resistance states that Courtney has been most assiduous in the performance of his duties not only with regard to the sick but in the entry of boys for HM Navy
19 Mar	1870	Forwarded copies of 'Remarks on present system of recruiting and examining boys for the Royal Navy'
8 June	1870	Forwarded form for recording 'Particulars of the Physical Examination of Boys for the Royal Navy'
18 June	1870	Informed by the DG that he concurs generally with his views as stated
25 Feb	1870	Requested to send certificates for HMS Resistance
6 Sept	1870	Candidate for HMS Excellent and HMS Royal Adelaide when vacant
19 Jan	1871	Candidate for HMS Cantor and HMS Eagle
16 June	1871	Granted 7 days leave by the Senior Officer, Portsmouth
6 July	1871	Reports his admission on 5th July into Haslar Hospital with poisoned wound of the right thumb from the discharge of the scalp of a patient he was dressing on the 1st July. Hand and forearm much inflamed. Treatment will probably extend over one month.
16 July	1871	Died. Their Lordships expressed regret of the melancholy Intelligence of this officer's death.

Appendix 2

Surgeon's account of the Battle of Camperdown 1797 by Robert Young, Surgeon

All of these were wounded in the action of the 11th of October, in which I had no mate having been without one for three months before. I was employed in operating and dressing till nearly four in the morning, the action beginning about one in the afternoon. So great was my fatigue that I began several amputations, under a dread of sinking before I should have secured the blood vessels. Ninety wounded were brought down during the action, the whole cockpit deck, cabins and wing berths together with my platform, so that at a time they were laid on each other at the foot of the ladder where they were brought down. I was obliged to go on deck to the Commanding Officer to state the situation and apply for men to go down the main hatchway and move the foremost of he wounded further forward into the tiers and the wings and thus make room in the cockpit.

Numbers about 16 mortally wounded, died after they were brought down amongst whom was the brave and worthy Captain Burgess, whose corps could with difficulty be conveyed to the starboard wing berth. Joseph Bonheur had his right thigh taken off by a cannon shot close to the pelvis so that it was impossible to apply a tourniquet. His right arm as also shot to pieces. The stump of his right thigh which was very fleshy presented a large and dreadful surface of mangled flesh. In this state he died in near two hours, perfectly sensible and incessantly calling out in strong voice for me to assist him. All the service I could render the unfortunate man was to put dressings over the part and give him a drink.

In many instances today, I had occasion to observe that vessels collapse and bleed little after gunshot or splinters. Melancholy cries for assistance were addressed to me from every side, by wounded and dying and piteous moans and bewailing from pain and despair. In the midst of these agonising scenes, I was enabled to preserve myself firm and collected and embracing in my mind the whole of the situation and to direct my attentions where the greatest and most essential services could be performed.

The man whose leg first amputated, thigh and traverse, had not uttered a groan of complaint from the time the was brought down and I swear exulting in the news of victory, regretted not the loss of a limb.

An explosion of cartridges, abreast of the cockpit hatchway, filled the hatchway with flame and in a moment fourteen or fifteen wretches tumbled down upon each other, their faces black as a cinder, their clothes blown to tatters and their legs on fire.

Appendix

After the action ceased, fifteen or sixteen bodies were removed before it was possible to get the platform cleaned. I have the satisfaction to say that of those who survived to undergo amputation or be dressed, all were found next morning in the gun room, where they were placed, in as comfortable a state as possible and on the third day were conveyed on shore in good spirits cheering the ship at going away, smoking their pipes and jesting as they sailed along and answering the cheers of thousands of the populace who received them at Yarmouth Bay.

Appendix 3

Diseases on board HMS Highflyer

NOSOLOGICAL RETURN OF THE SICK AND WOUNDED FROM JANUARY 1ST 1859 TO DECEMBER 31ST 1860

DISEASES	CASES REMAINING BY LAST RETURN	SINCE ADDED TO THE LIST	DISCHARGED TO DUTY	SENT TO HOSPITAL	DEAD	INVALIDED	NUMBER IN THE LIST	15-25 NO. OF CASES	15-25 DAYS SICKNESS	25-35 NO. OF CASES	25-35 DAYS SICKNESS	35-45 NO. OF CASES	35-45 DAYS SICKNESS	45-55 NO. OF CASES	45-55 DAYS SICKNESS	55-65 NO. OF CASES	55-65 DAYS SICKNESS	TOTAL NO. OF CASES	TOTAL DAYS SICKNESS
CONTINUED FEVER		4	3		1			3	144	1	58								
REMITTENT FEVER		9	7	2				7	105	2	32							9	137
INTERMITTENT FEVER		209	206				3	101	647	61	444	41	181	6	33			69	1305
EPHEMERAL FEVER		6	6				3	13	19	1	3	2	19					6	41
EPILEPSY		1	1							1	23							1	23
DELERIUM TREMENS		3	1	1			1					3	29					3	29
COUP DE SOLEIL		1	1							1	17							1	17
BRONCHITIS		6	4	1			1	3	66	1	12	1	7	1	15			6	100
PLEURITIS		1	1					1	69									1	69
PNEUMONIA	1		1										19						19
PHTHISIS		9	1	7		1		4	120	5	146							9	266
CATARRH		24	23				1	14	138	5	26							24	219
CYANOSIS		2	2					2	13									2	13
ASTHMA		2	2					2	21									2	21
HAEMORRHOIDS		9	9					4	40	4	55	1	5					9	100
VARIX		3	3									3	35					3	35
DYSENTERY		28	18	7	1	2		17	246	7	137	3	74	1	7			28	464
DIARRHEA	2	175	155	10	5		7	91	1059	62	853	20	319	2	13			175	2244
CHOLERA		3	2		1			2	39	1	1							3	40
FISTULA IN ANO		2		2				2	36									2	36
CONSTIPATION		1	1							1	12							1	12
GASTRITIS		1	1					1	57									1	57
HEPATITIS		4	3	1				1	4	2	29	1	28					4	61
SYPHILIS	5	87	83	5			4	50	1919	29	1000	8	343					87	3262
GONORRHEA		29	26				3	23	652	4	158	2	47					29	857
ORCHITIS		33	32	1				24	354	9	232							33	586

Appendix

Diseases on Board HMS Highflyer

NOSOLOGICAL RETURN OF THE SICK AND WOUNDED FROM
JANUARY 1ST 1859 TO DECEMBER 31ST 1860 - CONTINUED

DISEASES	CASES REMAINING BY LAST RETURN	SINCE ADDED TO THE LIST	DISCHARGED TO DUTY	SENT TO HOSPITAL	DEAD	INVALIDED	NO NOW IN THE LIST	15-25 NO. OF CASES	15-25 DAYS SICKNESS	25-35 NO. OF CASES	25-35 DAYS SICKNESS	35-45 NO. OF CASES	35-45 DAYS SICKNESS	45-55 NO. OF CASES	45-55 DAYS SICKNESS	55-65 NO. OF CASES	55-65 DAYS SICKNESS	TOTAL NO. OF CASES	TOTAL DAYS SICKNESS
STRICTURE		2	1	1				1	9	1	35							2	44
SYPHILIS		2	2					2	84									2	84
PHEUMATIS	1	44	41	1		2	1	22	290	10	167	7	85	5	242			44	784
OPHTHALMIA		35	35					21	81	9	33	5	15					35	129
SCROFULA		2				2				2	251							2	251
BUBO		5	5					4	98	1	42							5	140
PHLEGMON		129	125				4	83	984	37	333	8	56	1	3			129	1376
ABSCESS		5	4				1	4	49	1	25							5	140
ULCER	1	24	24			1		16	603	6	204	2	106					24	913
HERPES		4	4					3	46	1	7							4	913
ONYCHIA		1	1					1	15									1	15
LICHEN TROPICAL		4	4					2	17			2	11					4	28
DYSPEPSIA		27	24			2	1	4	156	11	93	10	92	2	17			27	358
SCURVY		1	1					1	72									1	72
DEBILITY		1	1							1	25							1	25
WOUNDS		35	34	1				20	370	14	370	1	15					35	745
FRACTURES		1		1				1	2									1	2
SPRAINS		7	7					6	25									7	28
CONTUSIONS		68	64				4	37	581	21	250	9	162	1	19			68	1012
HERNIA		5	3			2		3	29	2	36							5	65
GUNSHOT WOUND		30	12	5	9	4		16	662	12	161	1	1	1	191			30	1015
SCALDS		3	2	1				2	16	1	6							3	22
BURNS		2	2					1	29			1	1					2	30
MORRUS COXA		1				1		1	36									1	36
TOTAL	10	1092	990	47	12	22	31	607	10017	328	5279	136	1695	21	543			1092	17534

APPENDIX 4

LIST OF KILLED AND WOUNDED BELONGING TO HMS HIGHFLYER DURING THE PEIHO RIVER CONFLICT

Name	Age	Quality	Remarks
Lieut Henry Inglis	23	1st Lieut	Killed
George Dawson	26	L. Seaman	Killed
Henry Nias	34	Cpl.	Killed
William Bassett	23	Armourer	Killed
George Macklacklan	32	L.F.J	Killed
William Daw	30	G.R.M.art	Killed
Michael Helmsley	27	G.R.M.art	Killed
Robert Moon	32	G.R.M.art	Killed
Christopher Irvine	36	A.B.	Killed
Captain CFA Shadwell	45	Captain	Compound comminuted fracture, 1st metatarsal of left foot
Lieut J Purvis	26	1st Lieut	Slight contusion of lower third of right leg by a round shot
Luke Crawford	28	L. Seaman	Compound comminuted fracture of the left ankle joint
James Fox	24	Seaman	Compound fracture of the ungal phalanyx of middle finger left hand
John Bullard	23	A.B	Contused wound of lower lip, several teeth broken
Joseph Jewett		A.B.	Gunshot wound of left temple, ball extracted
Fettes Higson	34	G.M. art	Wound of left leg immediately below knee joint, ball passed through limb.
William Alders	22	Ord	Wound over lower angle of left scapula, ball lodged
Richard Gardener	20	Ord	Wound immediately below external malleolus of left foot, ball passed through sole of foot
Joseph Tyler	19	Ord	Extensive lacerated wound of dorsum of left foot
Lenny Hampshire	20	Ord	Left foot shot away, foot amputated
Joseph Gunser	22	Ord	Wound of anterior surface of the middle third of right thigh, ball lodged
Albert Baker		Ord	Gunshot wound of right temple, ball lodged
William Burrell	23	Ord	Contused wound of right thigh immediately above knee joint
Frederick Richardson	19	Ord	Wound close to inferior angle of the scapula, followed by complete paralysis of lower extremities, ball lodged
John Harman	19	Boy	Arrow wound of middle third of right forearm, ball lodged
John Jackson	26	B.Mate	Gunshot wound, left side of occipital bone

APPENDIX 5

CLINICAL DETAILS AND POST-MORTEM FINDINGS OF TWO PATIENTS WHO DIED OF TYPHUS FEVER

Case I

Henry Woodford, at 32, Private in the Royal Marines belonging to the Provisional Battalion was admitted into Hospital at Canton in the 5th of April 1858 for Typhus Fever.

A strong able-bodied man about 5 feet 8 inches in height, dark hair who had been serving in the center of the city of Canton with the Police force for several weeks before this illness.

April 5th. On admission, face flushed, skin hot and dry. Pulse 92, tongue covered with a slight white fur in center. Bowels slightly relaxed. Stated that he had felt unwell on the previous day and that he had a rigor a few hours before coming into hospital. Was much exhausted by the walk of half a mile. Given medicines every 4 hours.

April 6th. Passed a restless night countenance much flushed; eyes suffused, skin hot and dry. Pulse accelerated. Fur on tongue becoming brown. Bowels open 3 or 4 times in the night.

April 7th. No amelioration of symptoms. Complains of giddiness and dimness of vision. Conjunctiva considerably congested. Beef tea, arrowroot and port wine. Quinine disulphate.

April 8th. Was very restless during the night, and did not sleep but he has a drowsy appearance. No diminution of heat of skin. Complains of pain on pressure in umbilical region. A rose-coloured eruption has appeared on body. Continued medicaments. To have 2 pints of beef tea during the day. Wine.

April 9th. No abatement of fever. Still feels pain in the umbilical region. Mustard cataplasm to be applied to abdomen. Continued medicaments. Has been delirious all the afternoon, Respiration hurried and oppressed. A cooling lotion to be applied to forehead. Saline effervescing draughts to be administered every 2 hours.

April 10th. The effervescing draughts were continued during the night and toward morning a solution of acetates of morphia was given which procured about ten hours uneasy sleep. He now takes no notice of anything but lies in a semi-comatose state, occasionally muttering to himself, but is perfectly conscious when roused. Has several times attempted to get out of bed. Complains of no pain and thirst, but drinks with avidity when any fluid is applied to his lips. Countenance still flushed and eyes congested. Skin moist. Tongue black and covered with sordes. The rose coloured eruption is very vivid over the body and extremities. Liquor of ammonia acetate. Vespere continues in a very drowsy state. A blister to be applied to each temple.

April 11th. Has had no sleep, skin hot and dry. Pulse 112 feeble. Drinks copiously, an inclination to stertorous breathing. Is passing faeces involuntarily. A blister to be applied to nape of neck. Caput medicaments, wine.

April 12th Has had constant hiccup all night. Great difficulty is experienced in rousing him. Has become very deaf and is continually muttering in his delirium. Abdomen tympanic. Continue nutritious farinaceous diet, beef tea and arrowroot.

April 13th is lying on his back perfectly unconscious. Drinks when fluid are applied to his lips, but never attempts to open his eyes. Breathing hurried; Pulse 120, slight subsultus tendinum. The eruption is visible all over the body and is persistent on pressure. The catheter has required to be used to draw off his water. From this time he gradually sunk and died on the morning of the 14th of April at 1 o'clock am.

Post-Mortem Findings

A well made body 5 feet 8 inches in height with dark hair. Faint marks of a macular-eruption visible over the whole surface. Very considerable gravitation of blood to the dependent part of the body.

Head. There is considerable vascularity prevailing in scalp and skull, and after their removal the dura mater appears highly congested, its blood vessels being distended with fluid blood. The pia mater and arachnoid also show a high degree of active congestion without, however, any further changes. Form size and structure of the brain natural. Grey substances show a reddish tint; White substance, exhibits very numerous dots of blood. Consistence of both very firm, ventricles regular. Commissina mollis large. Choroid plexus and liquor cerebro-spinalis natural.

Mouth and neck. Sordes on lips and teeth. Tongue covered with a dry brown crust. Fauces and pharynx cyanotic. Oesophagus natural. Larynx slightly hyperaemic.

Thorax well formed. Pleural cavities free and lungs collapsing with the exception of the upper lobe of right side which is slightly adherent. Trachea and bronchi perfectly permeable, their lining membrane presenting a peculiar appearance being throughout studded with small dark petechiae.

The upper lobes of the lung oedematous; also the corresponding lobe of left side, but in a lesser degree. Middle lobe dry, natural, but posteriorly entirely collapsed. Surface depressed, dark blue, substance dry, perfectly void of air. Solid, but without any infiltration on other structural changes. The quantity of blood in the lungs and their blood vessel is on the whole considerably less than natural.

Pericardium and heart. Pericardium natural; containing about 1 oz of clear serum, heart of natural size, flabby, collapsed, the cavities of right side perfectly empty the ventricle only containing a small stringy coagulum. Endocardium and aorta are slightly tinged with the colouring matter of the blood.

Abdomen. Peritoneum natural, intestines very tympanitic.

Liver. Slightly enlarged, very pale, anaemic: substance easily broken: blood vessel nearly empty. Fatty infiltration ascertained by the microscope. Gall-bladder containing a little dark grumous bile.

Spleen. About three times its natural size, very thick, capsule distended, edges rounded, substance bright red, rather dry; tolerably consistent, but readily broken.

Pancreas. Natural.

Alimentary canal. Stomach distended with hardly any fluid contents; mucous membrane throughout thickened, surface uneven and presenting throughout the characteristic changes of gastritis chronic potatorum, with a considerable degree of recent capillary injection in the fundus accompanied with numerous small petechial spots. Duodenum and ilium. Tympanitic and without contents, considerable gravitation of blood to the dependent portion of the latter, producing the most perfect injection of the same. The inner surface appears upon the whole perfectly natural; pale. Peyers patches are very distinct, slightly pigmented, but neither raised above the surrounding surface; nor do they show any higher degree of vascularity than the other parts.

Large intestines. Tympanitic, contain some greenish yellow faecal matter. Looks perfectly natural.

Omentum. Thin with hardly any fat. Mesentery enclosing a good deal of fat. Mesenteric glands perhaps a trifle enlarged, but without any increase of vascularity, or other structural change.

Uro-genital organs. Present a natural appearance. Pelvis regular, ureters slightly distended. Bladder distended with clear pale urine, generative organs natural.

Remarks: We have inspected the above as being the first one that occurred and as a good example having a strong resemblance to many of the others in its leading features. It will be observed that the rose-coloured maculated eruption was first noticed on the 4th day and remained persistent until after death, and that the pulse remained about 95 till a day or two before death when it rose to 120.

We now insert a second case differing sufficiently as regard to its complications to make it interesting.

Case 2

Robert Green, age 23, Private in the Royal Marines belonging to the Provisional Battalion was placed on the sick list on the 19th of June for continued fever and died on the 2nd of July. The following are the particulars of the case. June 19th a delicate looking man who had been under treatment three times while in Canton for diarrhoea and intermittent fever. On admission complains of languor, lassitude, general debility, nausea, vomiting and much headache. Skin moist. Pulse quick. Tongue foul, Bowels confined. Given medicaments.

June 20th Bowels not yet open. Febrile symptoms not at all diminished. Pulse 112. Nausea continues. Tongue furred. Quinine disulphate given.

June 21st Bowels freely open, but no amelioration of symptoms, coughed occasionally during the right. Hair to be cut close. Liquor ammonium acetate.

June 22nd Catarrhal symptoms very marked. Expectoration frothy, Respirations very hurried. Large crepitation heard over the base of both lungs. Skin hot and moist. A rose coloured eruption coming out on body. Pulse 100 weak. Tongue dry and black. Bowels have a tendency to constipation. Liquor ammonium acetate given. Wine 1 gill, beef tea and arrowroot.

June 23rd Fever still runs on. Skin hot and pungent. Pulse 96, very little headache, cough no easier, vomited once in the night. Tongue very foul and black in centre. Complains much of thirst. Bowel not yet opened. Liquor ammonium acetate. Soda-water, wine and beef tea.

June 24th Face flushed, Eyes suffused, Respirations hurried. Has frequent cough and some expectoration. Skin warm and moist. Eruption vivid. Pulse 112. Liquor ammonium acetate.

June 25th Face less flushed. Skin cooler. Pulse 108. respiration not too hurried. Tongue moist with brown fur in centre. Bowels open.

June 26th Complains of pain in umbilical region. Skin moist. Pulse 120. Tongue brown and moist. Bowels regular. Sinapism to abdomen. Ipecac and liquor ammonium acetate given.

June 27th Much the same as yesterday, skin moist. Pulse 120. Pain in abdomen still present. Liquor ammonium acetate. Quinine disulphate. Mist camphor. Beef tea arrowroot and wine.

June 28th Passed a quiet night, skin warmed and moist. Pulse 108. Respirations 36. Tongue covered with a brown fur. Bowel open. Cough and expectoration the same. Continued quinine.

June 29th Face somewhat fallen. Eruption fading. Skin pungent. Pulse 120 weak and difficult to count. Tongue dry; brown in centre. Bowels open. Urine free; specific gravity 1022 slightly alkaline. To have brandy and water frequently during the day.

June 30th Has been very restless during the night. Face becoming paler. Skin hot and dry. Thermometer in axilla 100. Pulse 120. Tongue covered with a blackish fur and dry in centre. Respirations 44. Has no pain anywhere. Continued brandy and water.

July 1st Appears quiet, lies continually on his back. Skin hot and dry. Pulse 139; very weak. Respiration 48. Tongue dry and brown. Sordes on teeth and gums. Thirst. Bowels open once in the night. Urine free. Continued brandy. Vespere, pulse about 126 small feeble and difficult to count. Respirations 60. Bowels open twice during the day. Moribund.

July 2nd Died at 12.30 am.

Post-Mortem Findings

A small body 5 feet 6 and ½ inches, reddish hair and beard. Countenance pale, sordes on lips and teeth. Body apparently wasted, gravitation of blood to the dependent parts very extensive. Marks of eruption very indistinct. Panniculus adipous moderately developed. Macular substance less dark and dry than usual in these cases.

Head. Integuments rather exsanguine. Dura mater slightly congested. Some coagulations of blood in sinus longitudinales, Arachnoid thickened and opaque, passive congestion of pia mater.

Size of the brain somewhat reduced. Substance firm; pale containing but little blood. Ventricle wide. Liquor cerebro-spinalis natural.

Mouth and neck. Tongue dark glazed. Tongue moderately enlarged. Cyanotic condition of all soft parts.

Larnyx. Slight congestion; large veins loaded.

Thorax. Pleural cavities free, lungs not collapsing. The upper 2/3rd of the lower lobe of left lung in a state of complete hepatization; remainder oedematous. In the right lung the corresponding portions also show hepatization, but here the inflammation is already in the transition to grey stage. The most perfect fibrinous cast is extracted from the corresponding branches of the pulmonary artery. Trachea and large bronchi natural. Inflammatory visitation of the finer bronchi. Bronchial glands very much enlarged and engorged. Pericardium: large tendinous patches on the cardiac surface.

Heart. Slightly enlarged; mitral valve thickened. Contents of right portion coagulated fibrin, thin fluid blood in left.

Abdomen. Liver of natural size, substance brown, of homogeneous appearance. No congestion. Microscopic examination shows a moderate degree of extra and inter cellular infiltration of fat. No melanotic deposits.

Spleen. 8 ½ x 5 x 2 ½ inches. Targescent, hard , edges round. Parenchyma dry, dark red, firm. Malphigian bodies large. No pigmentary deposits in its substance.

Alimentary canal. Stomach considerably thickened, some recent injection. Small intestines distended; the only sign of congestion is the dilatation of the subserous vessels of the ilium: mucous membrane natural. Solitary glands and Peyers Patches not raised. The latter but very little congested; central depression.

Uro-genital organs. Nothing remarkable.

Remarks. This case of typhus fever was remarkable for the great amount of disease found in the lungs after death, and the comparatively trifling symptoms of pneumonia during life; the absence of any remission of fever during the whole progress of the complaint, the presence of macular eruption; and the early death of the patient.

Appendix 6

Clinical Details And Post-Mortem Findings Of Dysentery

Clinical Features

1st Stage. Hyperaemia and retention of the blood in the mucous and submucous membranes. The flow of blood is diverted toward the mucous membrane, and the cellular tissue lying beneath it. The minute vessels are highly injected with blood, as is apparent even to the naked eye, and they dye the effected part light red.

2nd Stage. Deposit of the exudation beneath and in the mucous membrane of the colon. The deposit takes place particularly beneath the mucous membrane, between it and the muscular, in the shape of solid yellowish white, fibrinous masses.

3rd Stage. Softening and expulsion of the exudation. The originally solid exudation becomes softened. The softening commences in the centre of the exudation-mass, and proceeds from thence toward the circumference. The mucous membrane decays in the places in which it covers the exudation; its continuity is broken; the exudation is poured out into the cavity of the colon, and the decayed mucous membrane is itself expelled.

4th Stage. Cicatrization of the mucous membrane after the expulsion of the exudation, and mucous membrane, an overflow of plastic lymph takes place in the wound. A cellular-fibrous tissue is formed, which takes the place of the decayed mucous membrane and produces the cicatrix. No case of dysentery, in which expulsion of the mucous membrane has taken place, recovers, except by "cicatrization".

The acute form of the complaint is generally ushered in by rigors and diarrhoea although there is sometimes constipation and disorder of the stomach. There is increased frequency of pulse with heat and dryness of skin, or slight perspiration and clamminess. There symptoms are followed by frequent stools of a character peculiar to the disease which are generally accompanied with tormina and tenesmus, the latter being so urgent and distressing as to keep the patient almost constantly on the closet stool.

It is only by an accurate determination of the seat of pain that we can arrive at any conclusion regarding the particular portion of the large intestine affected, when the caecum alone is affected which is rarely the case, the caecal region is alone the seat of pain. When the colon is affected the pain is generally most severe along the course of the transverse colon and pressure made over that or over the ascending or descending portions will indicate the seat of disease. It seems probable that when scybala are passed that the colon is the part chiefly affected the scylous masses being formed by the irregular muscular contraction of the inflamed intestine. Should the rectum be much affected there is generally violent tenesmus and the patient makes frequent abortive attempts at defecation, and occasionally the complaint is accompanied with dysuria.

Should the complaint affect the entire length of the large intestine there is more or less diffused pain over the whole of the lower part of the abdomen. It may, however, be observed that the entire length of the intestine may be deeply affected and yet for many days together there may be no symptom of pain. Such cases are somewhat rare for as a general rule there is nearly always more or less pain or uneasiness.

With regard to the various stages of the complaint a careful study of the nature of the evacuations can alone determine the nature of the pathological process. When the faeces are mixed with mucus or are muco-sanguinous we may be certain that we are treating the disease in its first stage. When the faeces are mixed with pure blood, or pure blood alone is passed we may be certain that we are treating the disease is its 2nd stage. Should the stool be hemorrhagic and contain exudation flakes and shreds of mucous membrane this indicates that the exudation matter has softened and been expelled, the mucous membrane covering it having ulcerated and given way. In other words the disease is in its 3rd stage. The 4th stage or that of cicatrization is revealed by the previous history of the patient, by the stool becoming more normal, being freer from any admixture of mucous blood pus, and absence of pain.

Post-Mortem Findings

Post mortem examinations generally reveal more or less inflammation of the mucous membrane and the submucous cellular tissue, and the walls of the intestinal canal are usually very thick and vascular. In well-marked cases the superficial layers of the mucous layer are destroyed and in many parts removed leaving a raw dark red and easily bleeding surface. Where ulceration has taken place the mucous membrane is removed by a process of decay and sloughing, the decay of the mucous membrane being caused by the arrest of the circulation in its vessels and the softening and visitation of the exudation matter which advance through the opening in the mucous membrane and passed into the intestinal canal. Frequently the substance cellular tissue and the muscular fibres are equally hypertrophied and hypaeraemic and occasionally converted into a soft friable pulp in which there is hardly any structure to be perceived. Those portions of the mucous membrane which are intact generally present a pale and anemic appearance. The number of ulcers is sometimes quite extraordinary amounting to more than a hundred, and varies much in size and form. They may be either ovule or circular and may be very large or only the most minute spots.

In serious cases when perforation of the intestine has occurred the muscular and serous coats may be both in a state of gangrene and the contents of the intestine discharged into the abdominal or pelvic cavities unless this danger has been everted by adhesion of the peritoneal coat.

There is usually no trace of dysentery or inflammatory action in the small intestine, the disease not extending beyond the ilio-caecal valve, although occasionally there is slight vascularity of the mucous membrane. The contents of this portion of the canal are , however, not always natural. The stomach is frequently found somewhat distended with semi-fluid contents and the lining membrane somewhat congested. Enlargement and induration of the mesenteric glands is frequently associated with the disease. The liver though is occasionally found congested and is often frequently perfectly natural in form, size and appearance. Spleen often moderately enlarged but frequently healthy.

It seems very improbable that any method of treatment adopted could have saved life, but upon reflecting on the case and comparing it with others it would appear not improbable that life might have been somewhat prolonged if the plan of treatment had recourse to it at an earlier stage of the disease.

Disease, accidents and battle injuries in foreign climes have been the lot of naval surgeons throughout history and fortunately many accounts of extraordinary experiences survive, having been meticulously recorded in journals. This is one such example, the journal of Naval Surgeon Charles Courtney who served in the China Squadron in the mid-nineteenth century. It is a unique and hitherto unpublished account of his travels and observations in a rapidly changing and dramatic era in Chinese history.

The original journal is in the form of a leather bound book written in longhand that documents visits to ports along the China coast from Canton to Shanghai and also describes a short visit to Japan to install the first ever British Consul to Hakodate. The journal is an eyewitness account of significant historical events including the Canton campaign during the Second Opium War and of the failed assault on the Taku forts in 1859. In this brief period Courtney operated on sailors with dreadful injuries under battle conditions as well as keeping the ship's crew in the best possible state of health, literally 'fighting fit'. In addition he was required to manage a wide variety of illnesses such as malaria, typhoid, dysentery, typhus and the ever present 'gleet' and 'pox'.

Despite these onerous duties, Courtney found time to make regular entries to his journal which describe in detail the topography, medical environment, people and customs encountered along the coasts of China and Japan. The journal also contains essays on opium smoking and foot binding and also a treatise on Chinese medical literature written together with renowned sinologist Alexander Wylie during Courtney's sojourn in Shanghai. This treatise is one of the earliest contributions by westerners to catalogue and acknowledge the contributions of Chinese medical scholars to our understanding of the medical sciences. Having been discovered by chance, the journal is a rich resource for those with an interest in Chinese, naval or medical history.

Published by Atrabates Press, Hong Kong

www.ingramcontent.com/pod-product-compliance
Lightning Source LLC
Chambersburg PA
CBHW051052160426
43193CB00010B/1160